DIALOGUES WITH THE LORD OF TIME

Praise for
DIALOGUES WITH THE LORD OF TIME
~~~~~~~~~~~

"Some of us are hoping that human cultural evolution, amidst the enormous challenges that lie ahead, will produce an integral planetary spiritual vision capable of shedding the manifold dysfunctions of the world's religions while preserving their rich veins of psychological wisdom. For such a day to dawn we will have to tell many stories (for all worlds are made of stories) about how such a vision might feel and sound, preparing the etheric soil from which it may one day spring, revealed more than concocted. John Roger Barrie's Father Christopher and his probing conversations with men and women who have found their ways to his forest hermitage and who nickname him the Lord of Time, is one such story, an engaging and illuminating trek into the multiple religious understandings that foreshadow a new universalism."

—**Philip Novak, PhD**, Sarlo Distinguished Professor Emeritus, Dept. of Philosophy and Religion, Dominican University of California, and bestselling author of *The World's Wisdom*

"*Dialogues With the Lord of Time* is a thoughtful, engaging fruit of the spiritual imagination, a work of fiction that nonetheless bears within it many simple, powerful truths. It is beautifully written, concrete and free of pretense. Fr. Christopher, its central character, comes across as wise and unpresuming, something of a recluse who is nevertheless a precious guide for those who find him and come again and again to hear his words. Through it all, John Roger Barrie himself shines in his honesty, his own voice reaching us in his telling of Fr. Christopher's story."

—**Francis X. Clooney, SJ, PhD**, Parkman Professor of Divinity and Professor of Comparative Theology, Harvard Divinity School, Cambridge, MA, and author of numerous books and articles

"The frame story for this book is a set of talks given by Father Christopher, a retired Catholic priest living in California. His perspective is both mystical and universal, and the talks cover a wide range of experiences.

"His approach is both optimistic and thoughtful, and the book shows a very good example of interfaith dialogue, where ideas on religious experience from some major world religions are discussed and compared. It incorporates a mystical perspective into situations in everyday life, and it has a depth approach that is sadly lacking in much modern religious discourse. It would be useful for students of religion who have learned about the political and institutional side of religion, and wish to learn about the experiential and mystical side at its best."

—**June McDaniel, PhD**, Professor Emerita of the History of Religions, Dept. of Religious Studies, College of Charleston, SC, and author of *Lost Ecstasy* and many other books and writings

"John Roger Barrie's luminous text takes the reader on a voyage into the heart of the world's great religious traditions. Told with humor and gentle wisdom, Barrie's tale of the wise Father Christopher is at once deeply personal and utterly universal. It is a timeless parable of seeking, finding, and then integrating spiritual wisdom into human life, a task as urgent now as it has ever been."

—**Elizabeth M. G. Krajewski, PhD**, Adjunct Assistant Professor and World Religions Instructor, Humanities Dept., Colby–Sawyer College, New London, NH

"*Dialogues With the Lord of Time* is a refreshing and much-needed return to spiritual basics. Its main character, the larger-than-life Father Christopher, imparts a universal vision of religion that is right in the mainstream of the centuries-old mystical traditions, although colorfully and contemporarily presented. John Roger Barrie has produced a captivating, timeless story that should be required reading for any modern-day spiritual seeker."

—**William H. Forthman, PhD**, Professor Emeritus of Philosophy, California State University, Northridge, and co-author of the textbook *Religions of the World*

"*Dialogues With the Lord of Time* is part memoir and part guide for those seeking a deeper spiritual path in life—both beginning and experienced practitioner. Within these pages John Roger Barrie chronicles his quest for a life of deeper meaning: his explorations into various meditative disciplines, religious expressions from the east and west, along with his frustration at the highs and lows of his practice. Through his relationship with Father Christopher (the 'Lord of Time') he learns that progress and setbacks are all part of the process and that even one's teacher can be beset by similar frustrations. The solution? To look for what is positive and enlivening in all events on the journey. This text provides a beginning for a life of spiritual exploration."

—**Charles G. Krajewski, MDiv,** Ordained Pastor with the American Baptist Churches USA (retired)

"Inviting interfaith colloquies of enlightenment and connection to the universal. ... 'The true spiritual giants want nothing from you,' says Father Christopher, the fictionalized retired Catholic priest, teacher, and inter-faith mystic at the heart of this collection of searching spiritual inquiry and colloquy. 'They simply *radiate the light of God.*' That light—and that ideal of egoless spiritual instruction—shines throughout *Dialogues With the Lord of Time,* which offers a series of six discussions between Father Christopher and a group of seekers in the early 1990s. The form is novelistic, with a narrator who's not exactly Barrie recounting the conversations, his own spiritual journey, and the sustained effort that enlightenment demands.

"Throughout, among many heady concerns, Christopher and Barrie both emphasize the distinction between the 'two types' of spiritual leaders: 'those who spiritually empower others, and those who seek to control others.' As he lays out in clear and inviting language a path of his own that draws on a host of religious and spiritual traditions but is fully indebted to none, Father Christopher reveals himself as the empowering type of leader, one eager to guide others toward a 'responsible freedom' and a 'wholehearted love for one's chosen form of God, and unlimited, unconditional love toward others.' Achieving this, he posits, means that one must recognize and respect our place in 'the limitless interconnectedness among all things,' pray with ceaseless devotion, and not take the material world and its concerns as 'real'—it is instead a 'platform where we enact our desires and emotions, likes and dislikes.'

"Readers whose minds bustle with questions or objections after an assertion like that will appreciate that, throughout, Father Christopher entertains his interlocutors' concerns. Admirably, he leans into the complexities and paradoxes of such beliefs, explaining that 'one can be inwardly surrendered while outwardly assertive at the same time.' These rich, engaging discussions, alive with fresh insights and challenges, will reward readers eager for connection to 'a universal spiritual self—God—that contains all individual souls and every particle of the universe.'"

—**BookLife Review** by *Publishers Weekly*

Artist's Rendition of Father Christopher's Cabin
*black-and-white version of the original watercolor cover artwork
hand painted by Lucie Mizutani
and digitally enhanced by John Roger Barrie*

DIALOGUES WITH THE LORD OF TIME

John Roger Barrie

Sky Parlor Publications™ · Nevada City, California

Library of Congress Control Number: 2022952450

ISBN: 979-8-9866506-0-9 (paperback)
ISBN: 979-8-9866506-1-6 (hardcover)
ISBN: 979-8-9866506-2-3 (e-book)

First edition published January 2023.
Second printing, with minor corrections/edits
to the chapter "A Spiritual Memoir," March 2025.

Original watercolor cover artwork
Rustic Log Cabin Amid Serene Woodland Setting
hand painted by Lucie Mizutani
and digitally enhanced by John Roger Barrie.
Copyright © 2022 by John Roger Barrie. All Rights Reserved.

Cover design and layout by Sky Parlor Publications™.

Sky Parlor Publications™ is a registered trademark
in the United States of America.

Sky Parlor Publications™
P.O. Box 252
Nevada City, CA 95959
skyparlorpublications.com

Dedicated with much love
to those who inspired this book,
and to those who encouraged
my spiritual writings

AUTHOR'S NOTE

This book is inspired by my own real-life experiences, but I have fictionalized many accounts and have written it as a work of fiction in its entirety. All characters and their identifying characteristics, including the first-person narrator and the character called Father Christopher, are fictional or have been fictionalized, in whole or in part. Any similarities between the fictional and fictionalized characters in my book and real persons are strictly coincidental. The only exceptions are as follows: the individuals whom I have gratefully recognized by name in the Acknowledgments, including Nick J. Weber, whom I also mention in the narrative; and the actual names of real persons that are mentioned incidentally in the narrative. The names of actual persons, places, businesses, events, incidents, and entities that appear incidentally in the narrative are used fictionally, as are the names of fictional characters. No sponsorship by or affiliation with the owners of trademarks that are mentioned in passing is claimed or suggested.

William H. Forthman, PhD, provided his generous endorsement in June 2021. Sadly, Prof. Forthman passed away in August 2022.

Various meditation, devotional, and similar practices are mentioned in the narrative. However, the reader is encouraged to seek expert personal advice and individualized instruction, and medical advice if and as warranted, before undertaking any of these practices.

All endnotes reference both scriptural and bibliographic citations found within the text. There are no instances of explanatory comments in the endnotes.

None of the scriptural quotations from the Judeo–Christian Bible, the Koran, the Bhagavad Gita, the Hatha Yoga Pradīpikā, the Khaggavisāṇa Sutta, and the Tao Te Ching are drawn from a single source. In each instance, I have consulted several translations to compose a composite version. I have similarly rendered my own composite versions of citations from *The Cherubinic Wanderer, The Cloud of Unknowing,* and *The Way of Perfection.*

Finally, whenever "he" or "she," "him" or "her," "his" or "hers," or "himself" or "herself" are used as nonspecific pronouns, this usage is not intended to indicate any specific gender.

—*John Roger Barrie*

ACKNOWLEDGMENTS

My heartfelt appreciation goes to Nick J. Weber for reading and approvingly commenting on the section of the manuscript describing my real-life encounter with him during the December 19, 1974, Royal Lichtenstein Quarter-Ring Sidewalk Circus performance in Los Angeles, as I sought to ensure authenticity of this milestone event that occurred so many decades ago.

I am especially grateful to Elizabeth M. G. Krajewski, PhD—theologian, contemplative, and adjunct assistant professor in Humanities at Colby–Sawyer College—for reading and commenting on the manuscript. Professor Krajewski specializes in early medieval hagiography and teaches courses in world religions. Her incisive and authoritative observations significantly benefited the text. Thank you, Elizabeth, for so generously providing your astute, informed, and valuable suggestions, and for offering such eminently helpful feedback during the manuscript's final stages, and for your numerous professional courtesies.

Professor Francis X. Clooney, SJ, PhD, of Harvard Divinity School, a leading figure and noted author in the field of comparative theology, provided insightful comments that greatly improved the narrative. I am most grateful to Professor Clooney for his thoughtful, valuable contributions.

Professor Emerita June McDaniel, PhD, whose academic specialties and writings have focused on mysticism and religious experience, especially in the Hindu tradition, provided critical comments that considerably benefitted the text. I especially appreciate Professor Emerita McDaniel for sharing her many constructive suggestions.

I express my deep gratitude to prolific author and noted attorney Jonathan Kirsch, Esq, for his thorough, expert review of the manuscript and his extremely beneficial comments on certain sections of the text. Mr. Kirsch serves as an expert witness on publishing-industry matters. He is a distinguished lecturer and consultant on publishing topics and has written two leading reference works on publishing law.

Author and editor Rob Bignell provided incisive editing suggestions, which greatly improved the readability of the text. I am most grateful to Mr. Bignell for his many helpful recommendations.

Finally, I extend my deepest heartfelt appreciation to my wife Deborah, whose ongoing, unfailing support afforded me the dedicated time to bring this manuscript to fruition.

John Roger Barrie
Nevada City, California
January 22, 2023

CONTENTS

PROLOGUE

These writings primarily consist of talks given by a reclusive, enigmatic spiritual teacher whom I first met in 1990. Over the course of a few years, a group of seekers occasionally visited this unpretentious man, known as Father Christopher, who spoke eloquently on the spiritual life. He lived in a modest and fairly inaccessible cabin in the wooded coastal region of Northern California. Father Christopher was a retired Catholic priest and university scholar whose broad-minded and eclectic approach incorporated teachings from the world's great religions and mystical traditions. His vast and timeless perspective led me to refer to him as the Lord of Time. What follows are transcripts of nine dialogues with him, which I captured during six visits I made to see him between 1990 and 1992, interspersed with personal recollections and musings from events in my life.

We all move on the fringes of eternity
and are sometimes granted vistas
through the fabric of illusion.

—Ansel Adams

FIRST VISIT (June 1990)

Introductions

IT WAS BARELY SUMMER. My friend Heather urged me for some time to see her spiritual teacher, a man named Father Christopher. She knew my own spiritual awakening began in the autumn of 1974, but it was unfulfilled at the time, and since then I had been practicing various spiritual disciplines to rekindle it and bring it to fruition. "Come along," she said, "This man is different. He won't contradict any of your other teachers, and he may have answers for you." Her words roused my curiosity, and one Saturday morning in late June 1990, I drove from my apartment in Ukiah to the Northern California coastal town of Mendocino.

Mendocino is where I would locate if I didn't have my current life to live. An artist's colony of sorts situated in a picture-perfect setting, the area's ocean-scaped ambiance lifts it from the realm of the ordinary. Just don't visit during peak tourist season as I did.

After arriving in town and securing a much-coveted parking spot, I met Heather around noon at a local health-food store. We walked to a nearby eatery for a meal. While sitting outside enjoying a sweeping vista of the Pacific Ocean, she and I rekindled an acquaintance that began in Los Angeles, the city of my birth in 1957 and the place of my exodus in 1978. Heather, a graphics designer, had never married, although she'd been in three serious relationships over the years. She's as close to me as any woman I've known, though we've never been more than good friends.

"Father Christopher is seventy-six years old," she said. "He cares for himself, and he sees few people."

"But why is he willing to see me?"

"I told him about you and your dedication to the spiritual path. He's eager to meet you. A few of us visit him during the times he makes available. But he ruthlessly shuns publicity. He sometimes lets us bring others to see him, but only with prior arrangement. And he forbids photo taking. So you'll have to play it low key."

"Don't worry. Maybe I can take some notes. But I'll leave my camera in the car."

Heather knew of my previous stint as a newspaper reporter and my penchant for capturing events by noting or photographing anything of particular interest.

After lunch, I followed her to her home—a funky, albeit clean, post-hippiefied bungalow on the outskirts of Fort Bragg, where she lived with her oversize tomcat Snowcap. I unpacked my belongings from my large rolling duffle bag before resting in her extra bedroom, which would serve as my living quarters for the weekend.

In the early evening, we ate a scrumptious dinner Heather prepared, mostly macrobiotic, and afterward rode in her silver Civic north along Highway 1 until we exited onto a local county road. A series of gravel arteries branched off from this main thoroughfare, which wound along an increasingly remote area dotted with lonely stands of Douglas fir and occasional Coastal redwoods. We turned onto one of these byways, and as we climbed in elevation I could see the sun sliding in and out of the incoming fog, now hugging the coast. We slowly drove along this winding road, sparsely populated with houses.

After turning past a bend, Heather exclaimed, "There's his home."

Father's house was an older, timeworn, ranch-style log cabin, just as one would visualize. There was a seasonal creek running along the back edge of his land, a parcel that totaled perhaps three acres. I spotted a well-kept light-ivory VW Beetle in the nearby freestanding carport, and two other cars in the large dirt parking area adjacent to the cabin, where we also parked.

We walked up the porch steps and found the front door open. As we entered the screen door, Ginny, a massage therapist in her late twenties, warmly greeted us and invited us inside. There was Father Christopher. With a sprightly yet measured gait, his slightly wrinkled face and receding gray hair formed an impression of venerable dignity. He readily approached us, at once embracing Heather and smiling broadly at me. Heather introduced me to Father. After clasping my right hand with both of his, he placed his right hand on my left shoulder. What instantly struck me was the clarity and depth of his blue eyes, intense yet faraway.

Along with Ginny were her husband Tom and an unmarried couple in their mid-thirties, Stuart and Liz. Following our introductions, Heather and I sat on one of the two six-foot by nine-foot patterned wool rugs that covered the spacious living-room floor. Father Christopher disappeared into the kitchen area. I noticed a tray on a nearby coffee table, which contained herbal tea and assorted snacks, the type I call organic junk food. Ginny poured us all some tea. Then another car pulled up the driveway. Soon Brandon, a college-age man, appeared. The seven of us chatted in a friendly, subdued manner.

I learned that, before we arrived, Father had spoken of the need to elevate one's consciousness above the commotion of the world. His message: Don't get upset; don't allow situations to aggravate you; be patient; and never lose your poise. And never allow other people's actions to extinguish your love. Our topic then turned to spiritual life in the modern age.

Father Christopher reappeared. An unassuming man, he dressed casually in blue jeans, an off-white long-sleeve shirt, and sandals. He appeared thin and lanky, just over six feet tall. His voice was firm and confident; his motions, deliberate. He sat down in a well-worn, chestnut-brown fabric chair that faced us.

Father began, "I'm happy to see you all tonight." He spoke as intentionally as his movements, never hemming or hawing, although when he really became inspired he would sometimes articulate his streaming cavalcade of ideas in a kind of excitable shorthand.

He joined our conversation.

"Remember, spiritual life is now a democracy," he said. "We are indebted to the great religious traditions. We carry their influence into the present. But we are no longer beholden to follow every *single* mandate under their authority, as in centuries past. Not in this age. We have been liberated from certain constraints. For example, we are able to participate directly in the mystical experience, which is not just for a select few. If we attend formal worship services, we are now imbued with a newfound freedom unknown in the past.

"However, this does not include practicing or promoting spiritual anarchy, as some teachers advocate. And so, we are all the more bound to express this freedom in a responsible manner. It is incumbent on us to internalize the control that religions have historically exerted. Especially when following established religions. In this way, we strike a balance between obeying the obligations of the tradition and maintaining our independence. We thereby willingly adapt to certain conventions and observances, such as ceremonies and rites, rituals and initiations, but we do so consciously, not slavishly. That makes our freedom a gift, a privilege. Freedom on the one hand, and responsibly implementing that freedom on the other. What the Sufis call *tariqa*—following the path conscientiously. Or what the Tibetans refer to as *samaya*—a faithful commitment to one's spiritual journey.

"And why is this important? Because this age demands individual freedom. And psychological freedom. Freedom from some, but not all of the limitations imposed by outside authority. A self-directed autonomy. Possessing this kind of responsible freedom is the hallmark of an aspirant who is fully dedicated to the spiritual path. A path, mind you, not religious dogma! You can spout dogma ad nauseam, yet all it will make you is a well-trained parrot. In fact, you may reincarnate as a parrot! But, according to the Hindus, you'll have to spend many births regaining a human body, so you might as well do it right this time."

Liz asked, "Father, are you saying that established religions aren't necessary?"

Father replied, "Of course the established religions are necessary; they absolutely have their place. Much in the same way that traditions and institutions provide continuity to society. But for a spiritual aspirant who is walking the mystical path, superficially following the outer forms of religion can hinder one's progress and act like an adhesive strip that binds an insect. If one merely recites dogma, or if the outer customs and rituals of religion are observed at the expense of its mystical elements, religion loses its higher purpose. The word 'religion' is derived from the Latin *religāre*, which means 'to bind together,' 'to join.' The true purpose of religion is to join the soul to God, not bind a person to dogma. And this is accomplished by following the mystical path."

Father reached for a freshly poured cup of tea, courtesy of Ginny. He smiled, looked over at her, and said, "Thank you." Pausing after a sip, he continued, "Because this is a democracy, we all can participate."

Brandon, a dark-haired, bearded young Anglo sporting a Rasta hairstyle, who drove for more than two hours from his campus digs at Humboldt State University, spoke up. "I've been continuing my meditations. But sometimes my mind simply won't stop!" Others smiled and nodded in sympathy. "It races on and on, and I can never focus on what you said about stilling it."

Father, also smiling, responded. "The point is not to stupefy the mind. That you do when you visit the dentist and receive a healthy dose of nitrous oxide. Which you don't always mind!" Brandon and everyone laughed.

"Remember, the mind and its contents are part of the continuum of existence. They rise, then subside. Rise, then subside." Father made a wavelike motion with his hands. "The mind entertains different objects and undergoes different moods. The contents of the mind are always changing. They are never the same unless you are stuck in a groove. Which, by the way, most people are. Most people are living grooves.

"Two things must happen simultaneously. First, you must exhaust the contents of the mind. As you wax a car, the accumulated gunk comes off. What you are left with is the shiny protective sheen underneath. Second, you must transcend the mind's contents. Even if they aren't fully exhausted, they can be fully transcended. The danger here is transcending them and assuming they are exhausted. But they may actually be lurking in seed form, as Patanjali, the ancient author of the Yogasūtra, maintains. In which case the cord has not been cut; there still remains a tie. And ties are binding.

"Consequently, some spiritual teachers, especially those who are psychologically oriented, recommend ignoring the riffraff of the mind—the various moods, the mountains of memories, the endless inner chitchat. Don't get sucked into the whirlpool or you will drown!"

Tom commented, "I can only do that occasionally when I meditate. But even then, my mind drifts."

Father said, "That's the purpose of the *home object* as it's known in Theravada Buddhism. For those who are new, it's one of the tools we use that helps us to cross over, to transcend the insidious workings of the mind. Lose yourself in the home object, which is the focal point, the anchor, of your meditative efforts, while letting your mind steer its own course. By focusing exclusively on the home object— such as an image of a holy person, like Jesus, or a devotional phrase or scriptural passage—you won't even be aware of your mind, let alone its nonstop ramblings, which will eventually recede into a profound silence."

By using the phrase "home object," Father was not advocating a form of Buddhist meditation. He often used terms from different religions to describe various aspects of meditation and spirituality.

"But shouldn't I try to control my thoughts?" Brandon asked.

"Trying to control thoughts is like the boy putting his finger in the dike, frantically attempting to contain all the leaks. Let's say there are a hundred thoughts, emotions, and images swirling around in your mind. You sit down to meditate, and you want to take your spiritual cork and bottle up each of those thoughts, emotions, and images, one by one?

"The meditation process is one of evacuation. What goes in must come out. When all the stored mental crud starts to emerge, the worst thing you could do is suppress it and block the flow. With patience, allow it to come out, like a skilled midwife. First the water breaks, then the baby pops out. Only you will be giving birth to something of special value to you spiritually—your own liberation.

"So instead of attempting to control thoughts, try to concentrate on the home object. Focus your efforts *there*, and leave the mind alone. The thoughts will automatically subside when the state of concentration deepens. Over time, with continued practice, your accrued mental debris—ingrained personality traits, unconscious habit patterns, kneejerk emotional reactions, and unresolved psychological issues—will permanently begin to attenuate.

"Do I see some goodies on the table?"

At that point, the informal talk ended. I was secretly delighted, as my hand had begun aching from taking notes. Some in attendance partook of the snacks. Stuart and Liz followed Father into the kitchen and spoke with him in private, as I had learned that Father often met privately with attendees during breaks and after meetings to answer individual questions, provide personal instruction, and discuss their spiritual progress. The rest of us chatted about what he had discussed, much to my relief, instead of the pestilent gossip and worldly conversation that often follows such meetings. This was a giveaway to me that this group was serious.

So far, I was impressed: the attendees seemed intelligent; the leader advocated independence; he delivered his ideas with humor; and I heard references to Sufism, Buddhism, and Hinduism—all coming from a retired priest. Indeed, this man was living up to the word *catholic*.

After around ten minutes, we spontaneously reconvened at our previous places. Father sat down in his chair. As twilight was fast approaching, Ginny adjusted the two table lamps so the soft glow from their built-in nightlights illumined the room. Then she lit a single candle that was set on a simple corner altar containing several spiritual images, which were reverentially framed—Jesus, Buddha, the Star of David, Krishna, Lao Tzu, and a calligraphy print of a verse from the Koran, which translates as "Therefore remember Me, and I will remember you."[1]

Father then counseled us. "When we sit in silence, the important point is not to pay heed to the flow of thoughts and emotions. They lie in wait like an angler's baited hook. But you are a savvy fish, and you ignore the temptation to bite and continue swimming with the flow of the spiritual current. Soon you'll altogether transcend the workings of the mind and come to rest in your true nature, which is unalloyed peace and bliss. If you are using a home object, slowly introduce it into your mind, then focus on it. But remember, it is merely the outer wrapping. You open a package to find a Christmas present inside. Then you discard the wrapping paper."

So saying, Father Christopher fell silent. All of us began meditating. Before long, a tangible spiritual atmosphere filled the room. I'd only felt this powerful, deep energy, working its way from the inside out, in the presence of an extremely few spiritual beings I had met—the Dalai Lama, for example. Here it was overwhelming, and my mind effortlessly ceased to function. It was completely slam-dunked back into itself. Wow!

After what seemed to be a timeless period, a slight ringing sound was heard. Father ended our session by gently tapping a small meditation bowl. We had been sitting for thirty-five minutes before gradually coming back to "reality." Heather and I got up with the others and said goodbye to Father. As we left the assembly, I noticed I felt incredibly light. Not simply a peak emotional experience or the uplift one feels while on vacation, but a whirring of palpable spiritual energy coursing through my being.

On the drive back home, I asked Heather about Father's background. She explained that he was ordained a Catholic priest. At first, he was assigned to teach at a local high school, but he found it too restrictive to express the type of spirituality he felt called to practice. So he sought reassignment, then he got transferred and taught for a number of years at a university back east.

"He became an associate professor of religion," she continued. "He specialized in comparative religion. He chose not to promote to full professor, and from what I heard, he worked under a sympathetic department head who more or less left him alone. At one time in his life, he made a pilgrimage to the Mediterranean region and India. He went to Jerusalem and toured all the holy sites. He studied with a Sufi shaykh in Turkey who gave him the name *al-Khiḍr*, which means a universal teacher in Sufi lore. He spent time at an Eastern Orthodox monastery in Greece. I heard that he visited Ramana Maharshi and Sri Aurobindo while in India. He may have gone to Nepal as well. During the Sixties, he was involved with the Civil Rights and Antiwar movements. Then he retired from both positions in the 1970s, moved back to California, and has lived here reclusively ever since. We still call him Father, although he doesn't actively perform any priestly duties. You could ask Ginny, but you may not find out much more."

Back at Heather's, we sat on opposite chairs in a room bathed in gentle light. Heather, thankfully sharing the same retro-musical tastes as me, played all of *Blue*, side one of *Harvest*, then side two of *Abbey Road* as the night wore on. We caught up on our lives and discussed our meeting with Father Christopher earlier that evening. We talked past midnight, then bade each other goodnight before retiring to our respective rooms.

God and God Alone

The following day, I prepared and downed my usual meal of steamed organic vegetables for breakfast, which worked well for me at the time, while Heather munched on her granola. She then headed for town to run a couple of errands. I drove up the road to a nearby trailhead where I hiked for a few hours near a small creek. Sword fern and salmonberry grew along its banks. Even now I recall the musty forest-earth fragrance which permeated the air that day.

Later, Heather and I again drove to Father Christopher's, as he planned to hold another meeting, which he normally didn't do on Sundays. I learned that several regulars could not attend last night's gathering, so they arranged to be present this evening. There was no fog, so as we drove along we witnessed a very pregnant sun descending over the ocean, which we found exhilarating.

"Have you ever seen the green flash?" I asked.

"The green what?" Heather replied.

"When the sun sets across the horizon, there's a moment—a split second—just as it disappears from view, when it gives off a distinct green flash, which is caused by some atmospheric phenomenon."

"How cool! Have you ever seen it?"

"Once. South of Monterey along the coast. I've looked for it several times since, but I've never seen it again."

We pulled onto Father's property. In addition to the three cars I recognized from last night, we spotted two more on this night. We approached the screen door and entered his cabin. Father acknowledged us and invited us to sit. He was already speaking.

"You see, there are two types of gurus or spiritual teachers—those who empower and those who enslave. There are those among the former who are respectable and reputable. But as many of you know, I frown on self-styled 'gurus.' Some of them act more like autocratic cult leaders than illumined sages who can truly help you. Beyond that, everyone has the potential to awaken their own inner guru, so to speak. But only if they want God badly enough. If a person musters up all their passion and directs it toward God, they will be guided from within. God takes those with the most intense yearning by the hand, as it were, and leads them to himself.

"Yet we are sometimes assisted by someone from the outside who activates the Divine within us. Not a spiritual babysitter, mind you, nor a spiritual dictator. But someone who holds a mirror right up to our face and shows us that what we are seeking is right *here*." Father pointed to his heart. "Someone who quietly works to liberate rather than control us. Someone who fosters independence, not a childish dependency. If you meet such a person, you will feel an intimacy, a bond with them that's hard to pin down. They will know your soul like the back of your hand. And you will feel like you have known them all your life. Those are the signs.

"And that's the true teacher—you own spiritual essence appearing in external form. But not the form! Otherwise, it becomes yet another addiction. It's then another way the mind latches on to something external. Another place outside of one's own soul where a person invests hope and the elusive promise of salvation."

All absorbed Father's cautionary words, including Heather and me, who sat next to each other.

"That's why the Zen Buddhists have a most apt saying, 'If you meet the Buddha on the road, kill him!' This is utter blasphemy to orthodox Buddhists. Imagine saying to a Christian, 'If you meet Jesus on the road, kill him!'" (Father murmured to himself, barely audible, "Which in fact occurred ...")

He continued, "But, metaphorically speaking, this is the absolute truth. Anything external to your inner spiritual essence is but a ruse. God resides *within* you, as Jesus emphasized.[2] Looking outward

10

for spiritual illumination is the mind's pernicious attempt to postpone embracing the genuine path, which is wholly internal. And it can postpone this encounter for scores of lifetimes, if you believe in reincarnation. So, you must not become attached to any teacher with whom you study. It's what they teach that matters most.

"Moreover, it's best to make a concerted effort to complete your spiritual journey as soon as possible in *this* lifetime, lest laziness sets in and you become complacent, which will immediately halt your progress. So, don't squander your most valuable asset in this life, which is time. And the most valuable use of your time is the time you spend pursuing enlightenment."

Brandon jumped in. "I understand what you are saying about gurus. But gurus are supposed to be representatives of God, which is why people worship them."

"Provided the guru is genuine! There was a time in the 1970s when I picked up a New Age publication. I believe I counted no less than fourteen *avatars*—incarnations of God, according to Hinduism—vying for my allegiance. Not to mention my money! They all had display ads of some sort. Some undoubtedly had an enrollment plan. Which serves as a perfect example of how hustlers had overridden the spiritual scene.

"Now, if you are able to discern a genuine teacher among the plethora of self-professed 'masters' that are littering the spiritual landscape, all the more power to you. They certainly exist, but they must be sought using methods other than commercial means. Especially when a duke's mixture of third- and fourth-rate hucksters crop up, all shamelessly promoting themselves, their practices, and sometimes each other. Then a celebrity or some other influential person jumps on the bandwagon, lending superficial yet false credence by endorsing these charlatans. Then the masses are truly lost, following the false teachers like lemmings to their own spiritual destruction."

Stuart remarked, "You said to use methods that aren't commercial. What methods do you mean?"

"Let's first discuss the commercial ones. When advertising agencies bombard us with commercials to purchase products, they gain our attention and sometimes our patronage. This is a form of manipulation, a type of psychological coercion. They create a need that did not previously exist. Or else they magnify an existing need. Advertising conditions us to behave in certain ways, and it works.

"Many so-called spiritual teachers who come crawling out of the woodwork are nothing more than sophisticated marketers. They prey on human vulnerabilities. They exploit human needs. They use marketing techniques to attract followers. They have a product to sell—the allure of spiritual liberation—and the vulnerable, needy masses are a prime target. And so, the unwary multitudes fall for these advertising methods. Out pop their wallets and they purchase their hope, much in the same way a person buys Pepto Bismol to alleviate a stomachache. In my opinion, these manipulators comprise the bulk of popular "spiritual" teachers these days. This situation is nothing short of deplorable.

"But there is an entirely different type of spiritual teacher, one who shuns the limelight and bypasses the ordinary commercial means to attract disciples. If you are fortunate enough to be led by the grace of God to such a spiritual teacher, ideally one who is illumined or at least highly advanced, they will help you unfold your spiritual essence. Just don't settle for a shallow teacher who has no familiarity with the deeper mystical states. And don't prematurely give up your search. If your aspiration runs deep, you will find what you seek, exactly as Jesus had promised.[3] This is the noncommercial means to find a genuine spiritual teacher, tried and tested over the centuries: your soul must cry out for God and God alone. By so doing, you will lay the groundwork for a qualified teacher to appear."

~~~~~~~~~~~~~~

Three additional attendees joined the seven of us who had gathered last night. Huddled in a corner sat two younger women, Erin and Marta, close friends and housemates. Both co-owned and managed a wholesale fuchsia nursery on Highway 1 (where some months afterward I stopped by, and they generously gifted me with a potted Dark Eyes variety to bring home to my retired father, who was especially fond of fuchsias). And there was another man, Bill, in his mid-forties, who had a professorial look about him. I subsequently learned he worked as an accountant. He, along with one or two others, occasionally took notes of Father's talks.

Heather later told me that Bill experienced a somewhat rude awakening on his first visit to see Father. He gleefully bragged that he was reading one of the popular books on spirituality from that era. Father asked him about it. Bill attempted to explain the kinds of teachings it contained. But Father was not impressed. Apparently, he characterized the teachings as faddish, superficial, and commercially oriented.

Bill made the mistake of responding, protesting rather agitatedly and defensively, "I spent a lot of good money on their study materials and seminars!"

Father replied, "I rest my case. I've seen similar types of teachings make the rounds every decade or so. They often attract hordes of followers, typically rabidly dogmatic minions, akin to a cult. The teachings are characteristically a mishmash of genuine spirituality and gobbledygook. Invariably, a highly profitable industry springs up around them, which serves to line the pockets of the elite few who spearhead the movement.

"Look, any number of things can make you feel inspired for a while, but very few teachings can cause you to become enlightened. A permanent transformation is needed, not a temporary lift or a touchy-feely sort of mood enhancement, or jazzing yourself intellectually with pseudo-inspirational platitudes. Don't keep inflating a punctured tire then driving on it. Purchase a brand-new tire!"

Heather said that after a few months' absence, Bill returned to Father's meetings, but he never again brought up the topic.

~~~~~~~~~~

Father continued, "I encourage you to see things for what they really are. If you but once look at anything clearly, directly, without judgment or emotion, you will see the truth of that situation. This is the idea behind Buddhist Vipassana meditation, whereby practitioners engage in mindful, insightful observation. You can use all the events in your life to see clearly once you get your mind out of the way. By so doing, you will weed out whatever hypocrisy exists within you. Because right now you are two people: the you who screens everything through the filter of your emotions and prejudices, and the real you—your soul or spiritual self—which is buried under all that. When you eliminate the bogus you, what is left is the real you. And when there is only one you, there can be no hypocrisy, because hypocrisy must have two 'yous' in order to exist."

13

Erin asked, "How can we progress spiritually while living in the world?"

"The answer is simple. Look on every incident in your life as an instrument you can use to transform yourself. At present, you view the world through secular lenses. Tear off these worldly glasses to spiritualize all you see! You thereby transmute the contaminated to the pure, the mundane to the sacred, and the unrefined to the polished. If you can do this, you will come to feel a detached, unconditional love toward everything you now dislike.

"At the same time, detach yourself from your past. Pray a heartfelt prayer, seeking grace and mercy from the particular form of God you worship. Express remorse for any hurtful actions you have at any time intentionally, or unintentionally, committed in the past. As the prophet Ezekiel counsels, 'Cast away from yourselves all the transgressions you have ever committed, and make for yourselves a new heart and a new spirit.'⁴ Then release the memories of your past deeds and mentally divest yourself of everything you've ever accumulated by symbolically offering it to God. In this way, you let go of your attachment to all things. They will have served their purpose."

Father returned to his previous topic. "And so, you must always look at the reality of any given situation. When you can see clearly without blinders, without burying your head, which is what we usually do, then you will be free from the influence of your mind. You now filter your perception through a thousand needs, wants, and emotional reactions—all of which place an impediment between reality and you. Once freed from this filtering process, you will no longer be governed by attachments and aversions—the twin banes of human existence—in reality, two sides of one coin. In a flash, in the twinkling of an eye, you can rise above the drama in which you're living and attain a radical state of consciousness. Just like the green flash we sometimes see at sundown."

Heather and I looked at each other in astonishment.

"But it typically never happens that way," Father said. "While I'm convinced a person can experience illumination in one hundred days if they want it badly enough, spiritual unfoldment generally occurs over time. The mind is like a thicket of thorny weeds that must be slowly pruned until a tidy lawn is revealed underneath. Once

14

you've cut away the outer layers of debris from your mind, which are composed of random thoughts and a Pandora's Box of unruly emotions, then you'll be able to see the core of your being, where you'll find nothing but God."

Karma and Destiny

Father further observed, "Yes, that's what you undergo during spiritual practice—an intense purgation of emotions, all kinds of emotions. There is fear, greed, anger, despair, as well as hope, generosity, patience, and joy. Happiness and sorrow, love and hate, gratitude and spite—all swirl around inside you like a kaleidoscope. All these emotions, which are composed of various attachments and aversions, must come out. They are part of one's karma, which is deeply embedded in the mind.

"Do you all understand what I mean by 'karma'?"

A few nodded.

"Karma is a Sanskrit word meaning 'action.' Basically, it's a Hindu theory that parallels the law of cause and effect. Recall the words of St. Paul, 'Whatever you sow, that you will reap.'[5] Karma is fundamentally a doctrine of predetermination. It applies both individually and collectively. On a personal level, karma is the sum total of all we are: the cumulative result of every one of our thoughts, emotions, words, and deeds. One's karma continually manifests in the present and in the future. Any action based in an emotional, reactive frame of mind is a karma-producing action. Any thought based in desire, anger, or fear is a karma-producing thought.

"As with many technical terms, karma includes several specialized shades of meanings. It has no exact equivalent English word. In certain contexts, karma can be used interchangeably with 'destiny,' and sometimes with 'God's will,' especially when signifying predestination. Only it's hard to convince people that adversity stems from God's will. The words 'karma' and 'destiny' don't strike the raw nerve that 'God's will' seems to. On the other hand, if you use too many Eastern terms, they dismiss you as a pagan or, heaven forbid, a polytheist! That's why I typically use the word 'destiny' when describing one's unalterable fate.

"Are there any more questions?"

No one spoke up.

"Very well. The effects of a person's karma can't be loosened and purged overnight. They linger like sticky molasses. That's what spiritual practice is for—to loosen and untie one's spiritual self from the knots of one's karma, and to expel the accumulated karmic residue by way of catharsis. This is why practice is so important. As Jesus asserted, 'Whoever hears these words of mine and puts them into practice is like a wise man who builds his house upon a rock.'⁶ Diligent and dedicated practice is the foundation of spirituality.

"Each person has their own individual means of catharsis, unique to their disposition. Some purge this inner debris silently, as it were, and some more boisterously. For example, some people may experience periods of irritability, while others undergo crying spells. Vivid, unpleasant images from the past may race through some people's minds, which might cause them to recoil in aversion, while others may experience restless meditations for days on end— the dry spells we read about. A vibrant stream of long-forgotten memories will often appear out of nowhere and drift through one's mind. All these experiences, which are at times similar to the inner trials reported by Christian mystics, hinge on each person's innate temperament and the karmic baggage they carry.

"The purgations usually comes in waves, over a period of time, depending on the intensity of one's spiritual practice. There are different strata of cleansings, ranging from relatively minor ones that result in the curtailing of a particular habitual reaction, to larger ones that address more deep-seated traits, such as eliminating longstanding, unproductive personality patterns and behaviors. Furthermore, each person's inner makeup is revealed by what is churned up through their spiritual practice. What has gone in must come out, be it positive, negative, peaceful, agitating, or any combination thereof."

There was dead silence in the room, not even a fidgety leg movement. Father's somewhat weathered face was fully animated. He simultaneously embodied the spirit of a playful boy and that of a wise old man. As he spoke, he glanced out into the room. He frequently made eye contact with each of us, and when his eyes met mine it felt as though nothing else existed.

"Spiritual practice thus facilitates the expulsion of one's storehouse of karma. On the psychological level, this storehouse consists of our various moods, personality traits, emotional reactions, and ingrained preferences—all of which obscure one's perception of their soul. Transcending the influence of one's karma is one of the main objectives in spiritual life. Your practice chisels away and loosens this accrued inner muck, which eventually gets discharged. This liberates the spiritual self from the obscuring effect it produces. This is why certain practices involving bodily movement, such as walking meditation, most commonly used in Theravada and Zen Buddhism, or vocal *zikr*, a form of devotional chanting used by certain Sufi groups, are so useful—they provide a cathartic means to release this debris by dissipating it on the physical level. But keep in mind, the karmic seeds are not always destroyed. They can sprout again."

Father paused, gazed across the room, then asked a second time, "Are there any additional questions or comments?"

After a moment I piped up, "Father Christopher, you said earlier that a person could realize God in one hundred days." Father's comment had resurrected memories of my own spiritual awakening in 1974, which lasted around one hundred days before waning. "Is this really possible?"

"Of course! 'With God all things are possible.'[7] But remember, most people don't want God. They want a comfortable, nonthreatening religion that sanctions what they *really* want—prosperity, worldly happiness, a satisfying career, a fulfilling family life ... and lots of possessions. Evidently some people also want a religion that sanctions prejudice, hatred, and war, and there are plenty such religious factions. Mind you, none of the worldly aspirations I mentioned— happiness, family life, prosperity, and so forth—are detrimental to one's spiritual life, provided a person doesn't become attached to them. These are all legitimate goals according to Hinduism. Except, I should add, for accruing possessions, which is not sanctioned in any sacred literature, except the sacred literature of capitalism. As Jesus observed, 'A person's life does not consist in the abundance of their possessions.'[8] You won't find God when you're lost in the labyrinth of worldly pursuits.

"Or else people make a hobby of religion. They become religious groupies. They go from sermon to sermon, ritual to ritual, ceremony to ceremony, hoping that something—anything—will happen. These people will never achieve enlightenment because they don't actually want it. They want to be entertained, nothing more.

"But the mystical path is personal, interior, private. Jesus said, 'When you pray, go into your room and shut the door and pray to your Father, who is in secret.'[9] A genuine aspirant will cultivate an inner relationship with God that is hidden from public view. And if they *adamantly, resolutely, and fervently* want God more than any- thing else, why, this in theory could happen in the twinkling of an eye. As Brother Lawrence pointed out, 'The shortest way to go straight to Him [is] by a continual exercise of love and doing all things for His sake.'[10] But the process of unraveling the inner karmic knots and refining the nervous system so it can sustain the higher states of realization typically takes place over time. In the Tibetan Buddhist tradition, one doesn't attain a 'rainbow body' in a day. Still, with this kind of intense yearning, the expulsion of one's mental de- bris rapidly intensifies. I guarantee you, when compared to eternity, one hundred days is nothing!

"Any more questions?"

No one came forward, so he continued.

"The greatest enemies to spiritual progress are fear, doubt, lack of faith, compromising to others, and conforming to the world's de- mands. Those are our weak points, and we feed them constantly each and every day. In reality, most of our problems originate from these shortcomings. St. Paul rightly declared, 'Do not be conformed to this world.'[11] You sell your integrity or compromise your soul for other people's sake because you fear various repercussions. Just re- flect for a moment and you will see this is the cause of many of your negative encounters in life. Or else you are overly concerned about how you think others will perceive you. All these factors act as im- pediments on your road to spiritual freedom. In fact, that's what you are trying to regain so desperately—your inner freedom. You have become a slave to others and a slave to your own emotions, espe- cially fear. Now you are trying to liberate yourself; specifically, your spiritual self. That's what spiritual practice is—self-liberation:

freeing your spiritual self from the clutches of duality. And so, to again cite St. Paul, 'Put on the new self, created to be like God ...' "[12]

Father again paused, "Okay, let's break."

Break we did, but there was little talk. I was already finding that whenever Father presented a new thought or, as he did tonight, a chain of similar thoughts, it sunk in. It was as though a new furrow were being etched in a deep part of my being. What's more, it was as though my mind were absorbing a picture, a photographic imprint of Father's underlying message, which was being conveyed on a level entirely other than words.

After a few minutes Father resumed speaking. "When meditating," he counseled, "try to focus on the home object, whether it be your breath, your heartbeat, a scriptural passage, or an image of a spiritual being whom you admire and with whom you feel an affinity, such as Jesus or Buddha. Just so it appeals to you and captures your entire attention. This will help you concentrate your mind so it won't wander and think of other things.

"It's also helpful to center your awareness in your spiritual heart when you meditate." (One's spiritual heart is located in the center of one's chest.) "When one is meditating, the Bhagavad Gita advises to 'focus the mind within the heart.'[13] The noted Sufi poet ʿAṭṭār recommends that a person 'seek for Reality within your own heart, for Reality, in truth, is hidden within you. The heart is the dwelling-place of that which is the Essence of the universe ...'[14] In addition, devotion to God or a spiritual being will exponentially benefit your practice and allow you to feel such an intimacy with the Divine that all your earthly concerns will melt away. So, let us invoke God's blessings and begin."

Following the same routine as the previous night, we sat and meditated just over half an hour. It was already becoming clear to me that meditations in this group, in Father's presence, were virtually effortless, as though he were meditating for us, or more precisely, as though his personal meditation were engulfing us, as if he had spread a spiritual net that caught us all. Regardless of how this occurred, it was a gift.

~~~~~~~~~~~~

By this time, I had formed a distinct impression of Father's meetings. Sitting in his company was like attending a festival of joy.

His great talent lay in transmitting a tangible atmosphere of happiness that swept over those around him. All were lifted from their cares and taken on a voyage far removed from their worldly concerns. Our daily troubles simply disappeared.

Father had an optimistic and upbeat outlook that complemented his razor-like intellect. He was always animated—quite vivacious—and he enthusiastically conveyed his various topics. His spontaneous joyfulness, subtle humor, and carefree, confident attitude proved contagious. Many in attendance would freely smile. We frequently laughed at his witty comments or when exchanging rapid-fire repartee with him. No one ever departed in a sad mood. We were transported to another realm altogether.

~~~~~~~~~~~~~~

After meditation, Heather and I took our leave from Father and the others. She drove us home, and following some small talk, we crashed in our rooms. The next day was a Monday, and after waking early and wolfing down breakfast, I hastily gathered my possessions before hugging Heather goodbye, petting Snowcap on his snow-white crown, and setting off to return to my simple two-bedroom apartment in Ukiah. Fortunately, my work shift on Monday mornings began at ten o'clock.

Over the next few weeks, I labored at my undistinguished job as office manager at a local medical-supply company. I earned enough money to pay the bills, but good God, what if I ever wanted to retire? I had avoided a stable profession like the plague, but as I grew older I developed a subtle envy of my peers, who had over the years forged steady careers for themselves that were replete with generous benefits and the promise of a secure retirement.

SECOND VISIT (October 1990)

Tibetan Buddhism, The Divine Presence

MY NEXT VISIT to Father Christopher took place a few months later. This time I drove the long way to the coast—southwest along Highway 253 to Boonville, then northwest along the Anderson Valley Highway toward Little River. This was the scenic route, made all the more picturesque by noticeable hints of the seasonal turn of colors, which framed many passing landscapes in a Currier & Ives–like portraiture. I stopped to buy some organic heirloom apples at a stand near Philo before heading over to Highway 1, then continued north to Fort Bragg to stay with Heather, who would again provide shelter.

I arrived in the late morning on a Saturday. Heather was staging an afternoon get-together with some of Father's regulars. When we convened, I again was pleasantly surprised to find none of the gossipy socializing or business-related networking I'd often witnessed in other spiritual groups. Equally objectionable is when the lonely look to spiritual meetings as a surrogate singles bar. Such worldly purposes only serve to trivialize the higher spiritual bond I'd often seen develop among members of such gatherings. This group was indeed different.

All of us drove to Mendocino for an early dinner at one of the local restaurants, and we surprisingly got decent seats without a prior reservation. The eatery was located upstairs alongside a street lined with several quaint boutique shops that catered to tourists. As there was no fog to be seen, we managed to secure a commanding view of the Pacific Ocean. We enjoyed a delectable meal. The home-made natural Dutch Crunch bread was a treat. Then off we caravanned, driving nearly thirty minutes up the highway to Father's modest cabin.

We all arrived at once, and Father, dressed in a pair of gray pants and a navy long-sleeve flannel shirt, warmly greeted us. He seemed happy to see me again, and he playfully tugged at the new, neatly trimmed circle-style beard I sported, which was fashionable facial wear at the time. Heather and I and a few others took our places on the patterned woolen throw rugs that covered the floor, while some used the black zafu cushions that were stored in a corner. Bathed in the subdued off-white glow from the softly lit table lamps, which accented the cabin's solid beams and knotty wooden planks, the group of us made ourselves at home in Father's large, though sparsely furnished front room. Spacious windows surrounded this area and provided views of the driveway and nearby vegetation. Perhaps three hundred books, mostly on religion and philosophy, were stacked inside short bookcases that lined two of the walls. I could best describe the ambience of that room, which would become an incubator of sorts for me, as warm, rustic, and cozy.

Brandon struck up a conversation with Father about Tibetan Buddhism. I listened in as Father spoke. "I agree, the idea of *terma* is entirely Tibetan. According to their tradition, it specifically refers to the so-called mind treasures that the legendary teacher Padmasambhava and his consort concealed for discovery in later times. Those mind treasures are actually spiritual teachings, which are said to be precisely adapted to the times and culture in which they are revealed. I don't dispute that idea one bit. I would only add that the concept behind terma—that of adapting spiritual teachings to the proclivities, needs, and aptitude of a given contemporary society—is not limited to Tibet."

Brandon quipped, "In addition to following Tibetan Buddhism, I've taken courses in *kundalini* yoga."

"Well, that certainly is an interesting combination."

"It seems to work for me."

Father observed, "Tibetan Buddhism is a remarkable and mysterious religion. I'm somewhat conversant with several of its main approaches. Its inner disciplines include a wide array of very powerful and, from what I could determine, effective spiritual practices.

"Just remember, when you follow this path, make sure your intentions are pure, and stay focused on enlightenment. Some aspirants become fascinated with tales of miracles by Tibetan yogis. They may have read accounts of high-speed Himalayan runners, known as *lung-gom-pa*, as well as Tibetan yogis flying through the air. Such stories often serve as justification for these adherents to develop and use psychic powers so they can perform miracles themselves. However, this fascination with miracles can occur with any religion.

"In fact, we see examples of miracles in most religions. In the Jewish tradition, we need look no further than Moses. Jesus, of course, is the archetypal miracle-worker in Christianity, and Catholicism positively touts the saints it has deemed as proven to have performed miracles. Russian Orthodoxy has its *starets*. Advanced Sufis are reported to dematerialize and rematerialize at will. In his Yogasūtra, Patanjali outlines numerous psychic powers that can be developed. Elsewhere in Hinduism, we read of evolved *siddhas*. There are also firewalkers, snake charmers and, among certain Pentecostals, snake handlers.

"The problem is that many people confuse spiritual advancement with the ability to manifest psychic powers. While such powers can be seen by some as a benchmark of accomplishment, in my view they are to be categorically shunned because they only fortify the ego. If these powers spontaneously occur without your consciously cultivating them, or if you attain to the same level of spirituality as Jesus and then God tells you to perform miracles, so be it. But the only miracle I advise you to perform is the miracle of attaining your own enlightenment. Otherwise, you will get side-tracked by the lure of developing psychic powers, and you'll quickly lose your spiritual focus.

"You may recall that Jesus performed miracles only to convince the skeptical: 'Unless you people see signs and wonders, you will never believe.'[15] Patanjali warned that psychic powers are obstacles to the attainment of spiritual union.[16] In Hasidism, advanced *tsaddiks* are said to perform miracles, but the most advanced among them recommend against this practice.

"Let's say you were to go down this road and become a well-known psychic. When you stand before the Pearly Gates, St. Peter will say to you, 'My child, what were you thinking? You wasted your time on earth learning how to read other people's minds, but all the while you remained a miserly, selfish rogue. You could have spent that same time cultivating love and compassion and developing a generous, giving heart.' So, if you really want to see miracles performed, I suggest watching a religious movie.

"In addition, the goal in Tibetan Buddhism, as is the case with most Mahayana Buddhist lineages, is not so much personal liberation but to become a *bodhisattva,* a being of pure compassion whose purpose is to liberate other beings. This undoubtedly is a noble goal, as is the Buddhist precept to love everyone equally, which Buddhists call *mettā* or lovingkindness, and which is synonymous with Jesus' instruction to 'love one another.'[17]

"But from another perspective, it can be the very height of egotism for any spiritual aspirant to presume they can liberate others. This is because, without proper training, it's actually one's ego that thinks it possesses the ability to liberate. When this occurs, such practitioners could end up creating more karma for themselves and for the poor beings whom they are attempting to liberate, who may in fact be better off without their intervention! Instead of trying to liberate others, a more practical approach for aspiring bodhisattvas would be to cultivate an *attitude of total selflessness* by placing others' welfare above their own, so much so that they get their ego entirely out of the way. Changing one's attitude is an achievable goal that would serve as a pragmatic means to help them attain this same objective, but without inflating their ego.

"Ideally, those aspirants intending to become bodhisattvas should be completely inconspicuous because they are striving to be egoless. When helping others, they ought to work quietly without calling attention to themselves. Because of their training, they should be inherently programmed to serve, sympathize with, and uplift others on account of their selfless words and acts of support and encouragement. In short, their entire focus should be on others. This should in fact be the ideal of any spiritual practitioner, not just bodhisattvas-in-training. By emphasizing others before themselves, such aspirants can quickly deflate their ego. And, as a byproduct of their selflessness, they spiritually benefit themselves."

Bill related the following. "I knew one would-be bodhisattva practitioner who wore their aspiring bodhisattvahood like it was some kind of badge of honor."

Father replied, "This can occur in any religious tradition. It's a kind of spiritual snobbishness. Those who proclaim themselves bodhisattvas or saints, or, more subtly, exude an air of superiority because of their spiritual practices, are either egomaniacs or exhibitionists. Has anyone ever read of St. Francis using a megaphone and declaring himself a saint? All the same, you can and should aspire to become a saint, but any would-be saint or bodhisattva must, by definition, be self-effacing, anonymous, and free from pride. Aspiring bodhisattvas and saints should train to become silent beacons of unconditional love and solace, not draw attention to themselves. They should never seek credit for their tireless, selfless work. To credit oneself with any degree of stature in one's spiritual unfoldment is one of the principal snares of the ego, and a telltale sign that one has gotten nowhere on their spiritual journey.

"It is also sheer conceit to think yourself superior to those who don't follow the spiritual path. This is merely another form of elitism. Moreover, it is out-and-out arrogance to proclaim that yours is the *only* path, yours is the *only* realization, which are hallmarks of blind fanaticism. However, with proper training, you'll avoid these traps. Ideally, you'll be taught to employ selfless love as a means to attain liberation, but without your ego getting in the way. Thus, your intentions will be principled and focused. At the end of the day, short of attaining illumination itself, it's an aspirant's intentions and actions that count the most on their road to enlightenment.

"So, I would simply counsel you to maintain the purest of intentions and proceed vigilantly on this path, because if not properly followed it can perpetuate and not eliminate your ego. As a high-ranking Tibetan lama once told me, the surest way to benefit others spiritually is to become enlightened yourself."

Father switched topics, addressing Brandon. "As for kundalini yoga, you must ask yourself what you're attempting to accomplish. In the context of this particular path, it is called the awakening of the kundalini. An entire branch of study in Hinduism called Tantra deals with this subject. The Hindu system has three schools, hence three pathways to liberation, which utilize techniques ranging from external to internal. The Tibetans incorporated the Hindu Tantra teachings into certain of their practices, although each approach has its differences. Both systems attempt, through mental visualizations, to generate, then transmute the sensation that we commonly experience as eros into a blissful, all-encompassing realization. However, this transmutation can and does occur in other religious traditions."

Brandon added, "Yes, I see many similarities, too, only the Tibetans don't always give credit to the Hindus."

Father smiled. "No, I don't suppose they would. But they have good cause. Tibetan Buddhism, along with a few mystical traditions, such as some schools within Sufism, Hinduism, and Orthodox Christianity, are carriers of living lineages. And so, they tend to become insular to protect the integrity of their teachings, and rightfully so.

"However, back to our topic. Suffice it to say that kundalini is a Sanskrit term meaning the profound spiritual energy that is said to lie dormant within us all. This energy is completely different from what the Hindus refer to as *prana*, which is the focus of hatha yoga. Prana is considered the energy that animates our psychophysical organism and fills us with vitality. It's equivalent to *chi* in the Taoist tradition. Kundalini, on the other hand, acts as a powerful vibratory, transformational current that scintillatingly engulfs us, tangibly courses through our being, and infuses our spirit with a blissful patina. It can manifest on both gross and subtle levels.

"Prana is immanent—associated with the body—whereas kundalini is transcendent—associated with the spiritual self. There is no concept similar to kundalini in the English language. I refer to kundalini simply as 'the divine Presence.' It is akin to *Shekhinah* in Kabbalistic Judaism and the Holy Spirit in Christian doctrine. And, just like the workings of the Holy Spirit, it opens up a whole new dimension of spirituality. When forcefully awakened, it produces many undesirable physical effects, which are well documented in the literature."

Stuart then asked, "If that's the case, then what's the best way to awaken it?"

"It's always best roused from dormancy as an unintended but very much welcomed side effect of devotional exercises and meditation. Trying to awaken the kundalini or divine Presence in and of itself by using external means, such as breathing exercises, physical or sexual practices, yogic postures and the like, is tantamount to putting the cart before the horse. These techniques may partially work, or they may work for a time, but they cannot permanently rewire the inner structure of your mind and thereby aid in transforming your innermost nature. If these techniques are used, it is best for a person eventually to wean off them, viewing them as temporary aids, like using training wheels on a bicycle.

"If you instead focus your efforts on realizing God through more subtle internal means, such as devotion and meditation, this intense spiritual energy will awaken of its own accord without your conscious effort, conferring on you an astounding multidimensional realization without all the unwanted physical manifestations. The divine Presence can also be roused from its dormant state through association with and blessings from advanced teachers, but this presupposes much preliminary purificatory work by the practitioner in order to effectively assimilate it. Otherwise, it's like plugging a 110-volt lamp into a 220-volt outlet."

"Father, what's it like once the divine Presence is awakened?" Ginny asked.

"According to the mystics, it's like nothing we've ever experienced. When induced by either of these means—inner practices or evolved teachers—this spiritual energy imparts a distinctive kind of joy and sustained ecstasy, often accompanied by subtle blissful inner tremblings. These sensations belong to a whole other plane of refinement, entirely different from what is produced through forceful awakening. One's soul is bathed in a sweet, expansive calmness that radiates from within, as if supplied from an interior generator. A wondrous, wonderful, palpable feeling of joyful peace pervades every fiber of the aspirant's being."

Following a brief pause, Father continued, "I should note this same 'cart before the horse' principle I spoke of earlier can also apply to hatha yoga. While some stretching postures are beneficial to help keep the spine limber and the muscles supple, to view this practice as a purely spiritual path is farcical. Many hatha yoga teachings go no further than shoring up one's physical wellbeing. They are completely lifted out of context from Patanjali's eight-limbed Yoga system, where they are merely a lower component.

"Has anyone heard of Patanjali?"

Stuart and I and one or two others raised our hands.

"Together with Buddha, Patanjali is considered a pioneer of India-based methodical meditation systems. He codified a sophisticated inner regimen consisting of four progressive stages of heightened spiritual consciousness that hatha yoga advocates do not always emphasize, which I'll outline.

"First, when a practitioner sits for meditation, they turn their mind inward by repeatedly focusing on one object until the mind becomes concentrated. Second, concentration is achieved when the mind becomes calm and is not swayed by wandering thoughts and distractions. Third, once concentration is stabilized, it consolidates into true meditation, at which point the mind becomes unwaveringly still and void of all thoughts for a protracted period. Maintaining this extended state of prolonged interior silence is the quintessential element of meditation. Fourth, and finally, the practitioner subtly dissolves their sense of identity until all self-awareness is obliterated. At that stage, they remain immersed in an ever-deepening state of nondual consciousness, which is impossible to describe." (The Sanskrit terms for these four stages are *pratyāhāra*, turning the mind inward; *dhāraṇa*, one-pointed concentration; *dhyāna*, uninterrupted meditation; and *samadhi*, deep indrawn absorption.) "This sublime practice is a far cry from standing on one's head!

"When yoga postures are used as ends in themselves, solely for health and longevity, they become watered-down practices because they are cut off from a higher, transcendent aim. Whereas a dedicated spiritual aspirant will only harness such exercises to augment their core internal practices, for example meditation and devotion, which they use for the sole purpose of higher realization, nothing more. Again, it is best to direct your energies toward attaining God and not become sidetracked by all these technical methods, which will not get you any closer to God."

Brandon admitted, "Well, I do hatha yoga, too. Are you saying I should give it up?"

Father smiled. "Not at all. I would, however, counsel you to put it in perspective. It is certainly desirable to conserve and increase your vital energy to assist in your meditation efforts. Undertaking spiritual practice presupposes an aspirant has at their disposal a tremendous amount of energy, which is needed to fuel their growing state of enlightenment. If you eat indiscriminately, numb yourself with drugs or alcohol—or drugs *and* alcohol—overindulge sexually, seldom exercise, or deplete yourself in various ways, including overwork and not getting enough sleep, you are draining your energy reserves. You thereby prevent your body from serving as a refined conduit that can express the subtler states of consciousness. The same is true with overindulging in worldly activities, which not only drains you like a sieve, but diverts your spiritual focus. All these activities tend to dull the mind and weaken the body."

I commented, "It's not always easy to maintain our spiritual focus while we're involved with the world."

"This is why the Buddha taught the Middle Path. You are all living in the world with jobs and schooling, sometimes families, and similar obligations. But first and foremost, you are spiritual aspirants, and your spiritual life is your topmost priority. So, you not only need to walk that fine line whereby you can maintain your spiritual focus while you live your secular life, but you also need to avoid overextending your worldly involvements so you don't get caught up in all sorts of minutiae that drag you away from your spiritual pursuits."

Father resumed his main topic. "In the course of your spiritual strivings, the divine Presence will come to permeate every fiber of your being. This reaches very subtle areas, which none of the mechanical hatha yoga postures could ever access. The inner spiritual practices, such as prayer, devotion, concentration, and meditation, especially when combined, act as a forceful integral process, affecting your entire constitution. They cut through blockages on every level—not only physical, but also mental and emotional, which are then purged and cleansed out of your system.

"When you can accomplish two goals, you'll transform the very contents of your mind. The first is curbing distracting thoughts. This occurs as a result of your meditation routine. The second is substituting old, unconscious behavior patterns with the fresh imprint of the divine Presence on your consciousness, and this is achieved through ongoing practice. This dual effort changes your essential nature, which never occurs when performing hatha yoga postures alone. In meditation you are connecting with your spirit, while in hatha yoga you are connecting with your body. It's the exact opposite approach. Trying to coax enlightenment by performing bodily contortions is not what the great spiritual teachers had in mind."

Father fetched a book from his library, then located a couple of bookmarked pages.

"Even the authoritative fifteenth-century hatha yoga text, the Haṭha Yoga Pradīpikā, insists that both hatha yoga *and* the internal raja yoga meditation regimens must be practiced together in order to achieve success.[18] Beyond that, the text clearly and somberly warns, 'Those who remain ignorant of Râja Yoga and only practice Haṭha Yoga are fruitlessly wasting their energy.'[19]

"Sometimes these practices are promoted by failed mystics and those who likewise lack this understanding. But this is a backward approach to spirituality. Such persons often haven't the aptitude to pursue a wholly interior path, so they develop superficial gimmicks such as manipulating the body or forcibly awakening the spiritual energy by using various techniques. But the benefits sought by practitioners of hatha yoga and kundalini yoga are, in truth, *byproducts* of spiritual realization. Jesus said, 'First seek God and all else will be added unto you.'[20] The promoters of these practices mistake the effect for the cause. Some are blind guides leading scores of others down paths that go nowhere."

Brandon did not appear to take umbrage at Father's remarks.

"The same holds true with the recent wave of New Agery that has enamored countless individuals. Interest in the occult and talismans and all types of psychic claptrap has cost numerous souls their ticket to God. What the New Agers really want to achieve psychologically, to use the terminology of modern brain research, is to live in a perpetual right-brain mode. This is the artistic, creative, and intuitive aspect of the mind, as opposed to the analytical, logical, and organizational part of the mind that is inherent in left-brain functioning. Alpha waves versus beta waves. This is certainly preferable to the left-brain corporate mentality that dominates our culture and perpetuates the contagion of materialism we are brainwashed to accept. But flitting around in a sort of ditsy right-brain haze won't get you any closer to God. It's just an illusion."

Jason's Impasse

Having concluded his talk, Father asked, "Does anyone have any questions or comments?"

A fairly new attendee, Jason, had arrived a few minutes earlier. He interrupted the proceedings with a personal issue. Which was too bad, as I had been increasingly impressed with Father Christopher's breadth of knowledge, and I would have liked to have heard more of his thoughts. I found myself absorbing his talks like a sponge.

Jason, in his mid-to-late twenties, worked for a geological-survey company. He seemed reserved and withdrawn. I later learned that he recently broke up with a woman named Pam following a two-year relationship. Or rather, Pam broke up with him (read: dump). He'd been somewhat distressed and unable to shake off his sense of loss. God, could I relate, as I, too, had recently "ended" a relationship.

"Father, I feel all I've known has been destroyed," Jason impatiently interjected, oblivious to those gathered around him.

Father apparently knew of his personal woes. He asked him, "Do you wish to discuss this in private?"

Jason replied, "No, it's not necessary."

"Very well. Look, there's always a risk in moving away from the familiar to the unknown. Your life from this point on is a voyage, a departure. You will leave your well-known moorings and drift in waters unfamiliar to you. Brace yourself for these changes. It is a stripping of illusion, a coming to terms with reality."

Father sounded apocryphal. I suspected this might lead to a profound discourse. As I shook the soreness from my hand and readied my pen for another round of notetaking, I set aside my reservations about Jason and strapped in for the ride.

"You are now unprotected. There is not one person or thing that can give you security. You must offer all your hopes and fears, aspirations and dreams—every one of them—to God. As St. Peter counseled, 'Cast all your worries on God, for he cares about you.'[21] So, too, you must give all your concerns to God. Don't hold on to a single one. Fill your mind with thoughts of God alone. Let go!"

"But it's impossible to let go," Jason rejoined. "That would be like walking the plank."

"Then walk the plank you must. Blindfolded. You are undergoing nothing less than a wholesale restructuring of your psyche. This entails the removal of all delusion, all of your ego's games, all your deeply ingrained patterns of behavior. You now stand defenseless, naked. You cannot go home. 'Foxes have holes and the birds of the air have nests, but the Son of Man has nowhere to lay his head.'[22] You cannot return to your former veil of illusion; it no longer exists. There is nothing to give you comfort, no place to run for support.

"Only God. God is your only alternative.

"Nothing—relationships, work, amusements—will cloak you with the illusion of comfort. Face it, you've been living a lie. Be *grateful* for every incident in which you lose or experience loss. It shatters your ego's armor, composed of a false sense of pride, and covered with sheathes of duplicity."

Father looked up from Jason and, after gazing across the room, expanded on his comments. "I might add," he said, as if to remove some of the sting from his observations that were directed at Jason, "the same situation can apply to us all."

After a pause Jason responded, "I feel hollow, as though my heart has stopped beating."

"You are feeling sad, bereft, alone...disoriented and adrift. All the layers of deception you've amassed to protect yourself from feeling genuine emotion, from feeling actual hurt, are being blown apart. Allow this process to happen. Do nothing to stop it. The accretions you've accumulated since youth, which fasten to your soul like barnacles, must be scraped away to reveal the innocent heart.

"Cling to God, my son. Make God the focus of your life, your top priority. More than your former girlfriend, more than your earnings, more than your ailing parent"—Jason's mother was then dying of breast cancer—"though you must at the same time serve her devotedly. The prophet Jeremiah proclaimed of God, 'You will find me when you seek me with all your heart.'[23] Your future will unfold, but only when you are deprived of all hope, freed from all illusion, and firmly and solely anchored in God. When these conditions are met, you will journey to where your heart so achingly longs to go.

"This is a time of loss, of divestment, not gain. You are losing your distorted views of yourself. You are being stripped of all the concepts you fed yourself until you became an unconscious automaton, functioning without feeling, without passion, without vulnerability. You've been acting according to fixed patterns and deeply embedded scripts.

"You will at times feel lonely and sad. This is a cleansing, a flushing of all the emotional debris you've stored up. This extraneous junk has served as a safety mechanism, a security blanket for you. But along with carrying this emotional baggage, you've abandoned your spiritual beliefs. You have lost your faith. You no longer trust in God. You love your ego more than God! To claim otherwise is to perpetuate your delusion."

Father paused. "It might be in your best interest not to run to another woman at this time. You will simply use her as a platform to enact your own dramas, as you have done before. This is your pattern, which you must wipe clean."

Jason replied, "Hopefully that won't happen anytime soon."

"My son, 'hopefully' is not an option. You must confront yourself before you drag out the same old you and sully others with your unhealed heart. Again, this same circumstance can occur and probably has occurred to every one of us."

I felt slightly uncomfortable, because Jason's deepest secrets were being spilled for all to see. And I felt elated, because it was as if

DIALOGUES WITH THE LORD OF TIME

Father were speaking directly to me, addressing my recent breakup with Sherri, a human-services specialist whom I dated for five whirlwind months. That relationship provided a meaning, an excitement, and a direction in my life I hadn't known for a long time. But Sherri broke it off because she didn't want a long-term commitment. And I'd been smarting ever since. Poor Jason was the sacrificial lamb, I suspect, for others besides me.

Father continued, "If you face the facts, you'll discover you've been living the life of a hypocrite. God will remedy this. Be prepared to have your dishonesty exposed. This process will be ruthless. In ways you cannot now imagine, you will be stopped dead in your tracks.

"Recall the Passion of Christ. Everyone who sincerely walks the path of God undergoes a similar period of humiliation and disgrace in their life, oftentimes completely unwarranted. But we must persevere, undaunted by the trials of this life. And so, the Book of Ecclesiasticus advises us to utilize both faith and fortitude when undergoing adversities:

> Calmly accept whatever befalls you.
> When sorrow arises, be steadfast,
> In times of misfortune, be patient.
> For gold is tested in fire,
> And those chosen to walk the path of God
> Are tested in the furnace of hardship and humiliation.
> Therefore, trust in God and he will help you.
> Never lose sight of him; have faith in God at all times.[24]

"We may find ourselves unfairly vilified even though we were entirely innocent. Or targeted as an object of ridicule and scorn. Or unjustly blamed and scapegoated for mistakes that were actually caused by others. Sometimes others ascend in their lives while our life nosedives, yet it seems to us that we are far more deserving. The situations are endless by which our ego is reduced to shreds and tatters. A guillotine blade can be fashioned into several sizes, shapes, and angles, but regardless of appearance, it accomplishes the same purpose."

~~~~~~~~~~~~~

I was reminded of one of several powerful spiritual dreams I dreamt during this period in my life. One vivid dream reflected my own occasional experiences of when others would use me as their emotional dumpster. In this dream, I was seated alongside a female American Tibetan Buddhist teacher.

In my dream, I said to her, "People slime on me all the time."

She instantly replied, "Good! That's part of your training."

As I had at times been somewhat complaisant when younger, this advice was quite appropriate, for it sought to instill in me a more assertive component to my character.

~~~~~~~~~~~~~

Liz chimed in, "Once a brownnosing, unqualified coworker lied, ingratiated, and bullied her way to the top. We all felt this was completely unfair!" Liz's revelation provoked laughter, which broke the somber tone of Father and Jason's exchange.

Not to be outdone by his significant other, Stuart related his tale of treachery and betrayal. "A colleague of mine knew I was working on a particular research paper. For two long years I labored until the end was in sight. Three weeks before my paper was published, this so-called coworker published his paper—on the very same topic as mine! He knew what I was working on, yet he intentionally beat me to it without once revealing his plans. To this day his paper is widely referenced at our corporation, while mine is viewed as a mere forgotten and, worse, plagiarized footnote. Not a day goes by when I don't think about this."

Marta shared her discomforting account. "Once at a trade show, I met with a few of our distributors. I boasted how meticulously we ran our company. I told them that we have an impeccable track record, that we rarely make mistakes, and to absolutely assure them, I said that if we ever did make a mistake, we ourselves catch 99 percent of any errors before they see the light of day. Then I had to excuse myself early for a doctor's appointment. So I gathered my papers and left. Erin took over to conclude the meeting.

"I arrived at my appointment, five minutes away. While I sat in the waiting room, the receptionist announced I had a phone call. It was Erin, who tried to sound as cool as possible."

Erin burst out laughing.

"But I knew she was coming unglued inside. She told me I had walked away with one of the distributor's file folders." Everyone gasped. "Sure enough, I hurried out to my car, and there it was, buried at the bottom of my pile. I had accidentally picked it up when I grabbed my own papers.

"I ran back into the doctor's office, canceled my appointment on the spot, then drove right to the auditorium and raced back into our conference room, where I was greeted by four men staring coldly at me in complete silence—one of the most uncomfortable experiences in my life. I handed over the one guy's file folder and apologized profusely. It was incredibly embarrassing!"

Bill asked, "Did you lose any of your distributors?"

"Fortunately no, but that one guy began doublechecking our invoices. He still does even now! I still second-guess myself when dealing with him."

Father continued unemotionally, "So you see, the exact situations whereby our ego is toppled most often catch us unawares. When we are blindsided by these incidents, they hurt all the more. Especially when we react to them in our old, accustomed ways. Then we are right back at square one.

"However, such events really serve as a mirror, revealing to us the exact nature of our attachments. These situations are hard pills for the ego to swallow, yet it is our obstinate ego that strangles our soul. So, you must look on these events as gifts from God. They have nothing to do with the perpetrators, who are merely puppets of destiny. These incidents are given solely to loosen the grip of your ego, to center you in your spiritual self, and to strengthen your faith in God."

Addressing Stuart and Marta, Father said, "On the surface, the experiences you shared were meant to teach you ego-crushing humility. But that was *not* the point. You are still carrying the memory and the emotional impact from these incidents. And therein lies the lesson.

"I'll tell you a story. Once two Buddhist monks were traveling by foot when they came upon a river. There stood a beautiful, well-dressed young woman who needed to cross. The older of the two monks at once hoisted her on his back, forded the waters, then set her down. The younger monk also crossed the river, then journeyed on with his companion. But inwardly he was fuming because the older monk had touched a woman, which was forbidden in their order. When he couldn't contain himself any longer, he blew up and scolded his companion. But the elder monk remained calm. He simply smiled at his friend and replied, 'Brother, I left that woman back at the river. It is *you* who are still carrying her.'

"This story reminds us not to react to any event, no matter how emotionally charged it is. Remain detached. Don't carry the memory of it; let it go! Otherwise, you'll resurrect it by continually ruminating over it. You thereby animate it into a living entity, as it were, where it resides inside your head and saddles you with invisible yokes. In this manner, you create your own shackles and chains."

Father directed his topic back to Jason.

"So, be prepared to lose large chunks of your ego in order to be peeled to the very core of your being. Don't be afraid when this occurs. It's only your ego that is dying."

Jason, simultaneously bewildered and moved, sat riveted, as though a divine radiologist were interpreting an X-ray of his soul. He then spoke about a nearly forgotten spiritual experience from when he was around twenty. He was raised in the Methodist Church and often sang in the choir. Singing helped him establish a devotional relationship with God. Some of the hymns powerfully affected him, putting him into a kind of ecstasy. He recounted a tale of innocent longing, of mystical yearning. No question, he experienced a deep love of God. But over time, he left the choir when the pull of worldly entanglements made increasing demands on his time. As he became more and more involved with the world, the spiritual connection he once felt with God proportionately diminished.

Father, who appeared peaceful and indrawn, matter-of-factly pressed on. "You have insulated yourself, numbed yourself from feeling pure, unguarded love. Remember when you were younger? Can you invoke and actually relive the spiritual experience you just shared with us? *That* was love. But you caved in to the mundane world of mortals and sacrificed the intimate connection with God you had established, forged by your intense, burning faith. You've since become a caricature of yourself, immunizing yourself from feeling genuine love. This is a travesty of all you once held dear."

Jason hung his head, gazing introspectively.

"Now, you must muster up the courage, the determination, and the perseverance to venture into the unknown with no map. You really have no choice but to move onward, breaking through your ego's barriers and transcending its limitations. If you are sufficiently motivated, prompted by your determination to be free, you can rid yourself of the binding influences that dragged you down and kept you chained to the world because of your compromise."

~~~~~~~~~~~~~

Father's comments reminded me of my own spiritual awakening, and how I forfeited it because I lost my faith when I, too, had compromised my spirituality by conforming to the world's opinions. This in turn triggered the memory of another dream wherein I walked up the steps of a male American Sufi teacher's home, which led to his front door. It was foggy and drizzling outside. I entered his house, which was warm and inviting. I found the teacher cordial, solicitous, and radiating the light of God. Once I was inside the meeting room, I prepared to sit down amid a small circle of longtime disciples. As I began to sit, I noticed a peculiar-looking cap dangling from the ceiling by a thread. It looked like a World War I leather flying helmet. I gazed curiously at it and asked the teacher what it was.

He immediately replied, "It's a fool's mask. All who come here must wear it."

I closely examined it, then briefly placed it on my head. I subsequently took my seat.

The teacher and I spoke softly for a while, gazing directly into one another's eyes, making a deep heart connection. Then I glanced over and noticed the severed head of an old man lying on the floor a few feet in front of the teacher. I looked up and saw, to the teacher's right and seated against the wall, the headless torso of the old man, as if it were deeply absorbed in meditation.

The dream ended. I interpreted it to mean that, in order to enter the innermost sanctum of God, a person must become a fool, figuratively speaking, by losing their head—their ego—which is set in its stubborn, know-it-all, self-righteous, self-justifying ways. As St. Paul observes, "If anyone among you considers yourself wise by the standards of this world, you must first become a fool in order to become truly wise. For the wisdom of this world is foolishness in the sight of God."[25] When playing the role of a fool, one must ignore what others think of them—this especially applied to me. And, by chopping off their ego, a person can enter into deep communion with God.

~~~~~~~~~~~~~

Father continued, addressing Jason. "When you fill your free time with trivia—obsessively pursuing various projects and becoming enamored of superficial things—you are really trying to bury your aloneness. But as Plotinus maintains, spiritual life is 'the flight of the alone to the Alone.'[26] No matter how much we succeed in preoccupying ourselves with inconsequential activities, we cannot forever hide from our aloneness."

Then Father stood up and perused one of the nearby bookcases. He pulled out a book and, returning to his seat, flipped through to a bookmarked page, then read a short passage. " 'In being stripped of an external object we stand denuded and see the intolerable abyss of the self yawn at our feet.'[27] This precisely describes this unbearable aloneness, which either drives people to surround themselves with a flurry of activities, people, and endless commotion, or else it drives them to madness. There is, however, another option, which is to pursue the spiritual path. It is on that isolated and thorny trail where one's aloneness must be confronted, embraced, and ultimately transcended. But this is no easy task.

"In your case," he said to Jason, "you've built walls that entomb your heart, and you involve yourself with pastimes that sidetrack you from getting in touch not only with your true feelings, but with your soul. In addition, when you have been rejected, it profoundly influenced the course of your life. This pattern of rejection has dictated your behavior. Whether you know it or not, you've been repeating that same rejection over and over with this or that person. You must ask yourself if this applies to your former lady friend."

Jason looked up. "But Father, she rejected me!" he protested.

"Oh, is that so?" Father countered without missing a beat. "I see it differently. You create situations whereby you re-enact that same rejection, which you've internalized at the deepest level. That has become your groove, your broken record. You keep replaying your wound. And when you repeatedly pick at a scab, it never heals.

"I tell the truth as I see it. What you really seek is God. But your kneejerk efforts to prevent another rejection fuel your every thought and action. In fact, your very effort to prevent rejection is simply a means you use to set up situations to bring about rejection. This is your theme, your motif. Until you free yourself from this pattern, it will continue to rule your life."

I noticed every so often one pair of eyes would stealthily meet another's with a look as if to say, *Can you believe what you're hearing?* I don't think anyone felt particularly at ease, because Father was exposing the little ruses that all of us employ at times, concealed under superficialities, affectations, and social pleasantries, which only mask our true nature. By the same token, Father didn't mince any words, and what he said resounded as only the truth can.

Father paused, then asked, "Does anyone know the story of the holy man and the scorpion?"

Several responded, "No."

"I'd be happy to remedy that. Once a holy man stopped to drink at a pool of water. As he bent down at the water's edge, he noticed a scorpion on a nearby rock. The creature suddenly fell into the water. The holy man immediately scooped it up with his hand and placed it on the adjacent bank. As he did, the scorpion stung him. Then it crawled over to the same rock, and again fell into the water. Upon observing this, the holy man helped it to safety a second time, but once again he got stung. This happened a third time.

"A nearby stranger, who witnessed this, came forward and asked the holy man, 'Sir, each time you save the scorpion, it stings you. Why do you keep doing this?'

"The holy man replied, 'Because it is the scorpion's nature to sting, and it is my nature to do good.'

"Similarly, you must heal from the wounds of your past and regain your spiritual innocence so that you may again love freely, without any limitations, conditions, or reservations—even when your trust has been shattered; even if you get stung repeatedly."

Jason confessed, "It's hard to love again when you've been stung by your girlfriend!"

Father calmly said, "But you must try." He reflected for a moment, then continued, "You project the feminine God—the *anima* of

Jung—on to these women, because you want to be touched, caressed, and spoken to in human form through them. The song of the mysterious feminine whispers to you, mesmerizing you. No doubt you crave that presence from the depths of your soul. Your girlfriend reawakened those stirrings, and you couldn't get enough."

Father glanced over at me, which caused me to shrink uneasily in my seat. "You allowed this infatuation to envelop you so thoroughly that you became obsessed by it. It consumed your thoughts and controlled your behavior." He mercifully turned his gaze back to Jason. "But, in reality, what you crave is God within them. You project the goddess on to them and isolate that aspect apart from their human features and the ordinary facets of their character. However, this is an impossible expectation to place on them. Seeing God in all beings is the ideal, but falling in love with a projection will only get you in trouble! Whether they consciously knew this or not, no one knows. And whether you were fully conscious of this or not, who knows. But now you are left alone with a gaping hole in your heart. Do you bury this feeling, or do you divert it to its real source—God?"

Following a brief pause, Father emerged from his inspired, albeit unrelentingly forthright stream of thought. Jason, far from being offended that Father had dissected and analyzed his psyche in public, thanked Father for his insights. (Jason in fact always spoke highly of Father and the enormous, positive influence he had on his life.) Father sweetly smiled back. Then Jason sat silently. He appeared to be mentally connecting Father's observations with his situation, taking it all in, and he seemed to be relieved. And Father, while delivering what appeared at times to be a frank admonishment, never once displayed harshness or animosity. Most of the time he beamed reassuringly at Jason. The teaching in Revelation 3:19 came to mind: "Those whom I love, I reprove and discipline."

~~~~~~~~~~~~~

Father's teaching touched a raw nerve in me, which I've not forgotten over the years. I am reminded of this talk whenever events conspire to reveal any underlying self-deceptions or duplicities that may unknowingly be influencing my behavior. The same holds true in instances when my ego becomes unreasonably defensive, or on occasions where my words and actions are at variance…or when I realize I behaved poorly toward others, or had made regrettable errors, or had acted awkwardly in the past. Such recognitions are never pleasant, because I am forced to come to terms with my own shortcomings and mistakes. I must humble myself and mend the mismatch between my words and actions by changing my ways so I can root out my hypocrisy. This unfailingly produces an acute, soul-searing realization that I am actually situated at the lowest rung of the spiritual ladder, which in turn invariably serves as a pointed lesson in humility.

This process of introspection is similar to the Vedic religious practice known as *svādhyāya*, "study of oneself," which is a subset of Patanjali's Yoga system. It also parallels the Sufi method of self-examination, termed *muḥāsabah*. However, it differs from a more rigid scrupulosity insofar as this kind of self-analysis is intended to benefit one's spiritual journey and produce positive advancement on the path, not merely cause a person to wallow obsessively over their imperfections or become guilt-stricken about their character deficiencies and engage in endless self-recrimination over their past misdeeds.

Years afterward, whenever I would speak with a member of our group who attended Father's meeting that night and the topic of Jason's talk came up, they unvaryingly related a similar experience as mine. They all underwent a comparable change. Father's discussion somehow managed to touch the Jason in each of us, which resulted in a profound inner transformation that none of us could fully fathom at the time. The effects of Father's talk that evening had mysteriously wrought something permanent inside every one of us. While drawing out the impediments that were hidden in Jason's mind, Father in some way lanced all of our collective psychological abscesses.

I later discovered that Father would perform this inner diagnostic procedure for some in public and for some in private. I never knew why, but I speculated that he somehow knew, perhaps intuitively, which mode of instruction was better suited for each person. Although he gave Jason the opportunity to discuss his personal issues privately, perhaps he was motivated to instruct him publicly in order to teach all persons who were present, as he alluded to when conversing with him.

For example, once Ginny cleared off the table nearest to Father before he began speaking. When Father saw her, he playfully remarked, "My daughter, I am most grateful for your thoughtful act. Now, I encourage you to focus the same attention on removing any accumulations that may be lurking in your heart." In this instance, Father's approach was lighthearted, prompting Ginny to laugh. Yet, Father made a spiritual point not only for the benefit of Ginny, but for us all.

~~~~~~~~~~~~

After a short break, we sat to meditate. A tangible feeling of love filled the dimly lit room. It was a powerful experience, more powerful than I could invoke during my meditations at home. A deep spiritual current flowed through my being, which involuntarily moved me to euphoria. After nearly forty minutes, Father chimed the meditation bowl, and Liz turned up the lights.

"All right," he said, "time to retire from this long night. When you sit for meditation, try to focus your attention on the home object. Once your mind is still, *feel* the divine Presence completely engulf you. That is your goal, because pulsating at the very heart of everything is God, the 'one God and Father of all, who is over all and through all and in all,'[28] as St. Paul reminds us. Remember to practice every day, especially when you don't feel like it. May God's blessings be on us all."

Father rose from his chair and promptly retreated into the kitchen. Bill followed him in for a private meeting. I bade the others goodnight, and everyone began to disperse. Heather and I drove away on that cool fall evening. I felt, for a moment in time, a suspension of every worry that had plagued me since I lost Sherri. The stars, twinkling bright and suspended in the sky, seemed to touch the earth.

~~~~~~~~~~~~

Heather gave me an additional insight into what may have prompted Father's talk that autumn night. I first met her in Los Angeles before she retreated from city life and relocated to Fort Bragg. As she had frequented the spiritual scene since the 1970s, she was familiar with many of the groups and gurus of that era. Some of those groups and teachers advocated spiritual realization through a kind of spontaneous self-understanding, thus bypassing the need for practice. Although Heather typically sat silently during Father's meetings, she once asked him—at a meeting that took place before I began attending—if there were really a need for spiritual practice in light of these types of teachings. She shared with me her account of Father's response, which I reconstructed and tidied up with her approval:

"Continual practice is crucial for one's realization," Father told her. "Occasionally sitting for meditation alone is not enough. Nor is getting a contact high from sitting in the presence of advanced souls. That's nothing more than pleasure seeking, a narcissistic self-indulgence that goes nowhere. I'm not in favor of passive or mechanical approaches, or of vicarious spirituality. Or of reading about mystical states, then presuming, falsely, that you have attained them. Or especially of armchair mysticism, whereby you assume, equally falsely, that by gaining an intellectual understanding of enlightenment, you are thereby enlightened.

"The fact is, a person must make a concerted, sustained effort to realize the truths of spirituality. This is the most effective way to uproot all the fixations, obsessions, habit patterns, and personality traits that dominate you, most of which you aren't even aware. Those unseen patterns dictate your life. This is why spiritual practice must be consistently and diligently applied in order to reach the goal. Otherwise, one's efforts are haphazard and unfocused.

"You must want this realization *above* all things, as a Hindu master once told me." (This holy man was Swami Ramdas, a popular Hindu saint, whom Father met on his trip to India in the late 1940s, and who is different from the American teacher, Baba Ram Dass.) "There must be a round-the-clock prayerful intent to change fundamentally who and what you are. This will bring about a complete restructuring of your psychological makeup. Such a wholesale change requires ongoing, fervent aspirations that are strong enough to override your ingrained behavior patterns. This incessant inner supplication—*at all times, above all things*—is the key to spiritual transformation. It must be more powerful than your present state of conditioning. It must be strong enough to retool the infrastructure of your innermost nature. Only then can it rein in your lower emotions and remold your behavior. Only then will you be rid of the

44

habituated illusion that causes you to identify with your encrusted, fixed personality. Only then will you be free."

~~~~~~~~~~~~~

Back in Ukiah, I gave notice at the medical-supply company. There was too much responsibility and too little reward, too much work and too little pay. I had already begun a job search and had two interviews scheduled. But naïvely, I didn't first secure a new position. I kept looking.

Following a two-month hiatus from dating, I began seeing Gail, whom I met at one of the two art-film houses in the greater region. We always seemed to get along, although we never moved in together. (At that stage in my life I often thought relationships were easiest at a distance.) She was my age, and she worked tutoring young children. She had been married once, but never had any kids of her own. Thankfully, she didn't judge me based on my job or income. We both loved nature and, even more important, spirituality. We enjoyed many happy moments together.

As time permitted, at nights I would assemble and edit the notes I'd taken of Father Christopher's talks. Heather and I chatted over the phone every now and then. My morning schedule at that time incorporated a regular meditation sitting, and the times when Gail and I stayed over at each other's homes, she would join me. However, I'd typically alternate among several different styles of meditations, including Father Christopher's, so I wouldn't become bored. This may have been confusing to her. But I desired variety in my spiritual palette, much in the same way one partakes of different cuisines at a buffet. I found that if my meditations from different traditions reached deep enough, they invariably led to the same inner place. Rotating among diverse paths kept the journey colorful and interesting.

Hurkey Creek

Around this time, in November 1990, I wrote to Father seeking guidance when I became disheartened over the prospect of leading an unfulfilling worldly life with nothing but drudgery in sight. I always seemed to be lurching from borderline discontent to outright unhappiness. I was hopelessly idealistic on the one hand, yet spouting complaints at the slightest hint of a dashed hope on the other. Why, I wondered, should I be joyful? My career had stalled, I was nearly broke, and my dreams of living a meaningful spiritual life had not materialized. I watched in silent anguish as those around me succeeded in their chosen field of endeavor, while that kind of success eluded me. Many of my contemporaries were of average intelligence but possessed shrewd self-promotional skills, which I entirely lacked. Some constantly socialized and excelled at the art of networking, while I preferred privacy and seclusion. In my spare time, I'd spend hours chasing any number of speculative ventures, which yielded nothing, while my peers effortlessly attained success simply by steadily working at their careers. I acutely felt many opportunities in life were passing me by. Despite my meditation routine, I believed I wasn't wholeheartedly pursuing my spiritual goals. Above all, I couldn't succeed in integrating my spiritual practices with my day-to-day life. As I would later learn, this issue was in fact the underlying cause of my discontent.

Further, I sensed my mortality looming on the not-too-distant horizon. Once during this time, I awoke to a powerful dream in which the figure of Death appeared, attired in a hooded black cape, as in Ingmar Bergman's classic 1957 film *The Seventh Seal*. Death stood on the periphery of where I stood, never coming closer, always keeping a measured distance away from me, yet always in sight. I somehow managed to stave off a direct encounter with Death's stalking presence. Yet the distinct and chilling element to my dream was Death's name, which I clearly remembered. His name was *Dominos Anima*, which is Latin for "Lord of the Soul." Thus, the unnerving message of my dream was that it is the approaching threat of Death which ultimately governs the fate of my soul...of all souls. Consequently, we must practice spiritual disciplines now while we still have time before Death lowers the final boom.

This existential crisis had become a recurring theme in my adult life. The last time I underwent a similar impasse was in late December 1988. I was then visiting my mother in Santa Monica. I needed a short personal retreat, and I required solitude, as was my wont.

When venturing into nature, I often camped alone. I would frequently splinter off and hike apart from any group I had initially joined. My occasional solitary flights into nature afforded me the opportunity to renew my soul. Just as a tripped circuit breaker must be reset, so I, too, would shut down completely during my solo treks into nature before starting up again, minus the cares of the world.

In such a setting, a person can shed their image—the persona we fashion in order to interact with others and suit society's needs. One is stripped of all nonessential elements of character. You can listen and feel and think. Your world becomes smaller, more manageable. You can observe without judging, and wonder without being judged.

I received encouragement to camp alone when, in my mid-teens, I would read of iconic naturalist John Muir's lone wanderings in the High Sierra. But the spiritual greats also practiced solitude. Many times Jesus retreated into the wilderness and spent time in seclusion, often to pray.[29] He would likewise advise his followers to remain in solitude: "Come away by yourselves to a solitary place and rest awhile."[30] Buddha similarly isolated himself during his spiritual awakening. In my later teen years, I found additional inspiration from a Buddhist verse I discovered in the mid-1970s:

> At home everywhere
> Quarrelling with none
> Content in all circumstances
> Enduring adversity unperturbed
> Wander in solitude as a rhinoceros.[31]

And so, on December 31, 1988, I felt compelled to travel from my layover in Santa Monica to the Southern California desert. I set my compass for Joshua Tree National Park. Apart from the outward purpose it serves as a nature preserve and rock-climbing mecca, Joshua Tree is a mythic destination, long associated with rockers the Doors, Gram Parsons, the Eagles, and more recently the Irish band U2. As with any haunt that has attained mythical status, whether fictional or real—be it Shangri-La or Joshua Tree—the whole of what it symbolizes exceeds the sum of its parts.

But first, I would stay overnight in the nearby San Jacinto mountains. I packed my car and drove east from Santa Monica, eventually passing through the quaint hamlet of Idyllwild. Nestled eight miles below this quiet village along State Route 74 lies Hurkey Creek Park Campground, situated at an elevation of 4,400 feet. Surrounded by the San Jacinto Mountains and set among impressive groves of Coulter, Jeffrey, and stately Ponderosa pines, this seemed a choice site. I arrived there midafternoon, well before any prematurely intoxicated New Year's Eve revelers might wend their uncertain labyrinthine paths along the precarious nighttime mountain highways.

After finding a suitable spot and setting up camp, I walked the course of the park's smallish namesake creek until sundown, when it quickly became very cold after the sun had sunk behind a nearby ridge to the west. Hurrying back to my campsite, I hastily built a fire and witnessed the evening sky descending blanketlike over the expanse. It portended to be a crisp, dark night, as the last-quarter moon had not yet risen, and many stars began shining above the nearly uninhabited campground.

Two years earlier, I decided I would try to market some fiction stories I had written. My plan was this: my stories would be published; the royalties would roll in hand over fist; and I would be independently wealthy by age thirty-five (at the time I was twenty-nine years old). I would then be free to follow my spiritual pursuits unencumbered by worldly obligations. In the event my stories were not published, I would give up my spiritual practices altogether and undertake an as-yet undetermined worldly career. Well, my stories were never published, and I was about to throw in the spiritual towel. Until that night at Hurkey Creek.

Weary from my daily work routine and contemplating an unknown future, I stayed awake in my tent as the night wore on. I periodically read from the spiritual books I had brought with me, including my pocket copy of the New Testament, finding solace in the uplifting, impassioned words of Jesus, as recorded in my two favorite sections: the Gospel of Matthew, chapters five through seven (the Sermon on the Mount); and the Gospel of John, chapters thirteen through seventeen (the Upper Room Discourse).

The air was biting cold, and when peering out from my tent, I could see countless stars twinkling in the chilly night sky. My heart soon became overtaken by a wistfulness, a certain yearning I hadn't known for years. I wanted badly to make some kind of breakthrough decision about my future. There, lying awake just after midnight, in the cradle of the incipient New Year, during a moment of inner reckoning, I experienced an epiphany of sorts. It didn't last long. But, unmasked of my social role and stripped of the pressure to meet any deadlines, I could see my life with absolute clarity.

In a flash, I realized I had been living a false life. My rolling obligation to participate in the world prevented me from seeing this; it obscured my objectivity. My worldly responsibilities had enslaved me. I had compromised my spiritual vision of life by capitulating to a mandate dictated by others. Yet, deep inside I knew that caving in to the status quo was the ultimate self-betrayal. And because I consciously carried out this forfeiture, I had inexcusably committed treason against myself. However, I knew better. I knew that, as one of my all-time heroes, philosopher Henry David Thoreau observed, "The greater part of what my neighbors call good I believe in my soul to be bad ..."[32] But I had slackened my vigilance by succumbing to and accepting the world's reality to the extent that it overshadowed my spiritual pursuits. I had become tethered to the world's agenda and entangled by its grip. And this sellout came at the cost of *my* soul.

At that very moment, as I was enveloped by darkness, aloneness, and bitter cold, a thunderous decision welled up inside me: I would not—*could* not—pursue a worldly career at the expense of my spiritual goals. I would not settle down and "adjust" to the world's reality. The deepest part within me cried out and refused to set aside my spiritual objectives by adapting to the world and kowtowing to its terms. Something had caught hold in me, and I clearly felt the truth of another hero of mine's ringing words: "There is a time in every man's education when he arrives at the conviction that envy is ignorance; that imitation is suicide; that he must take himself for better, for worse, as his portion ... Nothing can bring you peace but yourself,"[33] Ralph Waldo Emerson enjoined.

In the midst of a seeming eternity, as waves of inner revelation enfolded me, I realized that the spiritual reality was the only reality worth pursuing. This had been my dream, my vision ever since my life-changing spiritual awakening at the age of seventeen. To toss aside that vision or to compromise it in any way would be tantamount to abandoning the very foundation of my life. It would be like stumbling upon the Holy Grail of Christ, then spitting on it. It would be equivalent to scoffing at the very idea of God and spirituality. Or repudiating my own spiritual experience. I might as well become a born-again atheist.

During the middle of that propitious night of cascading insights, I realized that these indefinable, intangible goals meant far more to me than the empty promises of secular life. Vacant and hollow, the world and what it offered could not imbue me with purpose and meaning. Just the opposite—it can strip a person of resolve by breaking their spirit and forcing them to become a mechanized robot: nothing more than a soulless, talking mannequin.

I had been poised to dismiss my spiritual pursuits, embark on a worldly career, and live an average worldly life. Instead, I unequivocally and resolutely decided then and there that I would follow my spiritual ideals no matter where they led me. I would pursue them regardless of whether or not I achieved worldly success. All other considerations simply did not and could not measure up to this paramount goal: this was the only thing that mattered. Certainly more than becoming a slave to the system—working endlessly merely to make money and living as an undistinguished drudge—until death relieved me of the traitorous pact I would have forged with the devil by selling my soul if I were to have rejected my spiritual vision of life. But this inner calling was tearing at me, and I could not put it off any longer by diverting myself with a never-ending series of worldly distractions. I must heed it. I must follow my *dharma*, my inner nature, or else my spirit will suffocate.

So, I reprioritized my life on that eventful night, intent on severing any unnecessary participation with the world and focusing even more on my spiritual work. There, in a nearly deserted campground— a wayfarer's repose between the worlds of man and God—I opted for the less-traveled path: to follow my spiritual ideals regardless of consequences. At the pinnacle of my revelation, I felt a jubilant, victorious sense of emancipation for having mustered up the courage to face this realization rather than to continue hiding from it.

The resolution I made that night at Hurkey Creek marked a major turning point in my life. I still live off the vision from that experience. I had adopted a worldly mentality before then and had allowed my childhood spirit to become asphyxiated by the grindstone of life. But those timeless moments inside my tent became a crossroads for me; they had the effect of crystallizing my intentions and refocusing my efforts. I felt immensely empowered knowing I would no longer permit the realities of daily life to supplant my spiritual ideals. My youthful energy—embodying fearlessness, vivaciousness, temerity, and mettle; filled with passionate vision; unscarred by bitterness and cynicism; and not whittled down by cares or defeated by the frustrations of life ("choked by the worries, riches, and pleasures of life"[34])—had taken possession of my soul and had forcefully evicted my broken-down, soon-to-be middle-aged self. I was told in so many words: *You have no choice in the matter. You must live the spiritual life. There is no alternative for you in this lifetime.*

After waking early the next morning and promptly preparing breakfast, I packed my gear and headed out of the campground. Like the redeemed Scrooge, I felt the Spirits had completed their galvanizing mission during that single long, cold night. I felt an overwhelming, exuberant sensation of lightness, joy, and utter freedom from all encumbrances. Inspired by my renewed sense of purpose, I made a beeline for Joshua Tree. There I spent New Year's Day mostly in perfect solitude, meandering lazily as I drove along the main road that leads from Cottonwood Visitor Center to the West Entrance Station. It was a brilliant, sun-drenched excursion. I stopped every so often, taking in the magnificent sculpted landscape, hiking short distances, viewing majestic Joshua trees, and surveying the vast multihued desert terrain from the prominent Keys View lookout. In many ways nature had become my church, and I worshipped plentifully that day.

~~~~~~~~~~~~~

Thus, I'd often analyze and attempt to remedy this malady that periodically afflicted me, which I addressed in my November 1990 letter to Father Christopher. It seemed that something inside me, I wasn't quite sure what, was trying to sabotage my own efforts to pursue my various dreams in life, especially those of living a purposeful spiritual life. Meanwhile, I'd watch those same dreams die a slow death with each passing day. Yet only one person could motivate me to find my inner passion and direct it toward realizing my goals before it was too late. That person was me. I felt I must follow my own vision and create my own future. After all, I was just performing a dance, my own unique dance. Who cares what the audience thinketh? I must dance away in ecstatic delight.

I kept Father Christopher's lengthy handwritten response to my query, which I treasure to this day, and which reads:

> My son, consider this carefully. Your happiness comes from within. No outer change can affect this. It matters not if you marry, have children, win the Nobel Prize, work hauling garbage, become rich, or live the life of a bum. It does not matter whether you live in Ukiah or elsewhere. Not one of these outer circumstances affects your inner state. If you had everything you wanted in life this very instant, you would still be unhappy because of your own mind.
>
> You alone hold the key. You alone create your own happiness and unhappiness. So I advise you—do not brutalize yourself with litanies of imaginary demands that, once met, will give you your supposed happiness. You equate some fantasy state in the future with your peace of mind. But nothing could be further from the truth.
>
> You have duties to perform from which you simply cannot escape. Therefore, don't complain. Cheerfully embrace that which you cannot avoid. That is the key to your peace of mind. If you can but do this, your anguish will disappear. You create your own heaven or your own hell by your attitude. Change your attitude, and I promise that your current hell will turn into heaven. Much of your spiritual practice will be accomplished by this one simple act.
>
> True, you are impatient for a brighter outer destiny to unfold. This is natural in the secular sphere of life and for a young man of your age. But whether you are impatient or patient, it will occur only at the right time, if indeed it is to occur at all. So why not choose instead to be patient? That alone will give you the peace you so desperately seek.
>
> You are an instrument, and God will use you as he sees fit, whether you become a celebrity or a derelict. You cannot change one thing unless God wills it. So, don't rail in despair.

Maintain your peace of mind. Think of God at all times. Be of good cheer.[35] By so doing, you will be inwardly fulfilled, and your life will become radiant with peace and a blessing to others. Remember, God is with you always and loves you dearly.

Ever yours,
Christopher.

THIRD VISIT (February 1991)

Father's Constitutional

LAST NOVEMBER I was between jobs, as they say, with few prospects and even less cash. Not long after, I found work as an office assistant and occasional travel writer with a regional tourism publication firm located at the southern edge of Ukiah. I dreaded the brief Highway 101 commute, but it was a decent-paying position and, while challenging at times, it afforded me the periodic opportunity to engage in creative writing. All in all, it proved fairly stress-free. Gail and I still saw each other and, looking back, the time we spent together remained innocent and carefree.

Of course, I had spoken to Gail about visiting Father Christopher, and so we arranged for both of us to pay him a visit in late February 1991. We planned to car camp at Van Damme State Park so we wouldn't impose on Heather. We arrived at the park on a crisp, sunny Saturday morning, and I pitched our tent at the far end of the lower campground—not secluded enough—before driving to Heather's home. Happily, Gail and Heather got along. We ate an early, light lunch that Heather thoughtfully prepared, then sat about and chatted before heading to see Father later that afternoon.

I drove the three of us along the now-familiar road that leads to his cabin. When approaching his residence, I spotted Father standing outside, donning a wide-brimmed straw hat and carrying a walking stick. "Come along," he beckoned as I parked my car. "Join me for my daily constitutional. It's a most beautiful day." We hopped out of the car and, after I introduced Gail to Father, we began strolling along an old fire road that branched off the main roadway. Maintaining stride with Father was not altogether an easy task, as he managed a much brisker pace than I would have imagined. Out of the blue he spoke to me, almost reprising the theme of his recent letter.

"The frustration you feel is natural, yet you can entirely avoid feeling frustrated if you but change your outlook. Instead of feeling trapped, count your blessings and be glad you live the way you do. Try to recall all the things for which you can be grateful, even mundane things—your health, your job, living in a free society, so to speak. That way you can make of each day the best it has to offer.

"At times, you become discouraged in many areas of your life—all because you feel stuck or imprisoned. This is why little things bother you so. Again, change your attitude. Then you'll no longer feel any need to escape. Try also to practice perseverance and detachment. Remember, this is your destiny—Ukiah, your place of employment, your relationships, your various situations in life. Proceed through it all with emotional indifference, without becoming agitated, and watch the whole cinema show pass by quickly."

The scraggly underbrush soon opened up, and we came to a clearing where we could view the Pacific Ocean in the distance, which was sparkling. The four of us stopped, and Father spoke. "Just as the ocean is hidden, then suddenly appears in view once we rise above the shrubbery, the same is true of God. The ocean never at any time disappeared; it was only obscured. So, too, when the debris in our minds is removed and the muddying effect it produces over our soul is gone, all we perceive is the luminous being of God. Like the ocean, God is endless, infinite ..."

Father hesitated, as if reaching for words. Some unseen vision seemed to capture him. Perhaps moved by his attempt to describe the indescribable, a lone tear trickled down his cheek, something I hadn't seen before and would only witness two, maybe three times all told. He always managed to cloak whatever spiritual emotions he felt under a buoyant, happy-go-lucky demeanor coupled with a blinding, scalpel-like intellect. But beneath this facade flowed a profound spiritual current—still waters run deep.

After a few moments of silence, Gail spoke up. "I understand you were a university professor," she said to Father. "Why did you retire from teaching?"

Father responded, "As you can see, I'm not fully retired. I just shifted my focus. As Lao Tzu, the mysterious author of the Tao Te Ching, counseled, 'Abandon formal learning and all troubles will cease.'[36] So now I pontificate without tenure." We all laughed.

Gail continued, "I understand you also retired from the priesthood. So why didn't you marry?"

Father grinned, then looked over at me. Feigning exasperation, he said, "I see it's open season on my life!" My face turned red.

Turning toward Gail, Father addressed her question. "My daughter, there are certain individuals who are wedded to the Divine. Besides, on a very practical level, release from the obligation of celibacy is not granted during retirement." Father smiled. "And on an even more practical level, I was in my mid-sixties when I retired from both posts. As I was fairly set in my ways and quite content with my solitary life, the thought of getting married had not occurred to me."

"Did you find it difficult to obey the teachings of the Church?" Gail asked.

Father sat down on a nearby large rock. We followed suit and sat close by on a clean section of the forest floor.

Father graciously answered. "No, this was never an issue. I was granted a special dispensation to retire from both of my positions in the late 1970s for a very specific reason: so I could return to California and assist my ailing mother, who had become bedridden following a stroke. I was an only child, and my father had long ago passed away. There was no question about my need to assist her and my willingness to serve her, which the Church viewed as an act of compassion. Because of my age, I was granted emeritus status, so I no longer engaged in the formal functions associated with the priesthood after my forty years of service. I also elected not to continue performing any ministerial duties, although once in a while I was called on to perform an Anointing of the Sick. After helping my mother for a number of years until her passing, I relocated to Mendocino County."

Gail followed up, "When you taught courses on different religions, how could you integrate them all with your Catholic background?"

"First of all, Catholicism was the faith into which I was born and raised. Fortunately, it also happened to be the predominant Western Christian faith that advanced mysticism and accepted the supernatural and belief in the mysterious sacred, which is what most attracted me. It offered both contemplative and devotional paths to God.

"As I consider myself a traditionalist insofar as I advocate religious-based mystical paths to find God, including those found within the Catholic faith, my intellectual curiosity led me to discover many such paths existed in other religions. As it turned out, I developed a passion to explore different religions and investigate their mystical elements. Not only to explore, but to *experience*. Many times I would take my students on field trips so they themselves could undergo various hands-on spiritual practices, which I believe is what made these classes so relatively popular compared with mainstream theology courses.

"For example, we'd arrange to visit Buddhist monks. Students could sit and meditate with them if they chose, and I always joined in. We'd also perform *salat* alongside devout Muslims, and we would stand with devotees chanting *kirtans* in a Hindu temple." (*Salat* is prescribed Islamic prayer, performed five times daily. In Hinduism, *kirtan* is devotional call-and-response chanting.) "We'd witness expressions of joy and hope when attending Hanukkah candle-lighting ceremonies with my close rabbi friend. We would also join my fellow Christians as they worshipped in solemn awe during a Serbian Orthodox service. I always hoped my students would find a common thread in these various approaches to God.

"I'd also invite representatives from different religions to speak on their beliefs and practices, and to dialogue with my students. And so, the students' own personal experiences and their direct interactions with these various practitioners helped tremendously when I taught my classes, because they could relate to their firsthand knowledge instead of relying solely on abstract book learning. I thought of my courses as a laboratory of experiential religion, spirituality, and mysticism.

"Moreover, on a personal level, I felt absolutely no conflict with my religious eclecticism and interfaith approach that might have compromised my love of Christ. As it was Christ who moved my spirit and to whom I was beholden, I found I could personally encounter different religions and love Jesus at the same time. In fact, these experiences only served to enrich and strengthen my own interior relationship with Christ."

Seeking to capitalize on Father's rare moment of self-disclosure, I joined in Gail's interrogation. "Father, did you cut your ties with the Church when you retired?"

"No, I am still considered a priest in good standing. While I no longer exercise my position as an authority figure within the Church, I've always kept up my love of the deep, rich mystical traditions of Christianity, including those of the Church. That love runs through my veins. And I never burned any bridges. I simply built new ones. I've maintained intermittent contact with several of my priest friends, and over the years I've referred a few people to certain Catholic retreat centers. Until driving became an issue for me, I continued to attend Mass in person, most often at smaller rural chapels, but always from the other side of the pulpit. Yet, I never let on that I once served as a priest." Father paused, then modestly smiled before admitting, "However, along with attending Mass, I sometimes also attended Buddhist and Hindu and Jewish and Islamic services, and other Christian liturgies as well!"

Gail persisted, "You seem to be a guru by the way you teach and the way that others gather around you."

Father excitedly answered, "I *never* view myself in that manner, and if others perceive me as such, I beg to God for forgiveness for even appearing that way. I see myself as a fellow pilgrim on the path, though a very talkative one. I've had some experiences and insights that I enjoy sharing with all of you. I look on us as a small circle of friends who are jointly probing the spiritual realm of life.

"While I have met some legitimate spiritual guides, by and large I take a dim view of the traditional role of a guru as a kind of benevolent dictator who must mandatorily and unquestioningly be worshipped. In my estimation, a spiritual teacher should not be someone you are compelled to worship and to whom you sacrifice every last vestige of self-initiative, but rather someone who empowers your soul and who spiritually awakens you.

"Most gurus by definition demand autocracy; they require obedient followers in order to exist. This practice is commonplace in India, where it has its place; it's been part of the Indian culture for millennia. It certainly can be argued there is a need for a hierarchical structure in religious organizations, as well as a need for a central authority figure in monasteries, both Eastern and Western. However, I believe a rigid, authoritarian teaching style that demands absolute, unquestioning subservience is largely incompatible with our contemporary Western culture. A spiritual teacher should allow for their disciples' freedom of choice without crossing that fine line which strips them of their autonomy."

Turning back in silence, we soon approached Father's cabin. Father headed inside while Heather, Gail, and I remained in the parking area. Before we parted, I asked Father if I might tape record his talks, as I had brought along my handheld cassette-tape recorder. He unhesitatingly agreed, although he couldn't understand why anyone would be interested in anything he had to say. I felt much relief at the prospect of not having to strain while taking notes of his discourses. In addition, this ensured a more accurate rendition of his teachings and a more true-to-life portrayal of his personality.

Father previously gave us permission to picnic on his property, and despite a slight nip that had crept in the air, that late afternoon presented an opportune time. We had brought some food with us, so I unloaded my ice chest and eating utensils from my platinum Sentra and set up placemats, paper plates, and so forth, on makeshift straw mats that we spread near a downed log located adjacent to Father's cabin, where the three of us dined.

In answer to her mealtime question, Heather told an ever-inquisitive Gail what she had heard from Ginny. Along with his retirement income, Father inherited a modest sum from his mother when she passed away (she then lived in neighboring Lake County). This helped sustain him through the years. This may partly explain why he never asked for donations or accepted any offers of money. But I further suspected that he so abhorred the glut of self-appointed, profiteering, so-called spiritual teachers that he wanted to set an opposite example.

While we consumed our supper—vegetable brown rice, garden salad, and a savory tofu–walnut dish—a few others arrived, including Ginny and Tom, who brought their six-year-old daughter Rose. Stuart and Liz drove up in their Vanagon, and they appeared pleased to see our picnic gathering. After we finished eating, just ahead of sundown, we packed our culinary gear back into my car. As we walked toward Father's door, I recalled Christ's words, "Knock, and the door will be opened for you."[37] Sure enough, just as this thought occurred, Father himself opened the door to greet us, and we assembled in the living room.

Lightning in the Sky

After some chitchat, Father took his seat and, upon making himself comfortable, he began speaking. I later surmised our walk must have stirred him. He was inspired that evening. I turned on my cassette recorder.

"The situations you face in life are tailor-made for your spiritual growth," he said to no one in particular. "They are pinpointing the remaining shortcomings in your mind. Once you progress beyond the stage where they trigger your emotions, you will be free. Until then, they are merely props whose purpose is to reflect back your own deficiencies. With continued development, you will reach a point where none of these incidents affect you. You will remain immune to them; they will pass over you like water on a leaf.

"The outer circumstances of life do not matter—which person, what place. They are as illusory as a mirage. Their only purpose is to trigger the personality traits and emotions lying deep inside your mind. Outer events act like a magnet that attracts then activates those personality traits and emotions within you, both positive and negative, which are resonating at that exact same karmic pitch as the outer events.

"For example, you see a certain person and you become happy. Or you read of your former employer, and it reminds you just how miserable that job was. Or you learn of a rival's accomplishments, and it triggers your deep-seated emotions of insecurity and jealously. And so on. These situations all strike a responsive chord if they are on the same wavelength as your corresponding mental state. Whenever you are provoked to react to them, your inner Geiger counter goes off, as it were. Other situations don't register at all, and so you simply ignore them. It's the ones which register that count.

"So, when these reactions occur and raw emotions are kindled, no matter how much anger, resentment, embarrassment, or remorse you may feel, detach yourself from those feelings. Regardless of how painful or pleasant any sensation seems at the time, allow it to quickly work its way through your mind whenever it becomes roused. Again, practice detachment as it does so these emotions don't overtake you, because any wave of strong emotion surging through your system will quickly displace you from your spiritual roost."

Marta asked, "What if these emotions are so strong that they overwhelm a person?"

"When strong emotions, such as joy and sorrow, are stimulated during spiritual practice, your initial response may be to embrace the joy as it courses through you, or to escape the sorrow as it envelops your being. But as the residual impressions of these emotions are purged on account of your practices, do not identify with either sensation. Allow them to be experienced on the physical plane with as little interference as possible. It is necessary for all these states—joyful and sorrowful—to move through your mind. They must come out. Yet at the same time you must try to control your reactions to them."

Stuart piped up, "What exactly do you mean by 'purged'?"

Father responded, "When you use a drill, it produces shavings as it bores its way through the wood. Similarly, the act of meditation serves as a powerful drill that forges a path straight to your soul. As it does, it dislodges many crystallized emotional reactions, subconscious psychological complexes, and fossilized personality traits, which must get purged as a result. This is why it's so important to maintain your practice while undergoing these purgations. Then, no matter which way the purgative winds blow, your ongoing commitment to your practice will anchor you while these emotional storms pass by.

"Meditation can also revive memories, both pleasant and unpleasant. We might experience happy recollections of childhood, or times when we were hurtful toward others. It can also resurrect long-buried emotional wounds, such as if we were ridiculed by our peers or if we suffered neglect or cruelty as a child. However, you must avoid dwelling on these images from your past. You must deftly allow them to move out of your consciousness. Stewing over them will only derail your spiritual progress. They must go."

Stuart pensively nodded.

"For instance," Father continued, "let's say you are a perfectionist. You easily recall the top ten most embarrassing incidents in your life. You have them memorized by heart. When you undergo periods of purgation during spiritual practice, these incidents are stirred up and they swirl around in your mind. They are so realistically vivified that they actually seem to be occurring. You squirm and cringe as they float about in your consciousness. If we analyze this, we see two events concurrently taking place. First, the past is rearing its ugly head. Second, you are identifying with it. There is one proven remedy for both situations. When the past emerges from its crusty coffin to haunt you, you must witness it as though it belonged to someone else. This is an extremely effective antidote. By disassociating yourself from your past, you will send it scurrying back to its moss-covered tomb.

"The fact is, you must make peace with your past. Nothing whatsoever can alter it. But you compound the problem by thinking that you are the actor in this drama. You become fascinated with your own movie. You replay the scenes you love the most. Then you replay the scenes you despise the most. You thereby turn your comedy into drama, then into melodrama. Or even tragedy. But to walk the spiritual path, you must entirely disengage from identifying with your past. The prophet Isaiah counsels us, 'Do not remember events of the past, nor dwell on what occurred long ago.'[38] To clingingly identify with your past is the very height of egotism."

Tom observed, "Father, I find it hard to let go of mistakes I've made in the past. Sometimes they haunt me."

"Remember," Father said, "the same principle about detaching yourself from your past applies whenever you become obsessed over mistakes you made in the past. Just as the most effective way to love one another is simply to stop hating one another—to cease all the back-biting; all the belittling comments; the petty grudges; and all the nasty, negative thoughts and snide remarks that are steeped in venomous ill will—so too the one surefire way to overcome the shadow of your past mistakes is not to repeat them. And the best way to forget your past is to live in the present. If you are married to your past, or if you had a particularly unsavory past with lots of skeletons in your closet before your religious conversion, it is useful to remember the words of Wilde, 'Every saint has a past, and every sinner has a future.'"[39]

"So when the past gets churned up during your practices, allow for the ensuing catharsis. Just don't let it dominate you or dictate your moods. Try to control your reactions whenever any snippets of memories become dislodged and surface in your conscious mind—the flittering, half-formed images and bygone spectral voices that no longer exist. As a result of this purgative process, a profound cleansing will occur. As the Psalmist jubilantly sang, 'Create in me a clean heart, O God, and establish a new and right spirit within me.'"[40]

Gail weighed in. "You're telling us to express these hidden impulses and to control them at the same time. That's contradictory! It sounds like an impossible task."

Father laughed. "No one ever said that practicing the spiritual life was easy! Let's just say a person strives to monitor their mental junk while attempting to mete out the manner and degree of its expression as it's being purged. This is more of an art than a science. It's not an overnight process, and it requires constant detachment—a relentless disassociation of the contents of your mind from your spiritual self. As St. John of the Cross maintains, spiritual life is loss, not gain. We lose what we never possessed in the first place."

Liz remarked, "This sounds like a difficult stage in a person's spiritual practice. I wonder if it would help to talk with someone when all this mental stuff comes out?"

Father answered, "Of course. The very best person to speak with is whichever form of God you worship, and the very best means of conversation is fervent prayer. To pour out your heart in passionate, spontaneous utterances while fully attuned to your divine Beloved is the single most intimate communication a person will ever experience. This act in itself has a profoundly powerful cathartic and healing effect.

"But remember, when you converse with God, don't dwell on your shortcomings or overly scrutinize your mistakes. 'Who can know all of their own faults?' asked the wise Psalmist, who then beseeched absolution from God for any of his character flaws that may have been lurking unawares: 'Cleanse me from my unknown faults and weaknesses.'[41] Likewise, we can seek to restore wholeness with God and ourselves without morbidly fixating on our limitations or emphasizing our failures. Just have rock-solid faith that God will forgive your past mistakes.

"And so, when you pray, rather than dwelling on your flaws, focus instead on joyfully interacting with a caring, infinitely loving God. Visualize you and God exchanging volleys of innocent love. Or, as Ruysbroeck nicely put it, 'The exercise of love between ourselves and God flashes to and fro like the lightning in the sky.'"[42]

Liz clarified, "I meant talking with someone like a therapist."

Father, smiling, responded. "In my opinion, the last person with whom you should speak when you're in the throes of meaningful spiritual growth would be a therapist. That would be like Shakespeare taking one of his newly written sonnets to the local amateur literary critic, a self-professed expert, for a review. Imagine Buddha undergoing psychoanalysis on Freud's couch: 'Your overprotective father is the real cause of your antisocial tendencies.' Or Jesus: 'You are the victim of maladaptation; you also suffer from a savior complex.' Divulging such information and subjecting it to secular interpretation could have a chilling effect on your spiritual blossoming. It could create doubt and undermine your conviction. Unless, of course, the therapist professes a broader spiritual background or hails

65

from a therapeutic lineage that accepts spirituality and the mystical experience. Provided, however, they are not intending to indoctrinate you into some rigid sectarian dogma if they are religiously inclined.

"But I would rather you sought counsel from someone learned in the mystical path, be they Jewish, Christian, Muslim, Hindu, or Buddhist. Someone who can validate your spiritual experience and discuss it credibly, not clinically dissect it according to some secular criteria, as if it were an aberration and you were their specimen. This could cause you to second-guess your own experience. There is no single greater act of moral turpitude than intentionally causing another to lose their spiritual faith. If you are learning to sail, you want an experienced sailor to teach you. You don't take sailing lessons from a used-car dealer!

"However, as a general rule, it's best not to talk about your spiritual experiences with anyone, especially the secular-minded. The relationship you establish with God is highly personal. It produces intimate spiritual feelings that cannot be explained. These are not the same as ordinary emotions. Not only do you risk losing touch with these delicate feelings by articulating them aloud, but there is a further risk that you may invite scorn or ridicule, even mocking. Look at how Jesus was treated! You readily stand to lose your spiritual gains if you indiscreetly discuss them."

Simply a Facade

Just then a college-age couple arrived whom I hadn't met before, Nicholas—"Nick"—and Carla, both of Italian Catholic stock, and quietly found places for themselves. I learned that Nick was majoring in philosophy, while Carla was studying to be a psychotherapist. (Perhaps it was providential that Carla missed Father's comments about therapists.) Both were friends of Brandon, who at the last minute couldn't attend, but encouraged Nick and Carla to show up anyway. Father, who never chided latecomers, apparently knew they'd be arriving. He stood up and warmly greeted them as they settled in.

During their introductions, Father had introduced himself as *Christopher*, as was his custom. However, when Carla called him

"Father," he remarked, "I've grown accustomed to being called 'Father.' But my attitude is that of Jesus: 'Do not call anyone on earth father, for you only have one father, your spiritual Father, who resides in heaven.' "[43] Everyone erupted into laughter. Happenstances such as this flawlessly captured Father's at-once charming and self-effacing personality.

When all had taken their seats, Father resumed his previous topic. "The outer circumstances of life are perfectly suited for each person. They match a person's inner state and allow their destiny to unfold. Within each person's environment, specific conditions are created for their destiny to manifest. These conditions may be personal encounters, their job, family issues; situations involving health, stress, uncertainty; overcrowding, poverty, wealth—whatever they may be. These conditions are solely created to draw forth the personality traits that are lying dormant in each person's mind, like iron filings are drawn to a magnet.

"To give some examples, the experience of motherhood is a role that allows certain moods to be expressed, such as tenderness, discipline, selflessness, and maternal affection. A soldier engaged in battle plays out various emotions that are inherent in the experience of war—the survival instinct, a kill-or-be-killed mentality, fear, valor, brutality, and so on. In a dramatic performance, the players take the audience on a series of emotional ups and downs, which causes the viewers to experience certain moods and feelings—happiness, sadness, conflict, resolution. The same is true of all situations in life. The outer drama both reflects and stimulates one's inner makeup.

"This is the only purpose of the physical plane: to serve as a medium through which desires, emotions, attachments, and aversions in every conceivable form are enacted. This arena we call earth is the gross, dense medium that allows the subtle grooves that are entrenched in our minds to manifest. These grooves are composed of ingrained patterns and personality traits. Our body is the instrument and the world around us is the platform wherein all these grooves are played out.

"Many enlightened souls report that, in reality, this physical universe does not exist as an independent creation. It is inextricably linked to the mind. All things within it that appear to be independent exist only in relation to the mind. Therefore, in this context there is no independent existence apart from the mind. In this sense, the external world is a projection of our own mind, of our collective minds. The mind and the objects it perceives are on a conjoined voyage through the time–space continuum—forever bound together, at all times dependent on one another."

Nick interrupted. "If what you are saying is true, wouldn't the world disappear when we sleep, then reappear when we awake?"

"The answer is both yes and no, depending on which explanation of reality you believe. This in turn depends on your level of spiritual evolution. From a materialist point of view, the world exists insofar as it is a gross entity subsisting in time and space. Any number of people can confirm its existence independent of one another. From this viewpoint, the world exists while we sleep, and it continues to exist after we die. But from a transcendent spiritual perspective, everything is relative to the mind. This is a core component of Berkeley's philosophy of subjective idealism. It parallels the Vedantic concept of *drishti srishti*, which means 'we perceive the world as we are.' This also applies to the central motif of existentialism, which is encapsulated in Kierkegaard's proclamation, 'Subjectivity is truth.' And he is right. We are so culturally indoctrinated to accept what we see and touch and hear as the only reality that we lose sight of the subject who perceives all this. Without the subject, the world does not exist. Does the evening news matter to a cadaver?

"Getting back to your question, from a spiritual viewpoint the world only exists if there is a mind to perceive it. And taking this one step further, the mind itself is relative to the spiritual self. The ultimate subject—the spiritual self or soul, and beyond that, God—cannot be objectified. It can only be *experienced*. This numinous experience occurs when the mind and ego are dissolved back into the spiritual self, and from there into the ultimate reality—God. This is analogous to what the Buddhists refer to as *nirvāṇa*, which means 'to extinguish,' except that Buddhists do not believe in the prevalent Western religious concept of a personal God."

Father continued his earlier discussion. "So, the outer circumstances of life mirror back the inner state of each person. Two people may have dissimilar experiences of, reactions to, and interpretations of the exact same outer event, depending on their inner state. One person may react with indifference, while another reacts with emotional attachment. A spiritually advanced individual will not react at all because their mind has been liberated from all reactions; they remain entirely aloof from them."

There was dead silence in the room. Nothing else mattered. All eyes were glued on Father, who appeared calm and serene.

"This world is but a projection of what is occurring on subtle, nonphysical levels. It is nothing more than a theater wherein one's destiny is acted out. All actions on this plane of existence are merely *representational* of what is actually taking place on the subtlest levels of manifest reality. Our family, homes, jobs, relationships—all are physical manifestations of what is being enacted invisibly, transcendentally on a causal, nonphysical realm of existence. This is the dimensionless realm where karma is stored up until, little by little, it begins to unwind and play out, as if on scripts. These invisible scripts run of their own accord, much in the same way a player piano automatically performs music, or a movie projector plays a film.

"The material universe is simply a facade, a prop, an artificial exterior like we see on a Hollywood movie set. It is the medium for playing out all the scripts that are unfolding from this unseen realm. Everything we perceive and all we encounter in this worldly abode are but manifestations of karma unfurling on this earth, which is the final, tangible stage where destiny is carried out. Once you have a direct, personal understanding of this—that this physical universe is merely a symbolic representation—your experience of life will be forever changed. You'll never go back to your previous view of reality."

After several reflective moments, Bill asked, "Father, could you repeat that please?"

Father slowly paraphrased his earlier remarks: "The physical universe is the medium for acting out what is actually occurring in unseen, nonphysical realms. It is but a staged concept.

"To a spiritually illumined saint, this world appears as a phantasmagoric image, of no more substance than a dream. They may be smothered in waves of bliss, perhaps only peripherally aware of the world as a passing footnote. Look at St. Joseph of Cupertino. He wasn't in the slightest aware of his surroundings when on numerous occasions he became enraptured in prayer and spontaneously levitated in ecstasy, as witnessed by scores of people. In an extraordinary revelation, St. Catherine of Genoa described her non-dual experience of unlimited divine perception: 'I see without sight, I understand without intelligence, I feel without feeling, I taste without taste; I know neither shape nor dimension ...'[44]

"These saints function in their body solely because of the continuing momentum of their destiny, which is the result of years and years of habit and conditioning. They peer out at this fleeting earthly spectacle from the timeless vantage point of eternity. They perceive themselves living in a noncontiguous moment-by-moment re-creation of this physical universe, with which they are completely uninvolved. All around them the workings of karma form and re-form afresh each instant, but they remain detached from them all. They witness the goings-on of their life while remaining wholly unidentified with whatever transpires in their environment.

"Though they may seem to be fully present, their soul is not even situated in their body, but rather in an orb of pure spirit that is entirely disconnected from their physical form. In the esoteric parlance of Tantra philosophy, this is known as the seventh *chakra*, which is said to be one of seven subtle energy centers situated along the spine, and which, when fully opened, is located *above* the head, as is depicted by halos, not inside the brain." (This extracranial site is also mentioned in Taoist texts.) "The body is merely the temporal locus through which their soul manifests."

Father paused to collect his thoughts before resuming. He seemed totally indrawn, as if rapt in a sublime vision.

"It is the human mind that acts as a fulcrum between the worlds of spirit and matter by creating arbitrary lines of demarcation—categories and definitions, measurements and labels—which serve as symbols of so-called physical reality. Only, the mind mistakes the many categories it makes and the many definitions it creates for reality itself, thinking that these various representations are permanent and real, and that they exist apart from the mind. Yet these are only terms of convenience used to identify objects in order to facilitate communication among humans. But we believe them to be true. Then everyone is brainwashed into accepting the same illusion. We collectively mistake a rope for a snake, to use the well-known analogy by Shankara, who was the prominent exponent of Advaita Vedanta, the nondual branch of Hindu philosophy. This is the insidious web of delusion, which the Hindus call *maya,* and which spreads like a fisherman's net to catch as many as possible in the pervasive apparition of duality. It is, as the prophet Isaiah describes, 'the veil that covers all peoples, the shroud that is spread over all nations.' "[45]

~~~~~~~~~~~~~

At the very moment Father finished speaking, I experienced an uncanny sensation of déjà vu. I found myself enveloped in self-imploding waves of recognition within the deepest part of my being—an intense experience of spiritual clarity I had undergone but few times in my life. Once in my early teens, I became inwardly absorbed while I was staring out the bedroom window of my childhood home in Los Angeles, for how long I don't know. I had lost all self-consciousness. When I came to, it was as if I were transplanted back into my body, from who knows where.

Another instance occurred in August 1974, as a friend and I hiked the backcountry in Kings Canyon National Park. When approaching wild, spectacular Evolution Meadow (elev. 9,229 feet) while trekking south along the John Muir Trail, I gazed around at the breathtaking High Sierra landscape, utterly devoid of any artificial points of reference. All of a sudden, I involuntarily lost all sense of distance, as there were no humanmade spatial coordinates that might have helped me determine where I was in relation to what I was viewing. I had unwittingly proven Emerson's perceptive observation of 130 years earlier: "At the gates of the forest, the surprised man of the world is forced to leave his city estimates of great and small ..."[46]

The mountains cast an alluring spell, and the mental function that provides the framework for measurement and dimension simply disappeared. In 1979, I wrote about this mindboggling trip: "There I stood, slowly surveying the desolate, haunting, strangely otherworldly barrenness that lay before me. One can capture this dramatic landscape with a camera, but you must *experience* the wonder of these mountains by pausing near them and gazing at them until you become one with them. By observing this striking mass of geological chaos to the point where you can't analyze it anymore, one is taught its secrets. The mountains reveal themselves to you."

Another occasion took place in around 1976, as I was reading Alan Watts' *The Book: On the Taboo Against Knowing Who You Are*. I suddenly got his message on a visceral level, and for an unknown period of time the floor of reality completely dropped out from everything I knew. These heightened states of consciousness, more akin to a temporary *satori* (known as *kenshō*) than a permanent *nirvāṇa*, were far more real and vivid than anything experienced in normal waking consciousness.

~~~~~~~~~~~~~

Father stopped to sip some tea and clear his throat. I groggily snapped out of my reverie when I again heard his carefully modulated voice.

"The ego is deeply entrenched within each person's mind. Actually, the ego—our sensation of self—is composed of three intertwined processes that act in unison: our subjective sense of 'I'; our perception of an object; and the connection between these two. For example, in the sentence, 'I am looking at you,' 'I' is the subject; 'you' is the object; and 'looking' is the verb, the connecting link that joins subject and object together. This threefold process, which the Vedantists call *triputi*, forms the sensation of self—the sense a person has of being separate and distinct from the external world. This sensation of separateness sustains the illusion of duality.

"The ego, therefore, is a relational and not a permanent component of one's mind. The one constant in the interplay between the ego and the objects it perceives is *change*. Existing only in relation to this or that changing object, the ego is founded on impermanence, just as the Buddhists maintain. Thus, its sense of being real is but a pretense. It is merely a fabrication, a concept that is used so there is a focal point—one's 'I'—through which various karmic interactions are played out on this physical plane. The collection of illusory images consisting of form and color and texture that we call the world and the ephemeral entity that perceives them—the ego—are part of the same transitory mechanism. Both are locked in an embrace of illusion.

"What 'you' are is a solidification of your karma. One of the six traditional schools of Vedic philosophy is known as Sankhya. According to the Sankhya theory of evolution, everything that is visible to the senses manifests from more subtle nonphysical states. This is similar to what we discussed earlier. When these nonphysical states are condensed, they congeal and appear as the dense physical medium we call the universe. Recall your high-school chemistry class. Just as carbon dioxide gas is transformed into solid dry ice, 'you' can be likened to an ethereal gaseous being that has solidified into a physical human form. Your form—your body and mind—acts out all the karmic scripts that are destined to unfold in this lifetime. But you—the real you, your spiritual self—are not this form."

Carla asked, "Please tell me, Father, how can I relate all this to my day-to-day life?"

Father smiled and replied, "Okay, let's analyze your day-to-day life, but in the context of nondualism. You now think that you are a person who goes to college, lives in a dormitory, drives a car, and so forth. But, from a nondual perspective, these are merely superimpositions heaped on to a transitory, physical mirage. These labels bolster an identity that, from this perspective, is entirely false. You are not this fabrication. Once you shed this cloak of illusion, you will perceive your true identity shining in all its transcendent glory.

"Further, from this same viewpoint, all that takes place in one's life is mere chatter, like static heard on a radio. This is not to devalue your secular life, but rather to call attention to the fact that once you disassociate your spiritual self from all this external commotion, you'll see that none of it matters in the slightest.

"When, through repeated spiritual practice, a person stops identifying with their ego, liberation ensues. Gradually, a spiritual aspirant catches glimpses of an immutable essence that permeates all changing phenomena. Gradually, they cease to react with lower emotions to their destiny as it unfolds. Gradually, they come to identify so much with this blissful immutable essence—their soul, their spiritual self—that they are completely lifted above the influence of their karma. They transcend its realm altogether."

All in the room—Bill, Carla, Nick, Ginny, Tom, Liz, Stuart, Heather, Gail, and a spaced-out me—were intensely focused on Father's words. Even Ginny's little girl didn't fidget.

"It is the ego that obscures one's identification with their soul. It so constricts a person that their connection with their spiritual self becomes lost. They remain boxed within the strangulating confines of duality. They have lost touch with Infinity.

"Spiritual practice forcibly untangles this constrictive knot by purging the mind of its accumulated contents. The less of a hold these mental contents, including the ego, have on a person, the greater contact they have with their spiritual self. They need not go anywhere to experience, to *feel* the presence of their spiritual self, and, beyond that, God. Simply undo the overshadowing influence of the mind's contents and thereby usurp the primacy of the ego. This removes the dross covering one's soul. 'Blessed are the pure in heart, for they shall *see* God [italics added].'[47] The spiritual self and ultimately God then spontaneously manifest, because both are luminously present at all times and can be clearly felt once freed from these overlaying sheaths. St. Paul eloquently expressed this state of illumination: 'With the veil removed from our faces, we all reflect the glory of God, and we are transformed increasingly into his same glorious image.'[48]

"And so, once this first stage of spiritual practice is complete, whereby a person wholly identifies with their spiritual self, the next stage begins. Just as the universe contains all individual galaxies, so too there is a universal spiritual self—God—that contains all individual souls and every particle of the universe. When a person comes to identify fully with their soul, their spiritual self, then slowly, imperceptibly, on the subtlest of levels, they begin to perceive the same spiritual self everywhere. As the Bhagavad Gita asserts, 'An accomplished yogi sees God in all beings, and all beings in God; they see the same God everywhere.'[49] Their essence is perceived as the same essence in all outer phenomena. This is the endlessly interlaced, boundless experience of God—the formless aspect of God that Jesus described with utter simplicity when he proclaimed, 'God is Spirit.'[50] It is the limitless *brahman* of Vedanta. At that stage, a person perceives nothing but infinite Oneness. Because their ability to discern any difference between their spiritual self and this infinite Oneness has been obliterated, it would be more correct to say that they don't perceive Oneness, but rather they become Oneness."

Taking a deep breath, as if coming back to the normal waking state after witnessing a vision, Father wrapped up his talk. "So concludes our study of Vedanta philosophy tonight. But it could just as easily have been the Gospel of John. And perhaps some night it will be. Christ and Krishna—partners, so to speak, in divine crime. The 'crime' of exposing who you really are. Which society strives with all its might to conceal. Yes, we are here to expose the fraudulent lie that pervades every institution of society, from family to school, from business to government, and, alas, much of organized religion when it lacks the mystical element. It is our job to wake up from this sleepy cocoon of illusion and materialism; to cast off the layers of deception that are woven round our souls; and to break free from this prison of earthly life. Sabotage the conspirators and awaken to who and what you actually are!"

So saying, Father reached for his mug of tea and stood up, which signaled the end of his discourse. Then he retreated into the kitchen.

We all took collective deep breaths and began descending from whatever *bardo* Father had taken us. Descending, but not quite landing. I had noticed that whenever he spoke on these topics, some inner shift occurred. I was not the same afterward. Something inside me was being refashioned at the feet of this curious old man. Based on my discussions with other attendees, many underwent similar transformations when studying with Father and practicing the spiritual disciplines he prescribed for them.

Man Plans and God Laughs

Father soon returned and settled in his chair. Just then Carla asked him, "Father, these teachings are really out there. How can we experience these things?"

"The answer is very simple. You must want enlightenment more than anything else. And you must practice diligently. Then you will find what you are looking for. As King Solomon declared of God, 'Those who seek me will find me.'"[51]

Carla followed up, setting off an extended question-and-answer session that capped this meeting. "But there are so many distractions and obstacles that crop up in my life each day. It's hard enough to focus on my spiritual development, much less achieve the incredible goal you describe. It seems next to impossible not to lose sight of it when these distractions pull me away from it."

In my opinion, Carla hit the nail on the head. Her observation epitomized my own dilemma. I found many of Father's teachings and perspectives on the spiritual life neatly jelled with certain of my own experiences, as well as my general outlook and overall approach to spirituality. But still, the crux of the matter was how to integrate—and seamlessly integrate—his and other mystical teachings into my everyday life. This was the dominant issue I tried to solve for years. The spiritual and secular aspects of my life always seemed at odds with one another. I could never figure out how to combine and incorporate the two into my daily life.

Father replied, "My daughter, as Jesus said, 'You are not thinking the way that God thinks, but as humans think.'[52] You are claiming these distractions and obstacles prevent you from realizing your goal. In reality, whatever hindrances you experience exist within you. They do not originate from any outside source. Nothing ever comes from the outside. What we term 'outside' in this context is merely a projection of something—a concept or emotion that already exists inside our mind—on to an external object. Jesus also said, 'Nothing that enters a person from the outside can contaminate them, but the things that emerge from within them are what pollute them.'[53] The mind first latches on to an object, not vice versa. The mind then paints the object with definitions and further colors it with emotions. However, external objects are neutral; it's how we interpret them and react to them that matters.

"Let's say some homes are built several miles downstream from a dam. Someone notices a small crack at the dam's foundation. Engineers hastily conduct an inspection, and the dam shows imminent signs of collapsing. The residents of those homes are going to react, because they rightfully interpret this event as life-threatening. While no one would question the reasonableness of this illustration, it simply conveys factual information about an event, similar to the sun burning itself out billions of years from now or a lion devouring a zebra in the Serengeti. However, it is we who interpret these events as dangerous or unnerving or grisly.

"From a relative point of view, there is indeed danger that these houses and their inhabitants will be destroyed by the raging waters if they don't immediately leave." Father smiled. "But the owners of one house are advanced spiritual aspirants. They quickly but calmly set about evacuating their family and gathering their important possessions without once losing their cool. Whereas their next-door neighbors panic; they are utterly hysterical and have completely lost their mental composure. By maintaining their inner centeredness, the first family will have nimbly sidestepped the scenario that befell the second family, which occurred because they became panic-stricken and allowed the snowball effect of downward spiraling negativity to seize them in its grip. The first family merely acted in response to an emergency and maintained their spiritual bearings throughout.

"To better illustrate this point, let's say the dam subsequently collapsed. The first family picked up the pieces and rearranged their lives as best they could following the catastrophe. But the second family viewed everything as a curse bringing only suffering and upheaval in its wake. The first family gallantly accepted and adapted to its fate, disruptive and ruinous as it was, while the second family allowed their fate to victimize them—they saw the whole incident as an unwelcome and unwanted impediment... an obstacle. It was each family's attitude toward, interpretation of, and reaction to the same event that made the pivotal difference in their outlook. In this same manner, the origin of obstacles is in the mind.

"This is a dramatic example, but it shows us that at every step along the path some apparent obstacle will appear. Moreover, it seems that when we are on the verge of a spiritual breakthrough, the gods send us calamity, often compounded by misfortune, which is nearly always augmented by trials, not to mention a seemingly endless series of hardships and tribulations. But remember, when the outer world is going to pot, our reactions to it must stop. Our reactions originate in our own mind, never outside of us. If you stop to notice all the supposed nuisances of life and brood over them, they will preoccupy you and drag you down. Then you'll truly be diverted from your goal."

Nick jumped in. "It seems like sometimes we get involuntarily pulled away from God, like the devil was doing this."

Father responded, "If there is a devil, this *is* his most devious undertaking: causing you to turn your attention away from God so you become consumed by worldly concerns. Jesus authoritatively stressed, 'No one can serve two masters...You cannot serve both God and worldly things.'[54] Actually, we succeed so well at becoming side-tracked by the world that we need no demon to aid us. We distract our mind at every turn from resting in its inherent nature, which is pure unalloyed bliss and peace. We end up wrenching ourselves away from our spiritual self, our soul; no one is doing this to us. As St. James maintains, 'God never tempts anyone. Each person is tempted when they are lured away and entrapped by their own desire.'[55] The mind thus causes its own downfall.

"So, ignore these pesky thoughts and seeming obstacles. Pay no attention to them. Handle all situations with an unflustered mind. There will always be a handful of people or situations that play a predominantly antagonistic role in our lives. There will inevitably be periods of friction and conflict throughout our lives caused by vexatious people, trying circumstances, and the like. As Jesus cautioned, 'In this world you will always have troubles.'[56] To live an unruffled idyllic existence is but an illusion. Therefore, don't buy into the world. It is a false paradise. Remain inwardly fixed on your spiritual self, where you can entirely transcend the realm of thought and the sway of your emotional reactions. Don't get caught up in the fleeting dramas of life. Everyone else can become emotionally unhinged around you, but you must remain stable and spiritually centered. Really, the path is very simple and swift if you but refuse to cooperate with diversions and stay the course."

Liz commented, "But when a person hampers us or an unexpected situation arises that spoils our plans, it's a setback. We can't move forward in life because something from the outside intervenes and blocks our goals."

"From a *relative* point of view, you are quite right," Father said. "We can attribute this occurrence to the unalterable will of God, who in fact is running the show, as the Psalmist thus declares:

> The Lord thwarts the plans of nations;
> He frustrates the designs of peoples.[57]

"Or, as my close rabbi friend colorfully observes on occasion, 'Man plans and God laughs.' We can also fault the devil. Or we can blame these interventions on destiny or karma. We easily see how agents of karma and various difficulties crop up that stop us dead in our tracks. Our hopes are dashed; our expectations, shattered. Our dreams lie in ruins. Life delivers blows that pummel us with tidal waves of adversities and untoward events. Our spouse gets in a serious automobile accident. The conniving bully at work backstabs her way into the promotion that should have been ours." Liz smiled. "Some con artist swindles our life savings.

"But from a higher perspective, these outer situations act as physical personifications that trigger the mental attributes existing within our minds. These mental attributes consist of our personality traits, our habit patterns, and our proclivities, that is, our likes and dislikes. External situations merely reflect back what's already inside us. When we react to them, it magnifies our inner attributes. Because of this amplification factor, we tend to blame the outer object when in reality it is our own inner attributes that are being stimulated. When these attributes are triggered, we project them on to the objects we encounter in the physical world, such as this person or that circumstance. In a manner of speaking, these so-called obstacles are three-dimensional manifestations of what already exists in our own mind.

"That's why a certain incident will cause one person to react, while the exact same incident will not even register in another person. An avid hockey fan whoops it up when watching the Stanley Cup playoffs, while his wife is indifferent, if not bored to tears. Or else two people react differently to the same situation. A Democrat will cheer a certain political decision, while a Republican will jeer it. That situation, whatever it may be, stimulates our various mental attributes and elicits our response, thus causing us to react. These mental attributes act, as it were, as preexisting receptor sites inside a person's mind. These inner receptor sites are the hot spots that need addressing. They are the areas within us that go on tilt whenever we react."

Carla added, "They are our buttons that get pushed. And the people who push them are our button-pushers!"

"Precisely," Father affirmed. "Regardless of what the outer cause is, if an inner receptor site is stimulated, we create karma. When we are provoked to react with joy or sorrow to situations of gain or loss, success or failure, adulation or criticism, we create more karma. The insidious cycle of karma then begins, and we are forcefully cast out of Eden. Our reactions to such incidents must stop.

"This is why these outer situations and the persons who push our buttons are so valuable. They are in fact our greatest teachers and our strongest allies on the spiritual path. They point out our weak links—the areas inside us that need fortifying. Otherwise, our practice will have loopholes. If someone or something pushes our buttons, we first need to fix ourselves, not alter the outer circumstance.

"I recall a line from a movie I saw in the 1960s, which made a deep impression: 'If you're broken, it's because you're brittle.'[58] Similarly, in nature we find that insects will most often attack a weak plant but seldom a strong, healthy one. Therefore, we need to overcome the reactive areas within us by strengthening ourselves, which is accomplished by diligently and persistently applying our spiritual practices until we are altogether impervious to them.

"However, we must always be cautious. You may pat yourself on the back if you master your reactions during one bad situation. But what if you are thrust into another bad situation and promptly go to pieces? At work you behave like an angel, but at home you turn into Frankenstein's monster! This is why our practice must be consistently applied at all times. It is our unequal responses to various events that reveal our weak links; they reflect the fact we've not yet stabilized our spiritual realization. And so, we need to remedy these weak areas inside us. Then we'll be able to maintain an even keel under all circumstances."

The Fruit of the Spirit

Stuart asked, "How can we know if one of our weak areas is about to get triggered?"

Father replied, "Sometimes we have a sense—sometimes a very strong sense—that a given situation might trigger us. There are definite signs. The primary indicators are stress, worry, fear, and of course anger. These emotions reveal the vulnerable areas inside us that need shoring up. If fear dominates our mind or motivates our actions, it holds us captive, so we are not able to progress spiritually. If we react to any situation with stress or worry, that means we are not spiritually centered. The same holds true with anger. Instead of gracefully rolling with the punches of life, if we erupt and become upset at every little inconvenience and nettlesome situation that besets us, or if we become perturbed with each difficult person who crosses our path, we will have gotten nowhere in our spiritual pursuits.

"Keep in mind the unequivocal words of Jesus, which he repeated three times in short order for emphasis, 'Do not worry…Do not worry…Do not worry.'[59] Likewise, St. Paul instructed his followers, 'I want you to be free from anxiety,'[60] and again, 'Do not be anxious about anything.'[61] 'Worrying,' Jesus counseled, 'will not add a single moment to your life.'[62] In fact, modern research has demonstrated that worry, stress, and anxiety will *decrease* your lifespan. In other words, these emotions only serve to kill you. So, be on guard. Worry achieves no purpose other than constricting the soul. Whenever stress and worry catch a foothold, heed their warning and take some time to re-establish your spiritual focus. Anchor your being exclusively in God so you can free your mind from these toxins.

"Furthermore, it is precisely how we react to the unexpected situations in life that provides a litmus test of how far we have advanced spiritually. You are delayed one hour at the airport and miss an important job interview. You become stuck in traffic en route to the hospital, and your wife gives birth in the back seat of your car. Which, of course, only worsens the gridlock. You discover a typo in the opening sentence of your doctoral dissertation the day after you submitted it. Something comes up at work that demands your immediate attention and prevents you from finishing your routine duties. All the while, you know your boss will reprimand you for not finishing your routine duties. You try your best to remain unperturbed, but inside you are champing at the bit."

Tom remarked, "Once a coworker made a snide, below-the-belt comment aimed at me, criticizing my work ethic. It completely caught me off guard. I stewed on it for days on end. It rattled me so much, I couldn't shake it off. It felt like I'd been attacked."

Father said, "When we are blindsided by certain events or if we feel that others have attacked us or are maliciously harassing us, it can certainly get under our skin. This simply demonstrates that you are vulnerable to these influences, and the event or person has succeeded in activating your inner receptor site."

Carla interrupted, addressing Tom, "What Father means is that the guy pressed your buttons!"

Father said, smiling, "When this occurs, the best remedy is to pray fervently to God for help. Then give yourself the tincture of time to regain your composure. You have been shaken from your spiritual self, and you need time to recenter your soul in God.

"In addition, you may be sorely tempted to strike back, and your lower mind might work overtime at devising various means of vengeance. But, as you cool off by figuratively counting to ten, it is imperative that you take the higher road by being the better person. Otherwise, you'll behave just like the miscreant who insulted you. We must always strive to behave just as a saint would behave in any similar situation, even if we're only a saint-in-training at this point.

"Here's something else you can do. Bring the image of this coworker into your mind's eye. You can mentally, or, if alone, actually tell that person's likeness just how badly their insensitive words affected you." Father then requested of Tom, "For the sake of our discussion, may I ask you to share with us the spiritual teacher whom you most admire?"

Tom softly replied, "Jesus."

"As you continue venting your feelings to the imagined image of your coworker, visualize a picture of Jesus appearing in their heart. Begin sending waves of pure love toward this picture of Jesus, then visualize your coworker completely transforming into Jesus, who is now present before you in spirit. You can do this with any such troublemaker, nemesis, or enemy—with any person who has ever harmed you. You can also visualize them as Mary the mother of Jesus, or as Buddha, or any spiritual figure or noble person whom you admire. You are in effect transmuting your unresolved issues and healing your emotional wounds, first by way of catharsis when privately expressing your pent-up emotions, then by constructively applying the salve of unlimited love, which is a far greater force than animosity.

"Once you are enlightened, you will see God in all beings. Your heart will be cleansed of all enmity and all residual emotional scars. In the meantime, this simple healing technique will give you a head start, helping you to rise above your lower emotions. If you can do this to the extent that all ill will is wiped clean from your heart, an aura of peace will accompany you wherever you go, and others will be transformed by the love you radiate.

"Remember, these apparent outer circumstances exist solely as mirrors. They are neutral in themselves and have no power over our spiritual self. But they trigger our emotional reactions, seemingly goading us to lose our composure. They serve as windows into our mind, showing us which reactions we must overcome. If we are susceptible to apparent attacks, such as the one you described, we must fortify ourselves so they no longer affect us. Our job as spiritual aspirants is to defuse all such emotional reactions entirely and free ourselves from the crippling influence they exert over us. Whenever we react, we only feed our tendency to react even more. By refraining, we gain proficiency."

Ginny related the following. "Father, you mentioned anger. When I was studying for my license, I realized I had enrolled in a school that credentialed some questionable types of massage therapies." Tom smiled; evidently he had heard this tale before. "I felt this might hurt my career. It would be like obtaining a diploma by mail versus graduating from a legitimate college. So I quit and re-enrolled in another school. But I had to re-do from scratch most of the trainings I had already taken in the first school. This set me back several months and cost me double the tuition! I was really mad at myself. Sometimes I still fume when I think about this. So, could please address anger?"

Father smiled. "Let me first tell a story about someone who also had to start over again. In the Tibetan Buddhist tradition, a sorcerer named Milarepa repented his sins after he had, in an act of retribution, caused the deaths of several dozen of his evil relatives. He sought redemption, so he approached the great Lama Marpa for spiritual instruction. However, Marpa made him undergo a series of grueling ordeals to purify the mountains of sins he had accrued from his wicked past. Marpa initially ordered him to build a large stone edifice. When Milarepa had painstakingly assembled the building,

Marpa commanded him to demolish it, then return all the stones to their original places." Many sighs and gasps could be heard. "This happened a second, and a third time. Marpa then directed him to build a fourth structure, and Milarepa dutifully obliged. Soon after, Marpa finally relented and initiated his obedient disciple, transmitting to him the secret teachings of the path. So you see, my daughter, your trials could have been much worse!

"We typically react with anger and frustration to certain situations because we are inpatient or else someone or something thwarts our plans. The outcome does not conform to our hopes and expectations, and so we are balked. Or, as in your case, we can direct anger at ourselves when we make a regrettable mistake. Prolonged stress can also cause anger and irritability, especially when one is pushed to the breaking point. Anger can also be triggered if we were wronged and the wrong is never righted, and so a lingering sense of injustice festers inside, such as a murderer getting off the hook on a legal technicality, leaving the anguished family enraged at the miscarriage of justice they just witnessed.

"The cure for anger caused by frustrated goals is not to have any expectations in the first place. Don't become fixated on a particular outcome. If we do become angry with ourselves, the remedy is to forgive ourselves for our oversight and move on, trying henceforth not to repeat the same mistake. If anger due to unresolved hurt or injustice consumes you, offer it to God whenever it intrudes into your mind, and thereby free yourself from identifying with it. You can also use the simple healing exercise I just outlined. The main point, though, is not to react to the circumstances of life with anger. Spiritually speaking, the one person hurt most by your anger is you.

"These are not merely palliative suggestions designed to give you false comfort. Simple as they may seem, these are practical solutions that produce tangible results when put into practice. And so, try using these remedies to subdue your anger whenever it erupts. As Paul the Apostle wisely advised, 'Eliminate all bitterness, rage and anger, rancor, and reviling, along with every kind of malice.'[63] And don't feed your emotions by reacting.

"Yes," Father mused, "when we react to outer events, we only feed our lower emotions. And this has a snowball effect…

"Have any of you heard the story from the Native American tradition about the two wolves?"

Several responded, "No."

"Then now is the time. A Cherokee grandfather was telling his grandson about the tremendous struggle that takes place within each person. 'It is like a terrible fight between two wolves,' he said. 'One wolf is evil. This wolf represents hatred, anger, jealousy, greed, pride, and deceit. The other wolf is good. This wolf represents kindness, peace, generosity, patience, forgiveness, and love. They fight each other constantly.'

"The grandson thought quietly for a few moments then asked, 'Grandfather, which wolf will win?'

"The grandfather replied, 'Whichever one you feed.'

"So, quit feeding your mind anger, worry, and so on. Consuming these emotions will only poison you. They are like mental junk food. You are what you eat, so once you abstain from feeding your mind stress, anxiety, anger, fear, and all similar emotions, you will thrive spiritually."

Nick wondered, "How do we know if we're succeeding?"

Father replied, "St. Paul carefully defined the qualities that will manifest in those who live a flourishing, virtuous spiritual life: 'The fruit of the Spirit is love, joy, peace, patience, kindness, goodness, faithfulness, gentleness, and self-control.'[64] These virtues crown those who successfully walk the spiritual path. Conversely, if your spiritual practices do *not* produce these qualities, then remember the cautionary words of Jesus: 'You shall know them by their fruits.'[65] This pithy saying of Jesus is the ultimate yardstick that measures whether you've been ingesting the correct spiritual food, to return to the lesson gleaned from our Native American story. If you're not growing in these spiritual qualities and are not producing them in all areas of your life, you're following the wrong path.

"And so, do not fault the outer world or attempt to rearrange or reform it to suit your needs. This can rarely be done. There are often larger cogs at play, over which you have no control. Instead, work to rearrange and reform your own mind so these emotional reactions no longer occur."

~~~~~~~~~~~~~

Father thereupon touched on one of my philosophical gremlins over the years—free will versus destiny. If there is free will, then we must do all we can to improve our lot in life. But if all is predestined, a person can do nothing to alter their circumstances. Father would address this topic several times during his discourses.

As was the case with a number of issues he discussed, his answer would vary according to context. For instance, during one meeting, Bill sought clarification: "You said that we have free will, then you said we don't have free will. Which is true?"

Father laughed, then answered. "The former … and the latter! Both are true in the context of how they were used."

While his response during this evening's meeting leaned toward destiny, Father ultimately advocated a path that combined both free will and destiny, thus acknowledging both the relative and absolute—the secular and spiritual—facets of life. This perfectly matched his viewpoint, insofar as when we are unenlightened, we feel we have free will—we are driving the car. When we are enlightened, all is seen as destiny—we are a passenger in the car.

~~~~~~~~~~~~~

"So, you must learn to welcome incidents such as these," Father counseled. "They serve as tests, indicators of your own inner state. Befriend them; they are showing you where you must work. With repeated practice, you will tangibly feel the divine Presence, so much so that your emotional reactions will diminish to the extent that the little events of life will not disturb you. You can then easily shrug off their influence and remain immovably grounded in your spiritual self while chaos ensues all around you.

"Recall the reassuring words of Sirach, the wise Jewish counselor:

> If you dedicate your life to serving the Lord,
> Be prepared for trials.
> Keep your heart pure
> And never waver in your commitment.
> Remain unperturbed in times of adversity.
> Cling to God; do not abandon him,
> Then you will find strength all the days of your life.[66]

"We must likewise reside continuously in God amidst all the events of this life, both good and bad."

The Best of Teachers

Gail piped up, "Earlier I asked if you were a guru, and you criticized some types of gurus. How then would you characterize a spiritual teacher?"

Father replied, "According to the Sufis, the more well-known a spiritual teacher is, the less that teacher is connected to the Divine. So, the best spiritual teachers are characterized by anonymity. The desire for fame, or the wish to accumulate a church filled with parishioners or an ashram full of disciples is indicative of ego, which is an enormous blot. Such individuals are often egomaniacs disguising themselves as legitimate spiritual teachers—'wolves in sheep's clothing.'[67] Beyond that, the drivel that gushes forth from the lips of pseudo teachers mesmerizes the vulnerable and the needy into mindlessly following them to their own spiritual demise, much in the same way the Pied Piper of Hamelin used his magical pipe to lure away the town's children, who were never to be seen again.

"Bear in mind, there are two types of gurus or spiritual guides: those who spiritually empower others, and those who seek to control others. The best of teachers give freedom to their charges. They typically establish a deep spiritual relationship with their students, often by means of formal initiation, which can considerably aid in their students' progress. They work on very subtle levels to bring spiritual aspirants home to God rather than browbeat them into submission. They neither tether their followers to themselves nor chain them to arbitrary rules.

"Such ideal teachers subtly discern an aspirant's inner nature so they can offer customized instructions based on their students' innate temperament. They then gently work to elicit the same state of consciousness in their students that they themselves experience, which an advanced teacher can do, as they can actually see into their students' soul. If they are not fully enlightened, they then pass on the transmission of blessings from their lineage, which can be extraordinarily powerful, to those seeking guidance from them. They get themselves out of the way instead of placing themselves squarely in the face of their followers and imposing their will on them. They demonstrate respect for their charges and provide a supportive, spiritual environment for them that fosters their progress. In this manner, their students are able to advance optimally by following a path that's in harmony with their temperament and vocation. Lao Tzu said it best:

> The sage teaches but does not force,
> He guides but does not obstruct.[68]

"Only those teachers possess this kind of attitude who themselves have no attachment to the results of their instruction. They express unconditional affection toward those who seek help from them, feeling truly in their hearts that their students are very dear to them. It is similar to parental love. And similar to parental love, sometimes they need to hammer home a point!"

Father's comment reminded me of Jason.

"Yet all along they want their students' freedom more than the students want their own freedom. Such unconditional love is rare. But it stems from their nonattachment; their realization that God or karma does all things; their attitude of 'regarding others as more important than themselves,'[69] as St. Paul emphasized; and their conviction that they act solely as intermediaries through whom divine grace operates.

"In addition, the great teachers awaken the Supreme teacher within you. When this occurs, your inner voice becomes clearer, more defined, offering intuitive moment-to-moment guidance and promptings about what you are to say or do, always in a spiritual context. Through their blessings, grace, and subtle influence, these sublime teachers infuse their disciples with spiritual conviction by forging an inward path that leads straight to the aspirant's soul. This exponentially assists in their disciples' spiritual journey. Learn by their example to be nonattached, to rely on nothing external, and to feel the unlimited love of God at all times while maintaining the attitude that you are an instrument of God."

After a brief pause, Stuart asked, "Aren't these types of spiritual teachers the exception and not the rule? You mentioned that some teachers only seem interested in how many followers they can accumulate."

Father smiled. "Remember, any legitimate teacher and you both have duties. Their duty is to permanently fracture your ego and lead your soul straight to God. Your duty is to cooperate with this objective. Otherwise, if a teacher coddles you or merely encourages you to hang around them without elevating your consciousness, you will have wasted your time. You'll be chasing yet another illusion. And if you don't take the spiritual path seriously and apply yourself wholeheartedly to your practice, you'll end up wasting what they have to offer. Besides, relying on a teacher can sometimes foster a kind of enfeebling, infantilizing dependency. This can produce spiritual laziness or *acedia* by stifling one's incentive to make genuine spiritual progress.

"For example, some may think that, because they have a spiritual teacher, they won't ever need to practice, which is a misconception. Some may even expect the teacher to magically bestow enlightenment on them without their making any effort. In fact, it is *we* who must at every moment possess the impetus for liberation. This initiative and incentive must spring solely from within us. As St. Paul counsels, 'Demonstrate earnestness to the very end so that you may realize what you hope for, then you will not become indolent.'[70] It is essential that we make concerted efforts to realize God. Without such dedication, spirituality is a mere pastime for such people, and their relationship with any genuine teacher is nothing more than parasitic. Finally, always take time to investigate these teachers and their teachings so that you can validate their authenticity for yourself."

Carla asked, "Father Christopher, you mentioned temperament, which I've studied in my classes. What do *you* mean by temperament?"

"First of all," Father said, "temperament is one's aptitude, while the related concept of vocation is their calling in life. Temperament refers to one's innate nature, proclivities, skills, and psychological mindset. Some people are introverted, while others are extroverted. Some are intellectual, while others are more physically or emotionally oriented. Some are contemplative, while others are active.

"Temperament goes hand in hand with one's vocation, which is doing the work that one was born to accomplish. Both play a vital role in an aspirant's spiritual life. Hinduism refers to temperament as one's dharma, and it is critically important that a person's spiritual path and their vocation are in accord with their temperament. For example, it probably would not have been a good match if Jesus had worked as an accountant or a soldier; he was raised a carpenter and became a teacher. Imagine Buddha working as an air traffic controller!"

Nick exclaimed, "If I were a passenger on that flight, I'm not sure if I'd feel more at ease or be terrified out of my skin!"

Then I asked, "Could you please explain more about your meditation practice?" I had been more and more intrigued by Father's approach. His explanation of stopping all thoughts during meditation paralleled my own experience at age seventeen.

"I'd be happy to," Father said. "First, find a secluded space in your home that you can call your own and where you can meditate without disruptions. This will help to create a spiritual atmosphere whenever you meditate. Then sit comfortably. I recommend meditating with eyes closed. Beginning meditators need approximately fifteen to twenty minutes of diligently applied effort just to gather the mind, free it from distractions, and focus on the home object. This will help to still all wandering thoughts that drift through the mind, which are like 'clouds of mosquitoes in the summer,'[71] as the eminent Russian Orthodox saint, Bishop Theophan the Recluse, wrote. You may even attempt to focus on two objects at one time, such as your breath and any suitable image that represents God. This doubly captures a wandering mind, assuring it will remain inwardly fixed. Those with more experience will quickly be able to escape this gauntlet of wandering thoughts and rapidly lose themselves in the inner orb of silence they have generated through their repeated past efforts.

"Also, try to keep your awareness centered in your spiritual heart when you meditate. This will help to produce a flood of bliss which will permeate your being and make you forget that you exist."

Father slowed the pace of his delivery. "Remember when you sit to relax your body, limb by limb. Allow your facial muscles to go limp; let your jaw go loose. Focusing the mind on the home object will help to prevent thoughts from taking hold and developing into a

James Michener novel. These thoughts will gradually cease to per-colate, and you will experience a profound inner stillness. Then a deep spiritual current will overtake you. Soon, you will be trans-ported to an exalted realm. Hold the mind in *that* place until it effortlessly remains there. Dissolve your sense of self, and continue to dwell in the blissful divine Presence, which will course through your entire being. The very moorings that anchor you to duality will begin to loosen. If you correctly accomplish this, 'you' will entirely vanish for a timeless period. This is the essence of our meditation practice, and the best way to learn is simply by doing." (See the Ap-pendix for more details about the meditation practice that Father Christopher advocated.) "So, let us now dissolve ourselves that we may dwell in the infinite presence of God."

Father fell silent and Ginny dimmed the lights. In virtually no time, we were absorbed in a palpable Presence. Our sitting lasted some forty minutes, although it seemed to go on forever.

After concluding the meeting, Father wished us a Pauline bless-ing: "May the Lord of Peace grant you peace at all times and in every way!"[72] Then he bade us all a good night. Gail and I headed back to Van Damme State Park. The others who had gathered during that now brisk February evening also began disappearing into the cool, misty, fog-laden darkness.

FOURTH VISIT (July 1991)

Armchair Mysticism

IT WAS SEVERAL MONTHS before I again saw Father Christopher. On this, my fourth visit, I traveled alone, as Gail politely declined to accompany me on any more trips to see him. Our relationship had developed some underlying tensions that would remain unresolved. We'd been seeing less of each other, and I knew if I pressed the issue, it would force these impasses to the surface.

As I drove along, I listened to sides of my various Classic Rock cassettes: ELO's *Eldorado*, the Kinks' *Arthur*, and Roger McGuinn's recent gem *Back From Rio*. My loyal friend Heather again put me up for the weekend, but this only added to the uneasiness that had arisen between Gail and me. Gail felt increasingly uncomfortable that I had cultivated close friendships with several women, including Heather. I felt absolutely no conflict in maintaining these platonic relationships, but I believe she saw them as potential threats. Perhaps in retrospect, I could have been more sensitive in this regard. While I sometimes stayed over with male friends when visiting distant locations, my occasionally staying overnight in women's homes when traveling afar may not have been the most prudent course of action to follow when I dated Gail or other women, at least for appearance' sake.

Father scheduled this meeting on a Friday so we could accompany him on a nature walk the next day. I took off work that Friday and arrived early at Heather's. She and I each did our own thing. Heather ran some household errands, and I ... well, I meditated a lot and just plain vegetated. But I also cleaned her throw rugs, unclogged her bathroom sink, straightened her back screen door, and edged her front lawn. During each stay I would rotate chores, and she was genuinely grateful for my help. Whenever time permitted and the opportunity presented itself, I never missed a chance to hike on a nearby trail, as I did that day. The trail I took meandered through alternating views of moss-draped forest terrain and open expanses that were punctuated by a deep azure sky dotted with puffy white cumulous clouds, which lent a dramatic skyscape to my outing.

We left on a beautiful summer evening for Father Christopher's now-familiar cabin. I felt both happy and relieved to see Father again; it was like returning home. Several of the regulars had already gathered—Brandon, Jason and his new female companion Stacy (whom Jason, I was told, introduced to Father with some trepidation; Father, however, warmly and unreservedly greeted them both), Ginny and Tom, Erin and Marta, Bill, and Liz and Stuart.

Stuart had recently driven up to Portland to attend a weekend seminar at a healing center. He shared his experiences with us, both good and bad. The good: Powell's Books, a legendary bookshop massively occupying three floors and one city block in the downtown area. Stuart spent every spare minute exploring and mining Powell's numerous nooks, crannies, and lairs. A book nut, he claimed he returned with three grocery bags full of used books, and he silenced his critics when he produced a photo showing his couple hundred dollars' worth of purchases. The bad: the teacher, a Hindu lecturer living in an East Coast ashram, who was longwinded and overly complex.

One thing Stuart noticed at the healing center, not surprisingly, was their well-stocked library. We learned they had several books by contemporary thinkers, including trailblazing physicist Fritjof Capra, whose groundbreaking 1975 work *The Tao of Physics* opened the door to more serious scientific explorations into parallel East–West insights. They also had several books by some modern writers on spirituality. Stuart bought one of these books at Powell's and, for better or for worse, Father had been listening in on our conversation.

True to character, Father joined in and rendered his opinion. "I read most of this book when it was first published. I felt the content drifted more toward grandiosity than substance. It conveyed no sense of the subjective experience of enlightenment. I also thought it was a mishmash of unconvincing, abstract concepts and meandrous, sweeping generalizations, which I found at times largely undecipherable. Further, I discovered little of practical benefit for a spiritual aspirant.

"In a more general sense, these types of spiritual writings—wherein various concepts are presented—don't always lead you to God; rather, they lead you straight to the mind and ego of the author. Once you become caught in their tangled web of ideas, well, just try to extract yourself and find God. They won't let you go. I've encountered this same situation with any number of writers and philosophers. Especially anyone who constructs a system, such as an 'ology' or an 'ism.' Instead of encouraging you to think for yourself or to realize God, they impose their version of reality on you. Many write profusely, yet say nothing. These systems are designed to create followers, whether they are psychological systems, philosophical systems, or theological systems. When reading these writings, one tends to get lost in the tedious labyrinths of the authors' overactive minds. And spiritual aspirants in particular don't want to get caught in the crossfire of the flotsam and jetsam that runs through an overactive mind. Our goal is to transcend the mind."

Liz shifted the topic by asking what was arguably, along with the issue of how to live in the world while maintaining one's spiritual bearings, the most frequently asked question of Father Christopher during the meetings I attended. "Father, how can a person know a genuine teacher?"

Father replied, "The true teachers always point beyond themselves, never to themselves, unless they are of Jesus' or Krishna's caliber. Jesus once told us that he served as a spokesperson for and acted as a representative of his heavenly Father: 'For I have not spoken on my own authority, but the Father who sent me commanded me what to say and what words I should speak.'[73] Any viewpoint an enlightened soul presents is a map; the deep spiritual principles they espouse serve as guideposts. Enlightened souls act as portals and passageways through which the path to God is clearly revealed.

"The lower teachers are often grubby, sticky like glue, feeding off their followers to fuel their egos or line their pockets. But they are the most popular because, in truth, they mirror the inner makeup of their followers, who in turn are often tainted by greed, ambition, and similar base emotions. We are drawn to the similar; birds of a feather flock together. If you want power, you will seek a teacher who is on that same wavelength—a power trip, as the saying goes. If you want fame or money, likewise.

"Look at how many salespersons use manipulative sales techniques to sell you things you don't need. Many so-called religious teachers do the same: they peddle money, success, and worldly gain when they should be preaching love of God and of others. That's why genuine spiritual teachers are so rare and often so relatively unknown.

"In Jesus' case, his real message of unlimited, unconditional love is at times so obscured and distorted by these unctuous, self-serving preachers, who skew it to fit their agenda, that the true meaning is lost. Jesus' actual views are often rendered unrecognizable because of these charlatans' secularized interpretations of his teachings. St. John the Apostle summarized this class of teachers: 'They belong to the world; therefore, their teachings belong to the world, and the world listens to them.'[74] They overlay their worldly mentality on to Jesus, and the bleating masses follow suit. These petty teachers corrupt the essence of Christ's message. They crucify him all over again. Which is, of course, an absolute travesty of everything for which Jesus stood. And yet, they flourish."

Stuart chimed in. "So Father, are you saying these lower teachers are frauds? What about spiritual writers?"

Several of us waited with bated breath for Father's response.

Father unemotionally replied, "There were two classes of religious instructors that Jesus frequently singled out and criticized as disrespectable during his lifetime—the scribes and the Pharisees. In modern terms, and irrespective of religious affiliation, these are the pseudo spiritual writers and the pseudo spiritual teachers, the same kinds of 'hypocrites' and 'blind guides'[75] that Jesus so thoroughly denounced in his time. I just now discussed the latter, the so-called spiritual teachers—those who would be considered, let's say at minimum, *questionable* when compared with legitimate spiritual teachers. Before I discuss the former, the pseudo spiritual writers, I'll speak a bit more about these teachers.

"Remember, like Moses before him, Jesus fought against secularization, and he re-emphasized the true purpose of religion. Both of these spiritual giants pointed out the errors that had crept into their native religion. Jesus stressed that religion is not merely reciting tenets, performing rituals, and following tradition. It is living a goodly life and, most important, establishing a living connection with God. And so, being vested as a spiritual teacher assumes a critical level of responsibility. A true spiritual teacher's job is not just delivering sermons and propounding dogma. It is leading other souls to God. As such, these teachers should live the kind of God-centered life that parallels what they teach so they can serve as role models to those who look to them for guidance.

"In addition, the category of questionable teachers includes those who set themselves up as authority figures or, worse, as objects to be worshiped—generally speaking, the self-anointed preachers and the self-appointed teachers —but who have no deeper inner realization. As Jesus pointed out, 'They do not practice what they preach.'[76] They ultimately possess no authenticity precisely because they have no foundation—experiential spiritual realization—on which to stand. And yet, this is the key criterion! Thus, they lack the one spiritual credential that truly counts. I would also, with rare exceptions, be wary of those who are not connected with and recognized by a legitimate lineage.

"By and large, these types of unqualified teachers should not instruct others. Nor should aspirants follow them; by doing so, they will get nowhere on their spiritual journey. I should note—this criticism is applicable in all times and in all cultures and across all religions, not just in Judea and Galilee during the time of Christ.

"Now, concerning the dubious spiritual writers, I'm specifically referring to those popularizers who write about the religious experience, mysticism, and mystical states, but, as with the questionable teachers, have no firsthand knowledge of these states. I'm sure that many such writers may be well intentioned. Some may offer sound advice; they may be reasonably knowledgeable and make sincere efforts to pass along useful information." Father mischievously grinned. "But in a broader context, not everyone who picks up a pen and writes about spirituality, and particularly the mystical experience, can be considered legitimate, let alone credible."

Ginny asked, "Father, are you saying these writers are deliberately leading people astray?"

"If there were any misrepresentation it would be this," Father said. "Such writers often present themselves as spiritual authority figures, and they are often marketed as though they are experts. But I'll bet my bottom dollar that many of them haven't any idea, not even an inkling, about what they are writing, experientially speaking. Some weave elaborate theories or opinionate blindly about the mystical experience without once delving into its more profound aspects. They are more or less guessing about the interior states of spiritual consciousness. Sometimes they write half-truths—their own conjectures mixed with information that could be gleaned from any encyclopedia. Some of them mislead other people into believing they themselves have attained these states. They promote the illusion that they are authorities, which may not always be true.

"On the other hand, many credible scholars, learned authors, and other subject-matter specialists present accurate information, posit plausible hypotheses, and publish academic treatises and sometimes popular tracts about spirituality, mysticism, and religion that carry weight. And still others, such as recognized spiritual authorities from authentic lineages, produce reliable translations and practical guidebooks on spirituality and mysticism. All these types of spiritual writers rightfully deserve credit for the realistic grasp they have of their subject, and so their writings possess conviction and authority.

"For example, many reputable professors produce landmark texts and classic works that demonstrate a serious and respectful treatment of religious studies and mysticism. These visionary scholars take the time and make the effort to learn and to understand the inner dynamics of the spiritual quest and the tradition about which they are conveying information through their written word. Their laudable works form the basis of our factual, unvarnished knowledge on these topics."

Marta added her two cents. "I'm not drawn to these kinds of intellectual writings. They don't speak to me at all."

Father replied, "I agree that academic writings can readily cross over into dry theory when they lack an experiential basis or if they aren't grounded in hands-on fieldwork," Father said. "This is because the mystical experience cannot be scientifically proven, let alone explained or described in an empirical, connect-the-dots manner. It must be *subjectively experienced.* Any after-the-fact interpretation is just that. You are only dissecting breadcrumbs after the main course has been consumed. To paraphrase St. Augustine, 'If you think you have understood God, it is not God you have understood.'[77] The giveaway is this: spiritual realization brings about a steady diminishment of the ego. That quality is absent from many such writers and teachers. Any advanced aspirant will see this. You will clearly see this for yourself once your inner eye of discernment opens with continued practice, enabling you to view this and any situation with complete objectivity and detachment.

"Beyond that, there is a Hindu concept known as *drishti srishti,* which means that our perception of the world is identical to the perceiver. In other words, we interpret what we perceive according to our own inner state. We perceive 'out there' what we are 'in here.'" Father pointed into the room, then to himself. "Theories typically reveal more about the person doing the theorizing than they do about their subject matter. For instance, it could be argued that Freud's theories reveal more about Freud than they do about us. The same is true of any writer or teacher. By scrutinizing their underlying message in order to discover what they're really saying, you can quickly gauge their level of spiritual evolution. And, in the process, you'll discover what they're *really* promoting, which more often than not is themselves. Again, you'll readily be able to discern a person's underlying motives as your detachment increases. This ability in turn will help you determine if any given spiritual writer or teacher is legitimate, and if they can truly benefit you."

We all had been listening attentively, taking in Father's sobering observations. He gathered his thoughts before resuming.

"Some of the popularizing religious writers and columnists write about the religious experience for a living only," Father observed. "They are not following a spiritual path, and they wouldn't recognize a lofty spiritual emotion if it hit them in the face. They write about mysticism or provide guidance on how to live a spiritual life for a mass audience. In this manner, they merely superficially propagate beliefs or report facts. They could just as easily be writing about sports or fashion. It's simply a nine-to-five job or maybe a hobby for them. It doesn't in any way affect their lives. And neither will it affect your life! This is one of the countless drawbacks of theoretical spirituality and armchair mysticism. Let's put it this way. Would you rather learn how to play baseball from a sports broadcaster, or from Hank Aaron?

"And other writers, who harbor aspirations of making a name for themselves, put forth the ill-fated claim, as did Hegel, to explain all of reality. You'll see this in many 'know-it-all' and 'explain-it-all' types of writings. Any person who makes such claims has been bitten by the fangs of hubris, and that venom is lethal. Reality is best understood by direct personal experience, never by theory. If theory is presented, it must be accompanied by practice. As Jesus said, which I'll slightly rephrase, 'You must hear my words, then put them into practice.'[78] Therefore, you must carefully discern if there is an underlying ego that permeates their writings or, worse, if their intent is to indoctrinate you into a whole system of beliefs. If either of these conditions exist, you'd best steer clear.

"Beware as well, because many spiritual writers and teachers who tout themselves as guru figures tend to endlessly promote and publicize themselves, which is again indicative of a monstrous ego. They weave a narrative or build a mythology around their lives and their seemingly never-ending series of accomplishments. Some create an entire industry, often an enormously lucrative industry, glorifying themselves! These are telltale signs that reveal their actions are primarily intended to garnish their own ego and enrich themselves in the process; you are just a means for them to achieve their nefarious ends. As with an insurance company, many times their true motive is to make a profit at your expense in order to help themselves, rarely you. Recall Jesus' unambiguous warning, 'Beware of false prophets, who come to you disguised as sheep, but inwardly are ravenous wolves.'[79] Spirituality is not a commercial enterprise.

"Yet, you can fight fire with fire by learning how to 'consumer shop' in order to discern the good from the bad. If any of these telling factors are present—ego, deceit, greed, hubris, hypocrisy—it would be in your best interest to entirely avoid this ilk of questionable spiritual writers and teachers."

Bill rather boldly but politely asked, "Father, earlier you spoke about teachers imposing their version of reality on others. Aren't you basically requesting us to accept and believe what you present to us?"

Father heartily laughed. "The sooner you forget everything I've said, the better off you'll be spiritually!" All of us laughed. "Except maybe two recurring themes—practice regularly, and don't take the world as real. And perhaps a third: question everything, and only accept as valid that which you can prove to yourself. This includes anything you've ever heard here."

Father resumed his previous train of thought.

"Many writers along these lines try to convince others that their theories are spiritually significant, when in fact quite the opposite is true. Theories will never get you to God—only direct perception and firsthand experience. The ultimate determinant that will convince anyone the mystical experience is real is their own personal experience of it."

Father grabbed a book from the nearby bookcase and leafed through its pages. "As *The Cloud of Unknowing* eloquently states:

> No matter how much a person may intellectually understand the spiritual nature of creation, they can never, by using their intellect, understand its uncreated spiritual essence, which is God. As Dionysius said, "The highest spiritual knowledge of God is that which is known by unknowing."[80]

"Furthermore, it is best to use a simple, uncomplicated principle as your map to reach God. The simplest premise on practical mysticism I ever read was in *that* book, which we used in class." Father pointed to another section of his library, then retrieved another book, *The Spiritual Heritage of India,* before sitting back down and flipping through to a passage: " 'God is; he can be realized; to realize him is the supreme goal of human existence; he can be realized in many ways.'[81] That is to say: God exists; God can be directly experienced; to experience God is the goal of life; and many paths can be followed in order to experience God.

"Once you excise the many layers of theology and dogma, and wring out all the embellishments and superstition from religion, then delve into the very marrow of spirituality, minus all its peripheral outer trappings, this proposition encapsulates the fundamental idea behind every genuine mystical tradition. This simply stated, four-part premise is all a person would ever need to use as their roadmap to God. Provided, of course, they decided which path to follow, then stuck to that path with tenacity."

Stuart brought the conversation back around to the book he had purchased. "I had some genuine insights when I read it," he said. "I thought the author had a good grasp of their subject."

"But were they transformational insights, or did they just tickle your intellect?" Father asked.

Stuart's silence spoke volumes.

Father continued, "From what I read, I found the ideas were mostly dogmatic pronouncements and abstract concepts, some quite complicated. But dogma and theories are fundamentally impractical in terms of helping an aspirant to experience God. Theories and spiritual book knowledge often titillate and dazzle, but in the end, they won't get you to God. It's incorrect for a spiritual aspirant to think that theories, let alone complex theories, must be understood as a prerequisite to understanding God. Spirituality isn't a theory. It's a realization.

"Besides, from a wider perspective, any spiritual writer should simplify their canvas, not overpaint it. Spiritual writers should present their ideas as simply as possible, then invite their readers to think for themselves, not pound their own dogma into their readers' heads.

"We read in the Tao Te Ching:

Once simplicity is made complex
Then names and definitions abound.
Once naming has begun, it is time to stop.
By stopping one can continue.[82]

"Beyond that, I could never understand why people are drawn to theories *they themselves* can't understand. Because they don't understand them, for some unfathomable reason they think they are significant. They don't realize that these types of theories are fundamentally unintelligible. Such theories can be so opaque and confounding that they'd give any logician a fit of blind staggers.

"Moreover, I've seen instances over the years where some spiritual writers or philosophers who construct various systems also figuratively construct a monument to themselves, as if to say, 'Look what I can do!'" Father waved him arms, provoking laughter. "Which is, of course, indicative of inexperience or egotism, or both. Or, in the worst of cases, the act of building a hollow philosophical edifice merely to adorn one's ego can point to signs of megalomania. Just look at Hegel, for example.

"I'll tell you a story," Father said, smiling. "Once a theologian died. He was greatly honored and respected, and was considered a noted authority. But upon arriving at the Gates of Heaven, he was shown a 'no admittance' sign. He failed to understand why. Just then, he looked over and saw a simple peasant woman approaching the Gates. She was readily admitted. That left him thoroughly flummoxed. For forty years he had studied everything about God. He knew each theological theory and every philosophical point of view, which he propounded in his lectures and books.

"So, he submitted an appeal. Eventually, he received a reply. The letter was transcribed directly from God.

"It read, 'My son, indeed you knew every fact that could be known about me. You recited by heart everything you had memorized. Now, do you remember that peasant woman you saw entering Heaven? She lived in poverty her whole life, and barely had enough food to eat and clothes to wear. But through it all, she prayed

103

continually, and she made a shrine for me in her heart. She was always content, she radiated love, and she joyfully gave of herself to those around her in need. So, it's true. You knew every fact there was to be known about me. But, unlike the peasant woman who knew me very well, you never once knew the real me.'

"Needless to say, the theologian was denied his appeal."

Father wrapped up his topic. "I find these types of writings are, in the final analysis, intensely *un*spiritual because they never transcend the mind, never give it a rest. As Brother Lawrence succinctly declared, 'Useless thoughts spoil all ...'[83] It's such labored mental activity—a slide rule-and-caliper approach to God. So I personally don't find value in these writings. I read Christ and Lao Tzu and Krishna, as well as devotional mystics from Christianity and Sufism and all religious traditions. Those who offer simple, practical pathways to God and who most affect the heart. And those who use devotion as a springboard to God, which is what spirituality is all about. I become bored with the mind. I like to dive into the colorless pools of the soul ..."

The New Spiritual You

Father broke his cadence. "Look, you still don't get it," he abstractedly uttered to no one in particular. Father's countenance changed. He sat up in his chair. I could see him shift from engaging in an intellectual discussion, to preparing to transmit a teaching—an entirely different style of discourse. I would not describe his dialogues as channeled teachings, because he was clearly the source of whatever he discussed. Whenever he was overtaken by this mood, I would characterize him as enrapt in an inner vision, which he would unselfconsciously communicate. He was not transfixed in an abstracted stupor as if he were hypnotized or in a trance; he was fully conscious and would interact with us by making eye contact and glancing around the room. And he certainly wasn't theorizing or intellectualizing. He conveyed a distillation of all he had learned, coupled with his encyclopedic knowledge about and shrewd interpretation of the world's religious scriptures. In addition, he was speaking from personal experience, which lent credibility and conviction to his words, even if he sounded a bit abstruse or technical at

104

times. Although I had turned on my cassette recorder earlier, I checked it again to make sure it was still taping.

"It doesn't matter in the slightest what work we perform in the outer world. It matters not what part we perform in the cosmic drama, whether we live a life of fame or obscurity, struggle or ease. Try as you may to alter your destiny, God has ordained a role for you to play. If you attempt to improve your lot, it may actually worsen. If you run from your life, it will somehow catch up with you. So, let it play itself out. Just remember, you are not the actor in this movie. The real you has nothing to do with *any* of this.

"The area I'm pointing to is the inner world—the realm of the mind. That is the seat of all karma. It is the source of your life's script. All the events that occur to you are the fruits of your karma ripening before your very eyes—in the market, driving to work, attending school, eating dinner, visiting friends, cleaning house. Anywhere and everywhere these events arise then fall away. Meanwhile, every moment your karma is being delivered like a takeout meal right to your door, where it completes its mission. Its boomerang-like path has come full circle—from you, where it is stored in subtle form, then back to you, its sole source. When it returns to you, it remanifests as the various interactions and encounters in your life, masquerading as this person or that situation. This process never stops, never ceases, as it impersonally dispatches back to you what you and you alone created simply by reacting with emotions to the diverse situations that arise in your life.

"The prophet Jeremiah expressed this same idea in theological terms:

> I, the Lord, examine the mind
> And search the heart,
> Giving to each according to their ways,
> According to the fruits of their deeds.[84]

"Look at the karma that returns to you. You heartily embrace that which you deem as good, and you vehemently denounce that which you consider bad. One brings happiness and satisfaction; the other brings anger, revulsion, and sorrow. Either way, you react and react and react. I cannot emphasize strongly enough that by reacting you only create more karma. You amass more baggage for yourself, whereas the purpose of spiritual life is to divest yourself of all baggage.

"Right now, your mood is entirely dependent on external circumstances. If you feel well, if you accomplish your undertakings, if you get your way, if others are nice to you, then you react with joy. The external circumstances cooperated with your objectives, so you interpret this as good. However, if so-called obstacles appear and your desires are thwarted or if others treat you poorly, you interpret that as bad. It's your interpretation of events that causes your downfall. This is further compounded by virtue of the fact that the 'you' who does the interpreting is wholly fictitious."

I asked, "But isn't it beneficial for an aspirant to know how to discern good from bad?"

Father smiled. "Of course. Only psychopaths and saints lack that ability." Everyone laughed, including me. "In the case of fully realized saints, their ability to discern is suspended when they are immersed in higher, nondual states of consciousness. All they perceive is the underlying unbroken unity, of which they are a part. To them, 'Dirt, rocks, and gold are all seen as the same,'[85] as the Gita observes. But for ordinary aspirants, and also for those times when a saint is engaged in normal dualistic consciousness, the ability to discern good from bad is essential.

"I'm referring to how the very act of interpreting things affects your spiritual bearing. When you interpret this or that experience, or judge x, y, or z person as good or bad, your interpretation or judgment crystallizes in your mind as an opinion or a preference. Your opinion, your preference, then becomes fossilized, as it were, and creates a new groove, whereas before there was none. This groove sinks its roots deep into your psyche, and your mind references this same groove in similar situations instead of encountering each situation anew. It operates according to the dictates of that groove. This was the Behaviorists' insight, and they are correct insofar as most of us are living examples of Pavlov's dog. All the grooves we create in our lives form predictable reactions and patterns.

"Using the terminology of Yoga psychology, these grooves are called *samskaras*, or impressions. Repeated impressions form *vasanas*, or ingrained traits. We unconsciously revive and reinforce each groove so often that most of us tend to become fixed automatons after around, oh, our college years. Then we more or less become set in our ways until death. To paraphrase a familiar saying, most people die at age twenty-five, but aren't buried until they're seventy. Which means that these reactions and patterns are fully in control of our minds all of our lives. Even more insidiously, they camouflage our soul. This is precisely how our subjective interpretation of and reaction to external events lead to our spiritual undoing.

"When a person's peace of mind is so easily swayed by external events, it indicates they have little faith. Faith is the inner experience that keeps one spiritually grounded regardless of the impact of any external circumstance. An advanced aspirant's mind will remain unmoved by fortune or misfortune, justice or injustice, blessings or travails. Good or bad, as such, do not exist for them. Their spiritual grounding places them altogether on another plane. Life just unfolds for them, as if moving along an assembly line from one station to another."

Father collected his thoughts while benignly looking at those assembled. "When your mind turns inward and becomes firmly rooted by faith in the spiritual core of your being, you will no longer react to external events, be they 'good' or 'bad.' This is the true test of spiritual progress: making the mind turn inward until it becomes so deeply anchored in the fertile spiritual soil within that it will not react at any time to anything. You will eventually reach a point where the things that now perturb you will not only *not* give you any cause to react, but you will not even register them. You will know when this occurs. One day you will look in the mirror and, upon seeing the face in the reflection, you will ask yourself, 'Is this someone I know?' You will be utterly astonished as the residual old you fades into obscurity and the new spiritual you emerges in its place. You'll then live in a constant state of wonderment as you grow accustomed to the new you, which in fact is your true identity. A person attains this state through grace, effort, surrender, prayer, blessings from their spiritual teachers, blessings from God, and most of all a keen desire to be free."

Pray Without Ceasing

All remained silent for several moments, pensively absorbing Father's teaching. Then Father asked, "Are there any questions?"

Stacy spoke up, "How important is prayer in spiritual life?"

"It depends on what you mean by prayer, and to whom you pray," Father said. "Most people pray to the deity of their religion, pleading for events to be altered so they can get their way, or else they pray to acquire things. They view God as their sugar daddy, nothing more. But the essence of true prayer is yearning for liberation; it is longing for God alone. This is the fundamental prayer in spiritual life. The Hindus have a name for this, which I cannot now recall." (The Sanskrit word is *mumukshutva*.)

"The great Sufi mystic Rabi'a embodied this outlook in her memorable prayer in which she prayed to love God exclusively, untainted by motives of fear or hope: 'O my Lord, if I worship Thee from fear of Hell, burn me in Hell; and if I worship Thee from hope of Paradise, exclude me thence; but if I worship Thee for Thine own sake, then withhold not from me Thine Eternal Beauty.'[86] This deep yearning wells up from the innermost recesses of an aspirant's heart and becomes the cornerstone of their practice. It is the primary factor responsible for success in spiritual life.

"As the Psalmist similarly cried out, fanned by pangs of fervent divine longing:

O God, you are my God!
I wholeheartedly seek you
My soul thirsts for you
My entire being longs for you
As a dry and desolate land needs water.[87]

"It is also essential for an aspirant to pray so they can develop such yearning, as well as pray to develop faith and an attitude of surrender. If you are a devotee, prayer is the principal means whereby you establish an ongoing, intimate relationship with God. A sincere devotee's prayers can be so intense that God actually seems to come alive in their heart. The joyful bond and sweet communications they share with God tend to parallel and sometimes even dwarf those of our most intimate human relationships."

Stacy followed up, "Which prayers do you recommend?"

"If you are Christian, the paragon of all prayers is the Lord's Prayer, which touches on every key point in spirituality: There is a God, whom I revere; I will follow God's will, not my own; I will be receptive to God's grace, which sustains my very being; I will seek God's forgiveness, which purifies my soul; I will forgive others, which cleanses my heart of hatred; I will invoke God's aid, so I can avoid straying from the path. The well-known prayer of St. Francis— 'Lord, make me an instrument of your peace'—is another sublime and powerful prayer, which shows us selflessness and compassion, and washes away our sense of ego. But any similar prayer from any religious tradition is equally recommended.

"Just remember, a prayer cannot be repeated mechanically. You must breathe life into it so you can realize its transformative effects. A heartfelt prayer forges a path straight to God and cleans the mind of its accumulated dross. We can follow the example of Jesus in this regard, who 'offered up prayers and supplications, crying aloud and weeping to God...'[88] It is simply astonishing to envision Jesus praying in this manner!

"Alongside that, the ultimate purpose of prayer is to deprogram you so you can shed the burden of your false identity. This is accomplished when you are absorbed during prayer to such a degree that you are no longer influenced by your mind and ego, and you become one—fully merged—with your prayer. You thereby forget yourself altogether. As St. Anthony emphasizes, 'Prayer is not *perfect*, if the solitary still perceives that [he] is praying.'[89]

"And so, when you pray, your heart's aching for God must pour out so strongly that your ego is entirely eclipsed. Your prayer will overtake your entire being and dissolve your sense of self. John Bunyan wrote of this, 'A man that truly prays one prayer shall after that never be able to express with his mouth or pen the unutterable desires, sense, affection, and longing that went to God in that prayer.'[90] Such a prayer cannot be rehearsed. You must pray from the depths of your being so strongly and with such single-minded fervor that you are divested of all worldly thoughts and stripped of your adult mindset, so much so that you come to embody the innocence and openness of a child. This creates the climate in which true prayer can occur. In such a prayerful atmosphere, one's supplications originate directly from their soul, from within the shrine of their heart, entirely spontaneously, and with total attention. *God will listen to such a prayer.* When stemming from such passionate outpourings, prayer in itself is an extremely effective and efficient path to God."

"Are there any more questions?"

Bill asked, "How often should a person pray?"

"This is another critically important aspect of prayer," Father said. "It is certainly beneficial to establish a prayer routine, however brief, in the morning upon rising and in the evening before retiring. Evening is also an ideal time to examine one's conscience. These routines help to renew your spiritual focus and center you in God. But along with establishing a formal, structured time for prayer, it is also helpful to make room in your daily life for spontaneous, un-structured prayer, as we discussed. But ultimately, the very best practice, in the words of Jesus, is to 'Pray at all times.'[91] St. Paul like-wise counsels, 'Pray without ceasing.'[92]

"If you haven't read the spiritual classic, *The Way of a Pilgrim*, about the inner progress of a nineteenth-century Russian Orthodox nomad who continuously recited the Jesus Prayer, as inspired by these words of Paul, I would highly recommend it." (The Jesus Prayer is, *Lord Jesus Christ, have mercy on me*.) "St. Paul teaches us that we are to maintain an inner prayerful attitude that perpetually links us with God amidst all circumstances. We are thereby in con-stant relationship with God and in constant dialogue with him. Further, because each moment of each day *is* our spiritual life, every second that ticks by presents us with the perfect opportunity for spir-itual practice. Thus, the entire life of an aspirant who is seized with spiritual ardor and devoted to their spiritual growth becomes one of continuous, prayerful communications with God; their heart is kin-dled spiritually by a nonstop Godward longing."

~~~~~~~~~~~~

Father's last remarks prompted me to recall a passage I first read in the mid-1970s, attributed to Swami Brahmananda, a prominent dis-ciple of Sri Ramakrishna: "Show me the line of demarcation where matter ends and spirit begins."[93] In other words, there is nowhere God is not. This parallels the Mahayana Buddhist view that worldly exist-ence (*saṃsāra*) and spiritual enlightenment (*nirvāṇa*) are not separate domains; both realms overlap and interpenetrate one another. As Father similarly observed, our daily life is our spiritual life. From this higher perspective, there is fundamentally no division between one's outer and inner facets of life—the two are inseparable. It is we who secularize our life and cut it off from our spiritual core. But as Father taught, and as he particularly taught me—to separate one's spiritual life and compartmentalize it from one's daily life is a mistake. Although it is helpful to isolate oneself from the everyday hubbub during times of concentrated practice, and to sequester oneself from the world when on retreat, spirituality can and should be practiced anytime, anywhere.

~~~~~~~~~~~~~

Interrupting my reflection, Father continued, "It is through all these factors—faith, yearning, surrender, true prayer—that an inward transformation occurs whereby a person becomes so infused with God that their sense of duality vanishes. This comes about because the twin sources of duality—karma and one's ego—no longer hold sway. At that point, all they see is God, and all they feel is infinite patience and boundless, unconditional love. Their former self—based in desire, attachment, and fear—has died."

Brandon puckishly asked, "How can I become infused with God and still do my homework?"

Father, smiling, answered. "By being detached. At present, you are working for worldly purposes. You are still gauging and measuring your life according to the world's standards; according to the criteria of accomplishment, achieving goals, and the like. You want to realize the fruits of your actions. That is, you set out to accomplish a certain objective and obtain its results, in this case finishing your homework.

"But this very effort, as the Bhagavad Gita maintains,[94] keeps the soul in bondage, because you become so fixated on realizing your worldly goal that you lose sight of your spiritual self. As Jesus instructively asked, 'For what will it profit a person if they gain the whole world yet lose their own soul?'[95] And so, you must carry out your work, but it must be performed without attachment, without worrying about the results. In this manner, you will always feel the presence of God no matter what you do.

"Further, once a person is entirely free from attachment, their work takes place automatically, unselfconsciously. The Gita describes this in paradoxical terms: 'The sage does nothing, though engaged in actions.'[96] The Taoists also have a name for this—*wu wei*: 'work without working.' Lao Tzu accentuates this theme: 'By doing nothing, everything will be done.'[97] It doesn't matter at all what that work is—whether it's cleaning toilets, bagging groceries, managing employees, or doing homework. It simply does not matter.

"You must perform this work without judging its relative value in terms of subjective criteria, such as *this* is more desirable or *that* is less desirable. Once you affix such emotionally charged labels and preferential designations on to your work, it instantly creates karma. When you try to escape or resist your karma, it only compounds the situation and creates even more karma."

Plea Bargaining

It was twilight time. For a short while, I focused my attention away from Father's well-metered talk, where I heard crickets chirping outside and the occasional sound of wind rustling through the nearby grove of Douglas firs, which I could see from where I sat. Gazing back into the room, I saw a dozen people of varying ages sitting with their eyes fixed on this one man.

"You want to avoid certain tasks and engage in others," Father said to us all. "By so doing, you are involved with attachment and aversion. Moreover, you want to get your way and force it through with effort and determination. And when you are balked, you rail against God." Marta gave a knowing look to Erin. "But then you are caught in a vicious circle from which you can never escape.

"When the ego is thwarted and refuses to surrender and accept its destiny, it creates the cycle of delusion so aptly outlined in the Gita, which I'll paraphrase: 'By brooding on worldly objects, a person becomes attached to them. He then becomes obsessed with obtaining them. Any obstacle placed in his way frustrates him. Thus thwarted, he burns with rage. This rage obscures his judgment so completely that he forgets his spiritual goal. Once forgotten, his spiritual perspective is destroyed. He then loses his ability to discern the Real from the unreal. He thus brings about his own ruin.'[98]

"Always keep in mind that we're dealing with these issues on the subtlest of levels. We're not addressing the specifics of one's outer circumstances—this person or that situation. To do so, to dissect the outer realm, is an utterly fruitless endeavor. The fact is, you have your destiny that you must face. Therefore, accept it with equanimity. Never lose your poise, even if destiny upsets your plans. You must adapt to changing circumstances as they unfold. So, maintain your balanced state of mind under all circumstances. That is the main point."

Then Jason interjected, "But Father, what about the death of a parent?" Jason's mother had recently died after battling breast cancer. "Or what if my dog were run over? Are we supposed to react with callousness to these kinds of events?"

Father replied with a serious look. "Not in the slightest. There is a world of difference between callous indifference and emotional detachment. I've seen spiritual aspirants become insensitive because they make a stoic effort not to feel anything. They think that a cold veneer is the same as detachment. Nothing could be more mistaken! In our relative, personal sphere of life we undergo many hurtful losses, which rout us to the core. It is normal and natural to grieve and feel a void in our lives. So, allow these emotions to pass through you. But at the same time, try to remember that the real you—your soul, your spiritual self—is entirely untouched by these things. It's only your body and mind that are undergoing these situations. With continued practice, you'll come to embody such a state of detachment that the events of life will barely cause a ripple in your consciousness."

Marta asked, "You mentioned surrender. How can a person know if they're in a state of surrender?"

"My daughter, let's first look at what surrender is not. You make a commitment to surrender to God. Then, without warning, something totally unexpected happens—your power goes out during a winter storm, your child develops a serious illness, your boss takes credit for an idea that in fact he stole from you—and you go to pieces. That's because you really didn't surrender. Instead, you merely proposed a set of acceptable losses that conveniently excluded the ones that genuinely mattered. That is not surrender; it's plea bargaining.

"A person who has truly surrendered doesn't care in the least bit what occurs to them, for example, how many delays they endure, or what inconveniences beset them. A fully surrendered individual doesn't even notice the relative, valuational difference between one event and the next. They don't interpret events as good or bad, joyous or tragic—everything simply *is* to them.

"It was Jesus who taught the ultimate prayer of true surrender: 'Thy will be done.'[99] Because, Thy will *will* be done, willy-nilly! And it will be done no matter if you're dragged along kicking and screaming or if you go peacefully. If you are late for a crucial job interview—in the overall scheme of things, what's the big deal? If you lose your retirement savings in an investment scam—well, it didn't destroy your soul, did it? These types of circumstances, disastrous as they sound, are all part of your karma, which you alone created. And by reacting to them ..." Father waited for someone to finish his sentence.

Bill volunteered, "You only create more karma."

Father nodded. "Remember, there are not numerous outer circumstances, there is only one outer circumstance. But now there are numerous 'yous.' When you have developed a keen sense of spiritual detachment, you will be able to remove yourself entirely from the immediacy of your life's situations and circumstances. At that point, you will gracefully flow with whatever is intended to occur without interfering or reacting. You will then see that the person you think you are—at work, at home, attending classes, driving, shopping, eating, sleeping, cavorting with friends—is not the real you. The person you think you are is just an assemblage of karmic molecules going through the motions. You'll then see that the real you is completely uninvolved in the drama that unfolds between the body you occupy and the world it inhabits. The real you is pure unalloyed consciousness and bliss, which remains forever untainted by all this. The rest is a mirage."

A perplexed-looking Tom asked a question, perhaps prompted by his role as husband, father, and main provider for his family. "But Father, are you saying that we must not plan or try to improve our lot? I mean, your examples of surrender sound unrealistic, almost facetious. These events could really affect a person. If I were late for a job interview, I might as well withdraw my application. If I lost my life savings, I would...my family would be devastated."

114

Father's appearance turned grave. "I certainly did not mean for my comments to seem insensitive. Nor did I intend to make light of people's adversities." Then his eyes slightly twinkled. "But I do see that I successfully illustrated my point.

"When you ask about planning or improving your lot in life—that is the art which each of us must try to perfect. It requires more finesse than walking a tightrope. Ideally, we flow without resistance and without care in the direction where our destiny points. Yet, our destiny may point us toward loss, grief, and strife—even destitution, maybe the poorhouse. There may not be a happy ending. Or, we may be destined to lead a Charlie Brown kind of life, whereby we undergo a succession of bad-luck experiences, but ultimately end up sort of all right.

"But are we—meaning our ego, our lower self that is involved with the world—to give up our efforts to better our circumstances, our families, and ourselves when besieged by adversity? I think the following saying sums it up best: 'The key to success is the ability to go from one failure to another without any apparent loss of enthusiasm.' So, whether you experience failure or success in your life, cast forth your aspirations and never give up. But don't lose your joy of life if your plans don't materialize. If you do, you'll wallow in resentment, cynicism, and defeatism. Then you might as well give up. So the critical element is *attitude*, because a person's attitude will either raise or sink them."

Tom continued, "In my life an unhappy ending is simply not an option." Ginny smiled. "But you're right, we're often dealt many blows."

Father responded, "It's true that, from the ego's point of view, you go through life and, along with attaining goals and accomplishing objectives, you also suffer setbacks, misfortunes, and undergo assorted difficulties. The former cause you joy, while the latter cause you distress, or at least they give you reason, and sometimes ostensibly very justifiable reasons, to grouse and protest. Which merely points to the fact that when the ego is thwarted from achieving its goals—the fruits of its actions—it typically becomes upset. It tends to blame anything and everything other than itself for its inability to obtain them. Conversely, when you obtain what you want, you take full credit for it!

"Whereas a fully surrendered saint accepts every single circumstance and encounter that befalls them with the same state of mind they experience in deep meditation. Bear in mind the perspicacious observation made about Brother Lawrence, which indicated his profound inner realization: 'with him the set times of prayer were not different from other times …' "[100]

Adding to the volley of questions, I asked, "What if a person is in a difficult relationship? Or an oppressive work environment? Isn't it incumbent on them to change these kinds of situations?"

Father replied, "If you—meaning your ego, your lower self—can alter your circumstances, then do so if warranted and not overly difficult. If there's nothing you can do, then cope as best you can in the meantime with a cheerful disposition and a detached attitude until an opportunity presents itself to make a change. But remember, '*Homo proponit, sed Deus disponit*': 'Man proposes, but God disposes.'[101] All depends on God's will.

"I recall a story I heard in India at one of the Ramakrishna ashrams, which I believe was originally told by Ramakrishna himself.[102] I'll restate some of the Hindu terminology.

"Once a devout weaver lived in a village. All the villagers loved and trusted him. He sold cloth for a living. If a customer asked him the price he would say, 'By the will of God, the price of the thread is one dollar; by the will of God, the labor is fifty cents; and by the will of God, the profit is twenty-five cents. So, by the will of God, the cost of the cloth is one dollar and seventy-five cents.' People had such confidence in him that they would immediately pay the price.

"The weaver was a faithful devotee. After finishing dinner, he would spend hours sitting in an open hut meditating on God and repeating God's holy name. One night the weaver stayed up very late. Just then a band of thieves passed by and spotted him. They needed someone to carry their loot, so they dragged him away with them. Then they robbed a nearby house and tied the spoils to his head. At that very moment, the police arrived, and the thieves ran away. But the weaver got caught and was arrested and thrown in jail. The next morning, he was brought before a judge.

"When the villagers learned of this, they came to the courthouse and unanimously declared to the judge, 'Your Honor, this man would never steal anything.' The judge then asked the weaver for his testimony.

"The weaver replied, 'Your Honor, by the will of God, I was sitting in my hut late at night meditating on God and repeating his holy name when, by the will of God, a band of thieves came by. By the will of God, they spotted me and dragged me away with them. By the will of God, they robbed a house, and by the will of God, they tied their loot to my head. By the will of God, the police showed up, and by the will of God, I was caught and placed in jail overnight. Now, by the will of God, I have been brought to appear before you this morning.' The judge saw that the weaver was a devout man and had been telling the truth, so he ordered him released at once. As he exited the courthouse he said to his friends, 'By the will of God, I have been set free.'

"The moral of the story is that everything happens according to God's will. So, maintain your peace of mind and never lose your faith in God while the drama of your life plays itself out. After all, it's only your destiny ripening." Then Father impishly grinned. "I might add a second moral, which is contained in this exhortation by Jesus and most certainly would have benefitted the weaver: 'When you pray, go *into* your room and *shut* the door ...' "[103] Everyone laughed.

"You may use magic and cast spells and wear amulets, or call on the gods to help you get your way by removing your so-called obstacles. You can spend your money on psychics who will sell you hope. But you only fortify the false reality of your ego by making it think it can do this or that and thereby achieve its goals. This in turn redoubles its strength, and then you are really lost. Surrender, therefore, is the only viable alternative."

Father paused, then scanned across the room and said, "I know you all have duties to perform, obligations to meet, families to raise, and similar involvements in the world. These events are all your part of your destiny. However, your only *real* duty on this planet is emancipating your soul from the clutches of duality and reuniting with God. Jesus clearly asserts, 'Only one thing is needful.'[104] That 'one thing' is undivided devotion to and exclusive focus on God. And so, when the world seems insipid to you; when you grow tired, even disgusted, with the panoply of worldly diversions and allurements that

117

await you at every turn; and when your soul aches for God and God alone, then at that exact same moment you earnestly begin your spiritual quest and commence your journey back to your true home. Until then, you are blinded by a thick fog that surrounds you, which obscures your perception and judgment, and which causes you to roam aimlessly through life, lost in the labyrinth of endless illusion."

Then Stacy spoke. "Father, frankly, very little of what you're saying applies to my daily life. What about when I'm stuck in traffic and late to work? Or my credit-card debt?"

"True," Father acknowledged, "these ideas won't help you arrive at work on time or alleviate your debt. But they might help you retain your poise while undergoing these situations. There will always be complications in life. So, you have to use your savvy and be as practical as possible. Maybe leaving earlier for work and re-examining your expenses might help ...

"The higher course is what I present for your consideration. Do not fight your destiny. Do not resist what is to be. It only destroys your peace of mind. Your destiny will unfold on this physical plane. It *is* your life; you have no imaginary life apart from it. If you think you do, then you are deluded. Otherwise, when your life is coming to an end, you will look back in regret and say to yourself, 'I was forever wandering down the corridors of a life I never lived.'

"But most people create a fantasy life for themselves, or else they lose themselves in the fantasy lives created by others—movies, novels, soap operas, and so forth. They become addicted to these fantasies, and they often live their lives vicariously through other people, be they famous or fictional. Or else they seek out thrills and excitement and a continuous stream of entertainments so they won't get bored. They become infatuated with the sensation that novelty produces. They develop dependencies on external objects for constant stimulation. However, the only true escape is in their soul, which is their innermost core. As Jesus emphatically declared, 'The kingdom of God is *within* you [italics added].' "[105]

~~~~~~~~~~~~~~

This brought to mind a meeting I once had with a Native American teacher with whom I studied for a time. She was a mystic and a seer. She said to me, "You see, we first create the stage. Then we invite others to perform in the play we write. All these things are in our mind. Others are simply acting on the energy we send out. They participate in our drama because of our attachment."

After pausing, I commented, "If we don't construct the stage, then the play can't take place."

She replied, "Exactly. The key to everything is inside us. We are taught by society to seek outside ourselves. But the only place we can find all answers is within. We need to go within ourselves and find the truth there."

~~~~~~~~~~~~

There Will Only Be One

Turning to Tom, Father said, "So again, the answer is to surrender. As the Psalmist joyfully sang: 'Show me the path I should follow, for I surrender my life to you.'[106] Never forfeit your peace of mind for anything. Don't expend all your energy trying to change your life's circumstances. Don't try to remove all of your so-called obstacles or remedy every one of your conflicts. In reality, they will never entirely go away. They'll just as likely be replaced by a whole new set of difficulties and hardships. Rather, change your outlook by elevating your consciousness, and these so-called obstacles will immediately disappear. I'm not talking about physically disappearing. But from a higher level of spiritual development, you won't view them as obstacles; you won't even be aware of them. At that stage, your so-called obstacles and your destined activities will be one and the same. There will no longer be a division between the two, which now seem at loggerheads with one another. There will only be one."

Tom noted, "It's really challenging to accomplish this in my life. Especially not reacting. There's always a point of no return just as I react to something. I often catch myself, but usually after the fact."

"Well, the Sufis take this concept one step further. They view the exact moment, the very point in time when you react to any given person or situation, as a choice between God and everything that is not God." Father snatched a couple of books from the nearby bookcase then skimmed through several place markers in the first. He began reading, "'If you act a single jot of your actions for the sake of another, your thought and speech are corrupt, since your motive in acting for another's sake must be hope or fear; and when you act from hope or fear of other than God, who is the lord and sustainer of all things, you have taken to yourself another god to honour and venerate.'[107] Thus, by even once taking your mind off God and diverting it to others and the concerns of the world, you have substituted the world for God. What a delightful approach!"

Flipping through the pages of the second book, Father exclaimed, "Here's another outstanding reference from Sufism. 'Someone asked a saint, "What is an idol?" The saint replied, "Whatever diverts you from God is your idol."'[108] In my opinion, this is an example of a perfect spiritual teaching.

"In a similar manner, whatever worldly object you think about the most reveals your greatest attachment. This could be your job, your family, your pet, or your car. You may be consumed by money. Or an enemy. If you obsess about yourself all the time, what does that tell you? The worldly object that most preoccupies your mind *is* your greatest attachment! As Jesus emphasized, 'For where your treasure is, there your heart will be also.'[109] So, never once allow your mind to stray from God. Keep it fixed on God at all times. I should add, in anticipation of a likely question, that thinking about or contemplating on God cannot be called an attachment per se because the end result of continually thinking about God is liberation from all attachments.

"The Sufi outlook is one of absolute nondualism, because the Sufis maintain that nothing exists apart from God. This can be viewed as paralleling the nondual pronouncement in the Hebrew Bible, which is so often overlooked. Does anyone know what that is?"

No volunteers came forward.

"No one?"

The crickets from the nearby woods could still be heard chirping amid the ensuing silence.

"Bring to mind the first of the Ten Commandments: 'You shall have no other gods before me.'"[110]

A collective sigh of epiphany coursed through the group.

"Therefore," Father said, winding up his central theme, "embrace the conditions of life that are presented before you. Do the work that comes to you without effort. But, and I underscore this, don't ever once become emotionally involved. You must control your emotions before they control you. Remain unmoved despite all the commotion, negativity, and assaults of this life. Then you will come to embody the ideal that is conveyed in the Gita." Father recited the following verse while slowly, deliberately accenting each word. " 'Content with whatever comes of its own accord, free from perceiving duality, liberated from comparing oneself to others, remaining unshakably poised in success and failure alike—such a person, though acting, is never bound by their actions.' "[111]

Father came down from his inspired, airborne state and reached for his customary cup of herbal tea. After a short break, Ginny lit the single votive candle on the corner altar, which complemented the two larger white candles on the nearby coffee table that were sometimes also lit during meetings. Father then led us through an intense meditation, which took us to sublime heights. I felt higher than a kite, as if I were soaring. I noticed that several in attendance also seemed inebriated from the contagion of silent euphoria that blanketed the room. Afterward, Father bade us all goodnight, thanked us for coming, and said he looked forward to seeing us again "by the will of God," which provoked laughter. "I urge you to continue your spiritual practices," he advised. "You must practice diligently so you can realize these truths."

Most of those who had gathered dispersed in short order, while a few lingered to chat on the grounds in front of Father's cabin, which a recently installed large sensor light now fully illuminated. But all were left alone with their thoughts as they drove off into the encroaching night, ruminating on the insights that Father Christopher had so evocatively shared on that July evening.

Reflections at Lake Cleone

The next day, a Saturday, a small group of us joined Father Christopher for a morning walk at nearby Lake Cleone, a charming 30-acre freshwater lake situated amid a largely undeveloped natural setting close to the Pacific Ocean. Stuart and Liz picked up Father, who rode with them in their van. All of us descended on the lake at the same time and parked near the picnic area, where we settled in at one of the tables.

The area was surprisingly less crowded than I might have imagined, and fortunately the weather cooperated. Heather and I joined Father and the group as we leisurely sauntered along a short section of the scenic 1.3-mile trail that loops around the lake before turning back and spending time at our picnic table. As could be expected, Father was more than disposed to conversation.

Bill opened the discussion. "Father, last night you counseled us not to remove all the obstacles or remedy all the conflicts that occur in our lives. But what about, for example, combating injustice or following up with flaky people when they renege on their promises? Or what if someone's trying to take advantage of me? I certainly don't want to take that lying down."

Father responded, "The main point, always, is not to react. And I should emphasize that true surrender is not docilely acquiescing to every single event that occurs in your life. That kind of passive mentality makes you excessively submissive, even gullible. Then you become cosmic fodder, ripe to be targeted and manipulated by exploiters or bulldozed under by the impersonal hand of fate. God did not intend for his devotees to become weak-willed, naïve pushovers! This kind of apathetic, laissez-faire attitude borders on Quietism. If your arm is broken, you don't helplessly wallow in self-pity and simply resign yourself to living with it, pathetically sighing, 'Woe is me; there's nothing I can do.' Instead, you must act decisively and take care of it.

"So, too, calmly face the vicissitudes of life with fortitude, and respond as situations warrant. The fact is, sometimes you—your secular self—must stand up for yourself and, when called upon, you must act courageously in order to deal with various people and circumstances.

"When interacting with others, try following the advice given by the Hebrew prophet Jeremiah: 'Do not be intimidated by them.'[112] And so, if necessary, you must fearlessly, yet peacefully, confront those who would harm you.

"However, there is a happy medium that allows for both assertion and surrender. It's like paddling a raft that's headed downstream. We navigate the minor currents, but all the while our primary course is set; it has been predetermined by the river. Similarly, it's important to find that fine balance where you can be surrendered and assertive at the same time, so you can go with the flow but also paddle when necessary. You thereby interact with your karma instead of fatalistically allowing it to trample you under.

"I recall a quote from Mother Catherine, foundress of the Sisters of Mercy: 'Perfection does not consist in performing extraordinary actions, but rather in performing extraordinarily well the ordinary actions of every day.' In a similar way, you can deftly engage your mind's tools to successfully traverse the road of life. As you progress spiritually and come to identify increasingly with your spiritual self, these same mental abilities will begin to function automatically in the background. When this occurs, you'll remain detached from them as you simply witness yourself carrying out assorted tasks. St. Teresa of Ávila wrote of this state, wherein 'the active and contemplative lives are combined…Martha and Mary thus work together.'[113] At that wondrous stage, you will know that you—the *real* you—are not your mind or body.

"In addition," Father said, still addressing Bill, "there is no injunction barring you from confronting irresponsible people, seeking justice, or calling out others on their lies, hypocrisies, and deceits, especially if you are in the right and their malice is adversely affecting you. The same goes for standing up for yourself if others are taking advantage of you. Think of Jesus' many clashes with authorities, or his overturning the moneychangers' tables in the Temple courtyard.[114] But keep this in mind: always seek justice, never vengeance. The true meaning of 'turn the other cheek'[115] is not to retaliate.

"All these situations require that you not become emotionally agitated. Otherwise, you may get so caught up in any given situation that you become entangled by it. By the time this occurs, you've already lost your poise. So always remain unperturbed. That is the key."

Spending time outdoors with Father was thoroughly enjoyable. Cool breezes drifted in from the nearby ocean, and many species of birds could be seen in their native habitat. Ghostly snags of Bishop pines dotted one shoreline, adding an otherworldly atmosphere to our outing, as we soaked up Father's thoughtful reflections at Lake Cleone.

Liz inquired, "Father, you mentioned Jesus turning over the moneychangers' tables. But Jesus also allowed himself to be arrested, then he passively stood before Pilate without speaking one word in his own defense. Wasn't this the same type of excessive submissiveness you warned against earlier?"

"Not in the slightest," Father replied. "Jesus demonstrated assertiveness when appropriate, and he demonstrated surrender when facing his fate, which, it is assumed, based on the Gospel writings, he knew all along. At the Garden of Gethsemane, he prayed in anguish to be released from his impending death. But he ended up conceding to his destiny by poignantly uttering, 'Thy will be done.' Therefore, it can be soundly argued that Jesus' resignation stemmed from a position of strength and courage, not one of submissiveness or a crushing hopelessness. So, too, it's best for us, courageously and fearlessly, to utilize both surrender and assertion as situations in our lives necessitate, just as Jesus did."

Tom spoke up, "Father, you're advising us to be assertive and also to surrender. This sounds contradictory."

Father laughed, then remarked, "It is true that spiritual life can sometimes seem—and many times is—contradictory, even paradoxical, as Lao Tzu poetically describes. Then again, the very heart of spiritual realization is nonlogical and inexplicable ... ever mysterious. There is a reason why Chaitanya, the Hasidic masters, and the Dervishes all danced away in ecstasy, and why Hui-Neng is depicted as tearing up the scriptures!

"But, to address your comment, I believe that both approaches, surrender and assertiveness, are needed as warranted. Even though they seem mutually exclusive, one can be inwardly surrendered while outwardly assertive at the same time. Both approaches can and should be put into practice when traversing the spiritual path, which must be trodden as adroitly as if walking a razor's edge."

Just as Father concluded speaking, a nearby angler reeled in what appeared to be a decent-size largemouth bass, which spooked a great blue heron that was doing its own fishing in a neighboring marshy area of the lake. The fisherman released his catch from his net, having presumably caught his limit for the day.

We all paused when witnessing the scene, which served as inspiration for Father's impromptu, analogical comments.

"Spiritual life," he said, "consists of unhooking your awareness from all the disruptions that occur in our lives, just as that fisherman unhooked his catch. And ideally, like an even warier fish than that bass, you must never take the bait to begin with when worldly situations provoke you to react. In this way, your spirit remains open, unchained, altogether free; it is never caught in any kind of net that would entangle it. Then you can focus exclusively on your spiritual self, without being disturbed by outer events of any kind, unlike the magnificent heron we saw take flight.

"Outer events are like a series of transitory mirages that float through the mind, similar to the small flocks of snowy plovers we see darting to and fro. These outer events march along like a parade, sequentially traversing the screen of the mind. But these are only pantomime-like movements without substance, mere automated flutterings, like the passing images and faint voices of a fleeting dream, like the events of this good day.

"When you truly understand and come to *live* this realization—that external 'reality' is nothing but a glossed-over projection of the mind—then the events you undergo will no longer carry any emotive charge. You will then be entirely free from their influence, just as that section of sky"—Father pointed skyward—"is entirely free from clouds."

Bill piped up again, discussing a more down-to-earth topic. "Father, earlier you spoke about turning the other cheek. I once had my wallet stolen by someone I thought was my friend. I was livid beyond words!"

"Did that person return it?"

"Yes, ... I caught him with it."

"Are you still upset?"

"Only when I think about it."

Father said, smiling, "Then whenever this incident comes to mind, offer it to God. Literally, take that image and mentally turn it over to God. In this manner, you rid yourself of owning that memory because you've given it to a new owner—God. Your past doesn't exist anyway, except in your memory. So give it away for good and be free from the hold it has on you."

"I've never thought of that," Bill said. "I'll try it. What gnaws at me is that he was my friend. Sometime after, he was caught embezzling funds from his workplace. He spent time in prison."

Father observed, "Then cosmic justice was meted out with a quick turnaround time! This certainly proves Jesus' teaching, 'Whoever is trustworthy in small matters will also be trustworthy in large ones, and whoever is dishonest in small matters will also be dishonest in large ones.'[116] However, along with divesting yourself of this memory, it is necessary to practice what I believe is one of Jesus' most challenging teachings."

The Storms of Life

Father then narrated the following scripture: " 'Peter approached Jesus and asked, "Lord, how many times must I forgive a person who wrongs me? Up to seven times?" Jesus replied, "I say to you, not just seven times, but seventy-seven times." '[117] Anyone who can truly 'Forgive those who trespass against us'[118] and not harbor any resentment or hold any grudge toward others who have wronged them has gone a long way toward attaining sainthood. This includes forgiving ourselves for any misdeeds we may have committed in the past.

"You may ask how attaining a perpetual attitude of forgiveness is a mark of spiritual progress. Because the only way to achieve a state of total forgiveness is to become completely free from one's lower self. Hence, a person is capable of complete forgiveness if they have no ego to take offense in the first place. At that stage, they won't even be aware of anything to forgive.

"Yet, the spiritual benefits of forgiving others generally do not help the ones whom we forgive; those benefits help ourselves. We usually won't change those who harm us by simply forgiving them. Unless, of course, God intervenes. But praying for our oppressors aids in cleansing our *own* hearts of anger and hatred, as the Book of Ecclesiasticus declares: 'Forgive your neighbor when they wrong you, and your own sins will be forgiven when you pray.'[119] Jesus echoes these liberating words: 'If you forgive others who mistreat you, your heavenly Father will forgive you as well.'[120] Thus, practicing forgiveness helps to heal our own soul.

"Remember also, Jesus taught us to 'love your neighbor,'[121] and equally, to 'love your enemies.'[122] He never placed any limits on this love. He didn't teach us to bracket off this person or to exclude that group of people—to love some while hating others. Recall the Proverb, 'Better a small portion of vegetables served with love, than a fattened ox served with hatred.'[123] Jesus taught us to love others unconditionally and to forgive others unconditionally, without any boundaries or restrictions. We may not always condone another's behavior or lifestyle, especially if their actions adversely affect us, but we must see through their outer persona and love their inner essence with this same unrestricted spiritual love. 'Do good to those who hate you. Bless those who curse you. Pray for those who mistreat you.'[124]

"Jesus further teaches us by his own words and deeds to overlook all outward differences, such as race, color, gender, religious beliefs, and economic status when practicing unconditional love and forgiveness. A person cannot be considered enlightened if they still perceive differences. Enlightenment presupposes that one's consciousness is part of an undifferentiated whole. If you are still able to differentiate, you are not yet enlightened.

"Similarly, St. Paul eloquently writes, 'There is no distinction between Jew and Gentile, for the same Lord is Lord of all and richly blesses all those who call on him.'[125] The great founder of Sikhism, Guru Nanak, similarly taught us to look on all as equals.

"So," Father said, summarizing his main topic, "engage others without fear. Confront those who apparently live without higher principles if they trouble you. Battle injustice when it knocks on your door. But whether confronting your tyrannical boss, or coping with aggressive drivers, or navigating through hordes of impolite people at the supermarket, or trying to come to terms with a dishonest friend, never, I repeat, *never* lose your poised, balanced state of mind. Once you do, you will have compromised the integrity of your soul by caving in to your lower emotions. Then all your spiritual accumulations will drain out, much like pulling the plug in a bathtub.

"Therefore, never sacrifice your peace of mind for anything or anybody. Otherwise, your emotions win out over your soul. Once this occurs, they gain the upper hand and dominate you. Every time you give in to them, you reinforce their hold over you, which in turn strengthens your sense of duality. Thus, you must learn to withstand the storms of life and maintain your composure throughout each tempest."

Following some small talk, Father stood up and led us the short distance back to the parking area where we all bade goodbye to one another. We then headed our separate ways, filled with the happy memory of this uplifting day we spent with Father Christopher.

A SPIRITUAL MEMOIR

First Awakening

IT WAS OCTOBER 1991. Autumn is my favorite time of year. I deeply resonate with each change of season, and I become especially in-drawn and introspective during the fall months. I had been increasing the length of my meditations, and many times my mind would effortlessly cease to function and become absorbed in a deep spiritual current. Yet, this was causing me conflict. On the one hand, I had a necessary involvement with the world. But on the other hand, I wanted to sever all worldly ties and dive wholly into my spiritual practices. I could not seem to integrate the two worlds, which at times seemed poles apart.

    A high-school friend and I once analyzed what separated Jesus, Gandhi, Martin Luther King Jr., and certain other iconoclastic nota-bles from the crowd. "They never compromised," he observed. That insight has stayed with me through the years. I, too, had aspired to be in a position where someday I would not have to compromise. On that day, I would be able to live my spiritual vision without watering it down. But in October 1991, I felt haunted by the recurring thought that I had abandoned my spiritual roots. I'd adopted the customs and views of the society in which I lived. I'd focused on making money and, while I was satisfied with my then-current level of earnings, I'd also chosen to live a life of voluntary simplicity as enjoined by Thoreau. Yet, *all this* at the expense of nourishing my soul? At times I felt lost.

I drove from my apartment and headed north toward Father's cabin. I had spoken with Heather and told her that I planned to camp out at MacKerricher State Park rather than stay with her. Gail and I were drifting apart, and I didn't want to fuel the estrangement. Besides, I needed to be alone. I needed to unearth something inside of me that had been buried since my life-altering spiritual experience of 1974, my self-described First Awakening.

~~~~~~~~~~~~~

This was the pivotal, defining event in my life, lasting from early September through mid-December 1974. For slightly more than three months, the portals of heaven opened up. I consider all the incidents in my life as leading up and referring back to this one central experience. Even now, its living presence occasionally engulfs me. It only needs the proper setting to resurface.

A number of factors influenced and presaged this event. Beginning in my mid-teens, I saw how most of humankind had enshrouded itself in an artificial, contrived reality that is completely cut off from nature and the spiritual realm. I felt that people were programmed from childhood into accepting a worldview based on materialistic values. They embraced conventions, such as time and language, which only reinforced their conditioning. They created cities to perpetuate their artificial environment. I clearly believed that humans were in the grip of a mass, illusive lie. This line of thinking persisted and became my predominant mindset through my late teens and early twenties; it enlivened and inspired me. It shaped the very essence of my view of life.

During this formative period, I had serendipitously developed my philosophical belief system based on my limited life experience and my own observations. For the most part, it was unspoiled by formal education and, except for less than a handful of admired writers, largely unaffected by the thoughts of others. I had encountered the writings of those whom I considered the three classic nineteenth-century nonpolitician American philosophers—Emerson, Thoreau, and Muir, all of whom exerted a significant influence on me—together with a smattering of Eastern thinkers, but none too influential.

My mind was not filled with rigid preconceptions or dogmatic beliefs. I was open, unspecialized, raw. I intentionally avoided learning different intellectual and technical details about things, such as the scientific names of trees. I felt this would dilute and color my direct interaction with and immediate experience of these objects. I believed that outside knowledge only tainted people's minds with potential bias, and it predisposed them to accept information passively, unquestioningly, rather than actively and consciously acquiring it. Thus, I aspired to learn and absorb knowledge on my own wherever possible and not through books or by way of other people's accounts, which I generally shunned, as I distrusted so-called experts. I felt that too much reading provided a person with secondhand analytical information, which tended to overshadow a more direct, experiential mode of learning. I sought firsthand knowledge, free from intermediaries and extrinsic interpretations. In short, I needed to find out things for myself. I further believed that all people could—and should, ideally—similarly acquire knowledge on their own with minimal outside instruction. I felt this learn-it-yourself method of educating oneself was an innate ability that remained dormant within every individual.

~~~~~~~~~~~~~

When I began my senior year at my all-boys high school, there were four events that molded my outlook. First, I had recently undertaken an unforgettable wilderness adventure. I leisurely hiked the 55-mile North Lake to South Lake loop trail in the Eastern High Sierra when backpacking with a friend from August 3 to 13, 1974. This left an indelible impression on my young, sensitive mind. The all-enveloping presence of nature swallowed me up and drained me of human perspectives. I vividly recall losing all sense of distance and, even more important, of time. For eleven priceless days, I lived on nature's terms, completely removed from the endless concrete and droning roar of Lost Angeles, as I then called the unforgiving city.

This adventure affected me so intensely that it transformed me. I had never been so thoroughly wonderstruck in all my life. I endlessly marveled at the numerous jaw-dropping spectacles of nature I encountered in this sublime high-country mountain pavilion. I wrote about this outing in early 1979: "It took three or four days to divest me of myself. The magic then descended full force. The Sierra began engulfing me." This mood swept me up, and I couldn't leave it behind when I left the mountains. "I clung to it like a jeweled treasure chest—it revived me, rekindled me. I became fully alive with it."

Second, coupled with my awestruck experience of nature, I was confronted with the reality of having to go to college, learn a vocation, and become part of the establishment. I shuddered at the thought of losing my philosophical orientation, to say nothing of losing my close friends, and most of all, leaving my sacred personal world. I had watched others capitulate to the system. When they did, the luster disappeared from their eyes and the spark became extinguished in their soul. I did not want the same fate to befall me. I did not want the world to win. I would not succumb to the pressure of being fashioned into someone else's idea of who I should be. Neither could I do something for a living that I loathed by virtue of slaving away at some mindless, unrewarding job that would define my role in society. I would not live as a robotized zombie.

Admittedly, I was not exactly establishment material. In the fall of that year, a friend asked me what I wanted to do in life. I replied, "Wander from town to town and spread joy to all people." While my youthful idealism was admirable, it most likely would not have put bread on my table. I also dreamt of living alone in a small house in the Sierra Nevada mountain range, which also would not quite be considered a formula for worldly success. My unambitious goals were not those expected of a typical college-bound student, and they would not have particularly endeared me to any college-admissions board. The truth is that I refused to live a life I felt was totally foreign to me. Instead of adapting and quietly conforming to the average American way of life, which I viewed as conceding to the commonplace status quo, I desperately wanted to escape.

Third, a sobering event at my Catholic high school profoundly affected me. When driving out of the school parking lot onto the adjacent street one afternoon in early September, I saw a friend in the car behind me. True to our teenage horseplay, I raised my right hand and jokingly saluted him with the *digitus impudicus*, not once but two or three times, goading him on, fully expecting him playfully to reciprocate. But there was no response. When I looked more closely in my rearview mirror, I realized that he was actually a *she*, and she was fuming mad. She drove straight around the corner and parked in front of the administration office, then marched herself inside. And I, aghast and embarrassed at my horrible mistake, sheepishly followed her. Inconsolable and raving, this high-school mother let everyone within earshot know the debased nature of my crime, especially—alas—the principal. My repeated apologies did nothing to assuage her unrelenting tirade.

Crestfallen, I, too, met with the Jesuit principal minutes later, who no doubt could see my face oozing remorse, along with abject, palpable fear as to my fate. I expected him to sentence me to weeks of detention—the dreaded afterschool incarceration known as *jug*, wherein many a recalcitrant soul was forced to recite obscure Latin texts, or worse, memorize stanzas by Milton. Or he could have suspended me, which was well within his purview, for my regrettable and unintended offending behavior.

But he simply said, "Always remember, actions speak louder than words."

"Actions speak louder than words." This dictum proved far more powerful than any punishment. In that moment of utter receptivity, those words sank to the core of my being, so much so that they became a lifelong theme, an ideal worthy of emulation. The principal's profound utterance, stemming from compassion and insight, deeply planted in me a seed that radically altered my attitude. From that instant on, and especially during this autumn 1974 time period, I realized I could not compartmentalize my life. Thoughts, intentions, words, deeds—all must be brought into alignment so they match without discord. A person cannot preach one thing and practice another. One must root out all double standards within oneself. Consequently, after this incident and for the remainder of my First Awakening, I purposefully avoided talking much about myself. My actions became my primary speech.

Fourth, and lastly, three classes in my senior year deeply affected me. Despite my predilection to acquire knowledge on my own, the skillful teachers who taught these courses gently imbued me with understandings I could not have gained myself.

The first class consisted of a course that examined values, and what I learned turned me inside out. The young lay instructor adeptly goaded us to think about life, about the deeper meaning of events, about ourselves, and how all these issues intersected.

The second class was theology, based on the practical application of New Testament teachings. The ordained teacher imparted to us his impassioned sense of helping the poor. He focused on alleviating hunger, which greatly influenced me. This eye-opening introduction to hands-on spirituality made me painfully aware of the plight of poor people. At times, I felt more concern for them than for myself. Once during this time, I fasted for two days—which was significant for me in light of my fast metabolism—so that I could experience the same sensation of hunger they felt. I occasionally donated my extra lunch money to the cause. I began to identify with those who struggled in life. It pained me that so few people cared about their predicament.

My exposure to these newly uncovered psychological and social issues set into motion inner awakenings that were far more than spiritual. I went through a crash course in political, societal, and environmental realizations. Without fully understanding the system, I knew it was wrong by the effects it produced—inequality, injustice, mistreatment of many, a lopsided social structure, unfair economic allotments, widespread pollution, and ecological imbalances. These high-school courses served to kindle a larger awareness in me.

The third class I took was photography. For my homework, I would snap pictures of my favorite haunts: the spectacular view from the seaside cliffs high on the Palos Verdes peninsula overlooking the rippling blue, whitecap-tinted Pacific Ocean; Temescal Canyon and the surrounding lush Pacific Palisades environs; Brooktree Road and the adjoining magical streets that wend around Rustic Creek and Rustic Canyon Recreation Center in verdant Santa Monica Canyon; the sheltered enclaves in the Crestwood Hills neighborhood adjacent to North Kenter and Hanley avenues along the scenic Brentwood highlands; several expansive vista points off iconic, sinuous Mulholland Drive between Stone Canyon Road and fabled Laurel Canyon Boulevard; the stately residential areas east of UCLA and nearby Holmby Park; the winding hillside roads north of Sunset Boulevard between Beverly Glen Boulevard and Coldwater Canyon Drive that snake around lavish mansions and hidden bungalows; and the then-secluded Franklin Canyon Reservoir greenbelts.

This class made me conscious of how to look at the world around me. The lay teacher gave us some valuable technical pointers. I would no longer take for granted the interplay between shadow and light, or color. I became acutely aware of the vibrant multicolored hues that constantly surround us, if we only paid attention. When snapping a photo, I would intuitively learn to sight the best angles to optimally frame an object, and I'd instinctively account for depth of field when juxtaposing foreground and background elements. However, I wasn't just taking pictures. During my First Awakening, my camera became a lens looking not into the outer world but into my soul. Photography turned into a spiritual exercise that enabled me to capture externally what my soul was perceiving internally. Thus, I viewed the world from an entirely new perspective, and my newly discovered capacity to look at things from a different vantage point carried over into my daily life.

Hence, the amalgam of my unconventional, individualist mindset and my unorthodox worldview; my reluctance to conform to establishment norms; my entrenched resistance to becoming a collegebound functionary; my lingering, overpoweringly moving impression of nature; my genuine remorse at having inadvertently offended someone; my effort to rid myself of hypocrisy; my ability to see the world in a new light; and my newfound cognizance of macro issues, including identifying with the poor, reached a fever pitch in me. These combined events upended my world. They catalyzed me by squeezing my soul into one all-encompassing scream, an inner cry, which insistently implored: *I want out!* I madly sought refuge from the imprisonment of home, family, school, society, and self. This fervor, this unquenchable fire, rapidly grew within me.

No Use for This Body

I had been an average teen growing up in the early 1970s. I was raised in an upper-middle-class home. While I was brought up in the Catholic tradition, I was not overtly religious insofar as I did not regularly attend church. My activities and interests consisted of normal, ordinary teen fare. I underwent typical adolescent adventures—and certainly my share of misadventures—when learning about life. I neither presented myself nor thought of myself as pious, and I sincerely doubt that anyone would have singled me out as particularly spiritual or devout. But this inner crisis prompted me to turn to God. My behavior markedly began to change.

In the evening hours, I would shut myself in my room and seal out all light by drawing the shades and blocking the bottom of my door until the room was pitch dark, except for the light given off by my bedside floor lamp. Then I would randomly open my family Bible and flip through its pages until my eyes fell on a seemingly intended passage, often a reflective or inspirational verse from Psalms, Proverbs, or one of the books of the New Testament. I would fix my attention on that one passage, as if nothing else existed, learning whatever lesson it offered, absorbing the essence of its meaning until it alone resonated inside me. I would then turn off my bedside light and, amid the piercing darkness that enveloped me, I'd lie face up on my bed using no pillow, with my open Bible placed face down over my heart. I would thoroughly rest my arms and legs until they were entirely devoid of tension. Remaining as motionless as possible, I would not allow so much as a muscular twitch or an itching sensation to disturb my ultra-relaxed, comalike state. Then, I would immerse myself in what I later learned was meditation, although at the time I had no idea what this was called.

Often in combination with my Bible-reading routine, I would similarly lie on my bed and play sides of a select few of my favorite albums: most frequently the transcendent *To Our Children's Children's Children*, and the equally transcendent *Every Good Boy Deserves Favour*, both by the Moody Blues; and the largely introspective, empowering early RCA releases by David Bowie—*Space Oddity*, *The Man Who Sold The World*, and *Hunky Dory*. I had arranged my speakers on either side of my bed to achieve perfect stereo balance, and I would lie perfectly still and focus intensely on the music until my mind attained a state of deep concentration. I would force all stray thoughts to stop. In so doing, I heard each lyric and musical note as if for the first time, as my once busy mind was emptied of all thoughts and would no longer interfere with my direct perception of the music. I fused and became one with the music, as I felt no lingering division between the music and my sense of self. Unbeknown to me, I was using music as a means to meditate.

At times, I would also briefly perform vigorous exercise before lying down to meditate, which had the effect of releasing any surplus bodily tension. This short workout routine helped induce a state of physical calmness, which proved conducive to meditation.

These practices allowed my inner being to enter a timeless realm wherein my ability to distinguish outer from inner, object from subject, and music from listener, had vanished. My mind was concentrated to the utmost degree and became oblivious to all else. My sense of self-consciousness dissolved, and I became inwardly rapt in deep meditation. I soon craved this loss of self more than anything.

In addition to meditating, I prayed to God from the deepest level of my being, calling out for guidance and direction. I would kneel next to my bed and send forth spontaneous, heartfelt outpourings directly from my soul to God. I felt an unimaginable longing to immerse myself in the infinite expanse of God. I reacquainted myself with Jesus, to whom I had turned during previous times of crisis in my life. Jesus' teachings came alive in me. I began to view him as the anchor and foundation of my life. I would often visualize the Lord's Prayer and repeat it slowly, one syllable at a time, until each word became animated in my heart. When praying, I envisioned God as a formless, omnipresent entity. However, praying to Jesus was much easier because I would picture him as he is commonly portrayed in popular images.

My frequent tearful Godward entreaties washed away the darkness concealing my spirit. My soul was laid bare, stripped of all pretentions. I invoked the living presence of God through the sheer force of my prayers—the vague became tangible; the invisible, known; the unseen, powerfully felt. My prayers drew me outside of myself and, at the same time, drew God closer to me. When I prayed, every cell of my being was on fire. This had the effect of eroding layer upon layer of the encrusted sheaths of worldliness that had covered my soul.

I started to follow a very basic path, as clearly outlined in my New Testament readings:

What is my purpose in life?
  "Seek first the kingdom of God."[126]
What is God?
  "God is Spirit."[127] "God is love."[128]
Where can I find God?
  "The kingdom of God is within you."[129]
How can I know God?
  "Love the Lord your God with all your heart, with all your soul, with all your mind, and with all your strength" and "Love your neighbor as yourself."[130]
But what of other concerns?
  "Where your treasure is, there your heart will be also."[131]
What, then, must I do?
  "Whoever hears these words of mine and puts them into practice is like a wise man who builds his house upon a rock."[132] "Come, follow me."[133]

It was so simple what I was to do, and I proceeded to do it, forcefully throwing off all hindrances that would prevent me from following and applying these life-transforming teachings of Jesus and his disciples.

Night after night, I continued this secret activity. My room became my private shelter; its shrouding darkness provided a sanctuary to my soul, which was emerging as if from a long slumber. I had found my refuge, my escape. While the world slept, I remained awake during the benevolent nighttime hours, praying for release from my worldly fetters. When I finally did fall asleep, I drifted off quickly and slept soundly. If I awoke later in the night, I'd often repeat my routine of Bible reading, prayer, and meditation.

All the while, my high school work suffered; in fact, I was so completely seized by my all-consuming, round-the-clock craving for freedom that I neglected to do most homework. I wrote of my attitude toward homework at the time: *Why am I doing this meaningless crap?* I shunned anything that disrupted my inner connection with God. It was not worth selling my soul for the world. I pursued my spiritual discoveries at all costs, as nothing could compare to my inner explorations—an undertaking incalculably more meaningful than anything even remotely imaginable in life. My new nocturnal prayer and meditation practices so diametrically opposed and took precedence over both my scholastic obligations and my worldly responsibilities that any secular ramifications simply did not concern me.

After I meditated, I had no desire to engage in activity the next day. I felt I might lose whatever gems I had mined during my inner excursions the previous night. I wanted only to enjoy unruffled peace and bask in the blissful spiritual awareness that engulfed me. This pursuit had become my passion, drawing me deeper and deeper inward, regardless of consequences. Nothing was more important. All that mattered was this newfound something growing inside me, which I nourished to the exclusion of everything else.

I ate no special diet, although I soon gave up meat. This had the effect of de-stimulating my body and mind, thus creating a calm psychophysical condition that was even more conducive to my spiritual practices. During the most intense phase of my awakening, I hardly ate at all, at times barely tasting food in my mouth until an inner sensation alerted me to stop. For some reason, this paltry amount of nourishment seemed to suffice, and I don't recall losing weight. For that matter, I hardly slept. I somehow survived on pure spiritual energy that was derived from divine grace, and this would provide enough sustenance needed to maintain the intensity of my burgeoning realization.

Throughout this time, with the exceptions noted below, I didn't seek outside help, look for gurus, or receive any type of spiritual initiations. Because of my youthful, provincial outlook and my correspondingly narrow experience of life, it never occurred to me to search out, for example, Hindu or Buddhist explanations, which may—or may not—have helped to place my experience in perspective. Except for adhering to the words of Jesus and the other passages I had read in the Bible, I embraced no formal belief system as my guidepost. I only followed my inner promptings, which I felt originated from God. I was totally on my own, learning the mysteries of my soul through my personal journey of self-discovery.

At most, I sought out two spiritual directors I had known, although I also briefly spoke with two priests. First, I met with my Catholic grammar-school religion teacher at her home. I tried to articulate what I was undergoing. I spoke to her of experiencing a state with no pain, no worries, and uninterrupted peace. I tried to explain that not one event affected my true self, which I felt was composed of pure spirit.

She responded, "What you are describing to me is heaven."

I shared with her the following observation. "I feel if I were to be thrown off a building, some part within me would continue to live."

"Nonsense," she replied. "You would die instantly! If I were to pinch you, you'd feel that."

Thus, I felt she misinterpreted my experience. Because of the dramatic nature of my example, perhaps she thought she was talking me out of suicide. But I truly identified with the shimmering, joyous essence that was taking hold inside my being. I also felt that my soul was located distinctly apart from my body, and so I didn't fear death, which I equated with the death of my body, not my spirit. I came to feel that, regardless of whatever happened to my body, my real "I"—my soul or spirit, and not my personality—would not die. Once during this time I signed my name, "I eternally exist," based on my experiential insight that my true "I" was neither my ego nor my personality, but pure disembodied spirit. I again wrote a note on December 4, "I think I would be able to live forever because I would have no use for this body."

My former religion teacher recommended that I read *Hymn of the Universe* by Jesuit philosopher Pierre Teilhard de Chardin, stating that my thoughts tallied with his. However, I did not read this book, not particularly on account of any perversity or rebelliousness, but because I could not tolerate blanketing an intellectual overlay on to my inner experience.

I also sought out an instructor at my high school, a priest, who taught religious studies, and related my experience. But as I described my spiritual state, I could see a certain look in his eyes that occurs when a person feels threatened. He responded by bringing up various theological points, which were well beyond my comprehension. He thereby intellectualized away my experience, which was the last thing I needed.

Neither of these religious counselors had any real idea what I was going through. My experience was outside their frame of reference, their comfort zone, and the constraints imposed by their positions. They were both eager to explain away my situation, offering little if any genuine support and empathy that might have actually benefited me, or any insights that could have shed light on what I was experiencing. Then again, what were they to do with a young, wild-eyed, would-be mystic who was breaking all boundaries of convention? Other than sharing my experience with these spiritual directors, I did not convey my inner findings to anyone.

I was also quite unaware of how my spiritual awakening might have affected others, except perhaps on one occasion. One day, I sat with a friend on the steps of a building at our high school during a break. Steve was an accomplished guitar player. He began playing his acoustic guitar, and I allowed my spiritual mood to overtake me. I also had brought my guitar to school that day, and I played rhythm to his lead. I became increasingly engrossed in his playing, as though I were deeply meditating on it. Then, as if prompted by some mysterious inspiration, Steve began playing faster and faster. He perfectly, feverishly hit each arpeggiated note. When he concluded his frenzied solo, he looked at me with a broad smile and exclaimed, "I've never played like that before!" This is the only instance I can recall when my spiritual mood may have spilled over and in some way affected another person.

A Complete and Total Union Into One

Meanwhile, I continued my practices in solitude, feeling quite alone and isolated from others. At the same time, I felt the absolute truth of Jesus' counsel to "Love one another." Along with putting into practice whatever biblical maxim I had read the previous night, the crux of my daily practice became invoking and expressing this increasing spiritual love, which I felt palpably coursing through my being. I extended this unconditional love to others, not so much through any particular act, but through my changed attitude. I became more open, sympathetic, friendly, nonjudgmental, and understanding. I tried to see the world from others' perspective. I deliberately broke down whatever barriers I sensed that might have prevented me from establishing a connection with other people at this deep, heartfelt level. I felt called, as if on a mission, to share this boundless spiritual love with all.

For example, as part of my inner discipline, I worked hard to rid myself of any hatred, bias, and animosity that I even remotely perceived within myself. The very ability to define an enemy or designate an adversarial situation became uprooted from the core of my being. I started to feel a deepening sympathy with all persons, especially the destitute. I would vicariously experience the sorrows and afflictions of other people as if they were my own. I viewed strangers as my closest friends.

Because this universal love had such a vast equalizing effect on me, I felt I could mingle with rich and poor alike, treating them the same, unaffected by their social or economic status. I realized I was not superior to anyone, but rather equal with everyone. To think otherwise was the very pinnacle of arrogance—the presumption of the fallen angels. I came to realize that any condescending feelings I may have felt toward others were nothing more than a ruse of my ego. This stark insight had the effect of reducing my sense of self even more, as I continued to eliminate any arbitrary mental divisions that separated me from others. The graces that enveloped me enabled me to overcome these seemingly intractable elements in my character.

Relatedly, I saw only the best and most sincere aspects of people, imputing on to them the very noblest of intentions. I was able to express spiritual love toward everyone without restriction, and give with a full, open heart. I knew no limitations, no distinctions. I was completely self-contained, filled with inconceivable joy, absorbed in inexpressible peace, and fundamentally receptive to and in tune with the words and teachings of Jesus, whose spirit became vibrantly alive in me.

Once I consciously recognized any attachments or addictions that may have been affecting me, I made deliberate efforts to break free from them, such as an occasional cigarette dependency I unfortunately acquired during my first year in high school. I forcibly attempted to give up familiar habits, accustomed routines, and deep-seated patterns of behavior. For instance, my friends fully expected me to stay up late and watch David Bowie, one of my early 1970s musical heroes, when he appeared on *The Dick Cavett Show* on December 5, 1974. But, obeying my inner spiritual promptings, I went to bed earlier than usual that night after my meditation routine, and I missed the program, much to their subsequent chagrin.

No doubt my peers must have been mystified by my abrupt, un-characteristic behavioral changes. A couple of acquaintances criticized me. I don't doubt they looked on me as enigmatic, unor-thodox, and nonconformist—which I unpretentiously took as compliments. This was part of the general unsympathetic reception I received during my spiritual awakening owing to others' complete lack of understanding of what I was undergoing, coupled with their unwillingness even to attempt to grasp it. But I genuinely didn't care what they or my other friends thought. If they thought me crazy, I thought them even crazier. I was following a higher authority.

At some point, I reached a state wherein I experienced no anxieties and no worries. I embraced each event as it played out, without fretting, feeling that God was directing everything that was occurring. This realization humbled me. I felt, *Who am I to interfere with the ways of God?* As a result, I began to see perfection in all things without any need to intervene and change them. I realized there was very little I could do to alter most events anyway, so I decided: Why should I worry about them? It seemed fruitless to stew over this situation or that outcome. It was only my body—the seat of my ego—that was going through the various activities of life. Because God was in charge, I felt I should accept as God's will whatever developed unsought, on its own, without trying to bring about a different result that would be more advantageous to my ego. My watchwords from that point on became, as I had written at the time, "nothing matters," because I stopped assigning a hierarchy of importance—viewing some things as more favorable, and other things as less favorable—to the various circumstances of my life.

Thus, I neither strove to attain a particular goal nor did I miss whatever was absent from my life, including things I did not possess. I felt there was nothing more in life to be sought or achieved. Events either would or wouldn't come to pass, and so I purposely avoided dwelling on them. In addition, I disciplined myself not to complain, which imbued me with patience. It was infinitely more valuable for me to retain my inner calm than to disturb it for worldly purposes, such as complaining about this or that. I simply would not allow any such distractions to pull me away from my spiritual practices. One moment's diversion brought me the pain of a thousand hells. I viewed every circumstance as a trial in which I was challenged either to remain in harmony with God or else forfeit my inner relationship with him.

I also became receptive to anything that would help me grow spiritually. I considered everything—past incidents, encounters with people, current events—as *lessons* designed to bring me closer to God. Many times an appropriate lesson appeared out of nowhere. I viewed my past in a new light by seeing how all the elapsed situations in my life, both good and bad, were really learning experiences intended to help me find God.

During this period, I found very few outside interests with which I could relate. This was because my new spiritual world became increasingly disconnected from the secular world I once knew and inhabited. One day at home, I viewed a TV showing of the 1933 film version of *Alice in Wonderland*. I felt a deep connection with Alice's illogical adventures and the assortment of eccentric characters she encountered. Everything in her Rabbit Hole world was as topsy-turvy and nonsensical as what I was facing in mine. I fully empathized with Alice's identity crisis: "I can't explain *myself*, I'm afraid, sir," said Alice, "because I'm not myself, you see."[134]

And, like the Private Charles Plumpick character in the 1966 cult-classic *King of Hearts*, I discovered that those who were considered insane were often saner than those who declared them so and who themselves were considered "sane." Again, I could relate to Patrick McGoohan's ever-defiant "Number Six" character from the 1967–68 TV series *The Prisoner*, and also free-spirited Lucas Jackson from 1967's *Cool Hand Luke*, both of whom proved that those who refuse to conform are often the most rational of all. This same reasoning applied to David Bowie's powerful 1970 song "All the Madmen," whose protagonist is characterized as preferring the company of those deemed mad to the company of so-called normal men because he is convinced the madmen all share his same degree of sanity. I, too, was mad—mad for God—and I would not compromise my spiritual madness simply to appease the truly insane, who wandered free in the world and controlled the fate of the rest of us.

As my awakening continued to unfold, each day I awoke to a new level of understanding. Upon rising, I mustered up all my energy and forced my wandering mind back into focus, so I could return to the state of inner silence I had attained the previous night. I mercilessly thrust out all thoughts and summoned into my heart a tangible experience of the living Jesus. In this manner, I curbed all mental processes and firmly directed my attention back to my spiritual goal, which was, as I had written at the time, "a complete and total union into One ... a totally perfected state of Divine Love and knowledge of nothing else."

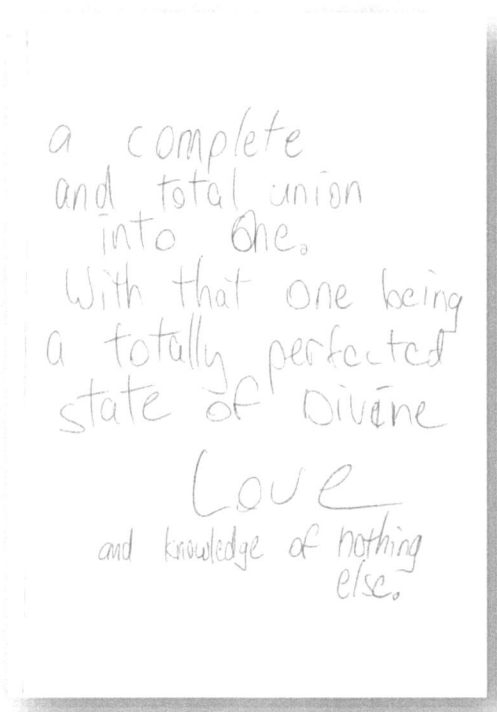

Facsimile of original December 1974 holographic writing

Using my willpower, I visualized Jesus as my constant companion, alongside me whenever walking, driving, or doing anything. (I could still drive when necessary, but it was an altogether different experience, as though someone else were at the wheel.) This sustained visualization of Jesus accompanying me everywhere vastly strengthened my faith, for it had the effect of smothering any doubts that might have crept in to undermine my spiritual experience. As my whole universe then centered around Jesus, my faith grew to the extent that I *knew* he existed. I strongly felt his invisible presence, and I would mentally converse with him in ongoing inner communications. Because of the deep relationship I had established with Jesus, it felt as though I were carried on a wave of pure incandescent love. Unending portals of joy opened up inside me.

~~~~~~~~~~~~~~

September soon turned into October, and I became even more intensely seized by a burning desire to be free. This passionate yearning gnawed at me to the exclusion of all else. It continually uplifted me. This had the effect of strengthening my intentions all the more. I maintained my fervent aspirations day and night, clinging to it tenaciously at all costs. I attempted to adhere round-the-clock to my spiritual ideals without once compromising them. My resolute intentions helped me to stay on track so I wouldn't be diverted. I would allow nothing to sabotage my resolve. I kept moving onward and upward, spiraling higher and higher, never settling for mediocrity or resting in smug self-assuredness. I honed myself on the whetstone of my undeviating spiritual goal, and I continuously strained and pressed forward to achieve it.

During this progressively wondrous time, I made every effort to be guided solely by God. A distinct inner voice emerged, which I sensed more as interior proddings than audible vocalizations, and I forced myself to obey it. The overarching theme it conveyed to me was to reject the world and undistractedly focus on God. In so many words, this message repeated itself throughout different situations every day. The guidance given by my inner voice frequently resulted in depriving me of what I might otherwise would have wanted to occur, or else it contradicted what I might have expected to take place. This created in me a keen sense of detachment by deflating my sense of ego and bringing what I once avoided on equal terms with what I once cherished. Thus liberated from my personal desires, I experienced a perpetual state of contentment. I felt inwardly fulfilled, ever at peace. I was never steered into any harmful circumstances when following the protective goadings of my mystical inner voice.

When interacting with people, I saw, related to, and communicated with their spiritual essence, connecting with the deepest part of their soul. I projected the spiritual awareness I experienced on to them and spoke to them with complete familiarity, as though they were my dearest, most intimate friend. I was not nervous, apprehensive, or anxious with others because I felt we shared the same consciousness. I identified so closely with their thoughts that many times I felt as if there were an intermingling of minds wherein any distinction between their mind and my mind did not exist. This was not caused by any kind of pathological psychological state, but rather a heightened supernatural nondual spiritual experience. I also felt that others were clued in on some grand cosmic secret, only they were merely acting out a role, pretending to be this or that person. It was as if they were already in sync with the spiritual core of creation—as if they were already fully enlightened—and it was only I who was catching on late.

When people spoke to me, I felt as though they were talking to someone else, because my personality had become so attenuated that I ceased to identify with my ego or body. When responding to others, I spoke and acted extemporaneously without first thinking or gathering my thoughts or mentally rehearing my words beforehand. One time, a high-school friend innocently wondered why I used so many "big words." But words, however big or small, spontaneously flowed out of my mouth when warranted, and sentences arranged themselves as if out of thin air throughout the time of my awakening.

Even though I went through the motions of attending my daily high-school classes, I rarely socialized during this time, and I was not dating. I tried not to taint my mind with worldliness, so I largely kept to myself. I shared my experiences with God when praying in secret, and I shunned anything that would draw attention to my spiritual practices. I did not strive for recognition, which I found repugnant. Just the opposite—I attempted to remain anonymous. I became very silent and inwardly centered.

During lunch at school or if I had spare time between classes, I would routinely wander off and hang out by myself on a secluded lawn area, amid scenic plantings of trees and a colorful bed of roses, on the far side of the school grounds near the rectory—the least populated section of campus—rather than mingle with classmates. Realizing there were essentially none who understood or supported my spiritual efforts, I was content with exploring my inner world alone and, for the most part, sequestering myself from other people wherever possible. My room at home served this same purpose. It had become my personal place of worship where I could unfold the secrets of my soul in solitude. My spirit required this seclusion. It journeyed on endless reverberations of ecstatic silence. God was reshaping my very being.

I Am All I See

November to early December 1974 marked the most intense phase of my First Awakening. I constantly felt alive in the bliss-filled state that enfolded me. Because of my ongoing practice of meditation, I soon left behind the realm of thoughts and concepts entirely. An inner stillness swept over me, which enabled me to perceive each instant, seemingly every nanosecond, apart from all mental filters, conjectures, and interpretations. I was immersed in a seizing in-the-moment intensity that results when the mind is freed of all thoughts. There was no continuity of experience from one moment to the next—all such partitions dissolved. Time as we know it did not exist. It was broken down into the minutest of particles, each a whole universe unto itself and unrelated to the particle just past or yet to come. Life was created anew each pulsating second. There was no linkage between moments; no two experiences, however similar, were exactly alike, as Heraclitus sagely observed when he wrote, "You cannot step into the same river twice."

Yet, paradoxically, I came to feel there was all the time in the world. I grew younger, became simpler. During my awakening, I had become imbued with feelings of the innocence, wonder, and wellbeing inherent in my early childhood. This tremendous sense of carefree contentment became integrated into my then-present consciousness.

Equally paradoxically, I felt older, ancient, timeless. I felt at home everywhere. Nothing seemed distant or apart from me; I experienced no sense of separation between the things I observed and my inner self. I wrote of my experience at the time, "I am one. I am ageless. I am all I see." I felt that, even though things changed, there was an underlying Essence that did not decay, and I was attuned to that essence.

Everything I came across appeared vibrant, alive. I often sensed a wondrous orb of misty, haloed light that shone around objects. When traveling about, I would see trees, rose bushes, and other living things vibrating with refulgent life, radiating the infinite light of God. My vision corresponded to the insightful verse by Elizabeth Barrett Browning:

> Earth's crammed with heaven,
> And every common bush afire with God.[135]

At times, I felt as if I were perceiving the innermost structure of things, composed of scintillating energy, and not their outer form. I would see the world around me as shimmering waves of bliss, similar to when watching tall meadow grasses swaying rhythmically in the wind, or when viewing a grove of weeping birches quaking gently in the breeze—each tree melding into a grand ensemble of translucent swells dancing in unison. These experiences were not caused by ingesting or inhaling any kind of psychotropic substance or by any other physical means; they stemmed from an exponentially purer and far more powerful source: they originated as graces from God, combined with a fully concentrated mind. I would witness similar serendipitous mystical occurrences, which I similarly attributed to God. I saw the world with new eyes. I felt I had encountered perfection.

I was deeply inspired and motivated by Jesus' directive not to judge or to measure, which made a profound impact: "Judge not that you not be judged. For in the same manner you judge, you will be judged. And with whatever measure you use, it will be used to measure you."[136] I looked up the words "judge" and "measure" in the dictionary and analyzed their deeper meanings. I concluded that Jesus intended for us to root out the very mechanism that is responsible for judgment and measurement. Thereafter, I made a determined effort to completely stop these mental functions.

Accordingly, I would command my body and mind to remain entirely calm when meditating. I would catch any thoughts immediately upon detection, then visualize them being hurled away from me. In essence, I figuratively prevented them from entering my skull. I concomitantly banished all emotions, especially toxic emotions, such as fear, worry, doubt, regret, and concern about what others might think of me. I thereby arrested all inner chatter by using the sheer force of my will to control my mind. This had the effect of subduing the talkative voice inside my brain and evicting any and all thoughts *before* they had a chance to fully materialize and catch hold. As a result, I largely lost the ability to classify and differentiate things, as the unseen boundary that separated my ego from the objects I perceived began to disappear. The mental faculty responsible for judgment and measurement thus became suspended during my meditations, and soon this carried over into my waking activities.

What in fact I was doing was dismantling the functional parts of my mind. I picked apart these components—intellect, memory, emotions, the faculty of judgment—and shut them down until I suppressed their ability to function autonomously. I unmasked any subconscious fears and other emotions that dictated my reactions. After I was able to detect then peel back and expose a particular emotion, it ceased to influence me. I thereby muzzled many unconscious reactions that heretofore ran on autopilot, and I suspended the operations of any number of deep-rooted behavior patterns. Likewise, I exposed many hidden assumptions, and I strove to uncover, then halt the workings of any fixed habits that were lurking in my mind. I also was able to disengage from the usual ways in which I interacted with others. I had thus effectively deconstructed and reverse engineered my own mind so it would no longer automatically function and control me. I did this in service of my soul, which I was liberating by wrenching it free from the clutches of my mind.

My nighttime meditations deepened. Increasingly, it would take very little time for me to enter my state of inner quietude, which I craved more than anything. Eventually, I acquired the perspicacity, the mental stamina, the focus, the resolve, and was granted the grace to dismiss thoughts at will, without all the effort formerly required. I monitored my mind, and if any thought arose, I immediately traced it back to its source and quashed it. Then I would bring this inner monitoring process to a standstill by stopping it so that no activity remained in my mind. Once all mentations and images ceased, I was bathed in a sublime silence. I had found a place inside myself untouched by any agitation, and I allowed nothing to breach this inner sanctum. I aggressively threw off all psychological hindrances and forced myself to abide in a state without thoughts while I simultaneously poured out an aching heart of innocent, untarnished love into the very soul of God.

At the height of my awakening, I felt completely elevated, transported to an otherworldly domain. I became steeped in a transcendent luminosity, consumed by the effulgent presence of God. This was an altogether different realm. My mind was stilled, my emotions quieted. I was cracking through and disintegrating the shell of my ego. I experienced unending, indescribable peace. The barrier between matter and spirit had ruptured, enabling me to peer at life from the other side of reality. Whatever tenuous grip the outer world still held on me started to loosen. I could not recognize my former self, which was receding out of existence. I was riding on the continuum of eternity. I lived in an abode of undiluted happiness. I felt that if others were to experience these same feelings of unmitigated joy, they couldn't withstand the accompanying euphoria. I became humbled, and I would thank God when these uprushing sensations of unutterable peace and ecstasy coursed through my being. I felt as though all my worldly travails had ended. I felt totally free. I had no goals or purpose other than simply *to be*. This state was incomparably superior to anything the world had to offer. I felt God had listened to and had answered my inner cry from early September.

I continued night and day with my love-infused, prayerful aspirations, anchored by my faith in God and Jesus. Soon, something began to stick. At first it was very subtle, but as the weeks rolled on it lingered with me into activity. I felt a thread of continuity continually connecting me with an unchanging inner sphere of resplendent spiritual awareness, unabated by any circumstance. I would enter this sphere and dissolve all sense of "I-ness." This sensation persisted throughout sleep; it lasted into my waking state. It was as though the spiritual part of me witnessed my body sleeping, then witnessed it going through the various activities of life when I was awake. I never lost touch with my spiritual core; it never left me.

This dazzling awareness was far more vivid and real than anything experienced in ordinary consciousness. Its essence was composed of an inexhaustible boundless ocean of pure love. As I carried on with my prayers, I would at times express deep remorse upon the realization that, when growing up, I had lost the capacity to feel this fathomless divine love. But during this exalted time, I was suffused continuously in this palpable love, a love that was unrestricted in its scope and unlimited in its distribution. When this loving awareness engulfed me, I was dumbfounded; I couldn't understand why *I* was being showered with it. I became overwhelmed with heartfelt outpourings of gratitude toward God, toward Jesus. This brought about in me a state of childlike awe and wonder. The more I drank of this love, the more I discovered there was of it. I came to realize that this infinite divine love formed the very matrix of the universe and encompassed all things known and unknown.

The Royal Lichtenstein Quarter-Ring Sidewalk Circus

On Thursday, December 19, 1974, a traveling troupe of three male performers calling themselves the Royal Lichtenstein Quarter-Ring Sidewalk Circus set up their show on our high-school campus. I joined around three dozen students, who had gathered during lunchtime to watch their midday performance, which was a delight. I laughed and reveled in their magic tricks, juggling routines, animal acts, antiestablishment comedy, and savvy light-handed preaching. But on that fateful day, I looked around and realized that no one saw what I saw. Most were caught up in their own worlds—rushing between classes, mentally preoccupied, unable to experience fully the joy of the moment. For some reason, this rattled me to the core, so much so that something inside of me collapsed. On that fateful day,

I realized that I was alone, completely alone. No one shared my experience. Not one person. Not only my joyful experience of the circus, but, more important, I realized with open eyes that no one shared my inner spiritual experience. For the first time, it strikingly occurred to me that my previous sense that others participated in the same spiritual epiphany as mine was an illusion, a complete out-and-out illusion. This startling insight imploded at the deepest level of my being and overcame me. I began to cry. I simply broke down in front of everyone assembled there.

Shortly thereafter, a colorful figure emerged from the circus backdrop and approached me. He was dressed in Tudor-era clothing and wore white face makeup. Looking like a cross between Jethro Tull's Ian Anderson and William Shakespeare, he reassuringly clasped my upper arm. Then he spoke.

"Hey, I'm the clown. What's going on?"

"They can't see what I see!" I tearfully exclaimed.

After pausing a moment, he replied, "Not everyone can see magic. Not everyone has the gift to experience wonder."

I countered, "But I can't *share* what I see. I feel all alone."

He again paused before speaking these words. "If you experience the beauty and joy of life, that's a special blessing. It's a kind of innocence. Maybe you've been graced to see what others can't see, to carry this gift inside you."

I looked at him; he smiled at me. I said, "Yeah, maybe."

He concluded, "God reveals his wonders at all times, but most people are blind to them. Yet miracles occur around us constantly. That's the reason for the circus—to make others aware of the miracles of God."

He looked at me with a look of utter sympathy. "Okay?"

No longer crying, I responded, "Okay." He smiled, then walked away and disappeared back into the circus.

I later learned that the clown was a Jesuit priest—Father Nick J. Weber, SJ, who subsequently resigned from the priesthood in 1993. His beneficent words, which resound in me to this day, provided consolation that assuaged my disillusioned spirit. His succinct, solicitous remarks had the effect of affirming the validity of my spiritual experience. Though our chance meeting was short, its effects were revelatory. He was the only adult who saw the essence of my being and my guileless spirit, and who accepted me at face value without judging me. How ironic it should be a traveling circus clown—an archetypal figure that can see beyond our personas and draw forth the unguarded innocence within us—who understood an all-too idealistic seventeen-year-old, and compassionately gave him permission to be himself. That brief empowering encounter, however improbable, conferred on me a priceless, lifelong gift.

But nothing could shore up my outer life. For the first time since my spiritual awakening began, I realized just how isolated I was. I had no support from my usual authority figures. No validation from my religious teachers. Practically no understanding from parents or friends. No context for my spiritual experience. And no future, because I had no footing on which to stand. I could not integrate my First Awakening experience into my daily activities on account of my uncompromising attitude. I did not even attempt to combine the two; this thought never occurred to me.

My extreme, unyielding approach proved both a blessing and a curse. On the one hand, it enabled me to experience firsthand this wondrous state; but on the other hand, it made it impossible for me to implement it in the real world. This and every similar roadblock I encountered showed me in no uncertain terms that I could not sustain my spiritual experience in the world of humans. These sobering realizations, which dawned on me more as intuitions than reasoned conclusions, marked the beginning of my separation from the invisible blessings that had carried me since September.

Even more consequential, because of the all-around lack of support I received from others, a seed of doubt had been planted in my mind. It grew to sabotage the single most meaningful experience of my life. Except for a solitary pivotal individual—a sympathetic priest/clown who arrived on the scene at the eleventh hour—not one significant person believed me. Worse, I began to believe their disbelief. This became the one chink in my armor. Exhibiting an extraordinary and ultimately ruinous lack of judgment, I started believing that *I* was living an illusion, and their world was the real one. I was being evicted from Paradise, and by tacitly collaborating with my detractors, I materially assisted in facilitating my own expulsion.

When St. Peter walked on water to meet with Jesus on the turbulent Sea of Galilee, he was overcome with fear, and he started to sink,[137] whereupon Jesus immediately saved him from drowning, accompanied by a powerful rebuke: "O you of little faith, why did you doubt?"[138] Similarly, when I lost my faith, I began falling from the sublime revelation I had been given. I, too, could have turned to Jesus, as Peter did. But I committed the one unforgivable sin, which I repent to this day. At that critical juncture in my spiritual awakening, God gave me a personal test of faith. However, I did not turn to Jesus, as I had so many times in the previous three months. Instead, I turned to the world and sought its approval, choosing to listen to and—far worse—heed its collective, disparaging opinion at the expense of the lone supportive voice of Jesus.

Hence, I failed my test.

~~~~~~~~~~~~

Years later, this brought to mind the words of *Peter Pan* author J. M. Barrie, "the moment you doubt whether you can fly, you cease for ever to be able to do it."[139] Sure enough, in the same instant when I doubted my own experience and lost the courage of my own convictions, my faith was shattered, and I lost access to the treasure that had been bestowed on me. At that very moment, my First Awakening experience started crashing to the ground. And so, by paying attention to the naysaying of others and going so far as to imbue their dismissive words with credibility, I forfeited the one complimentary passage I had been granted in this lifetime to visit Eden and to be chauffeured on a magical tour through its many wonders.

From that point forward, I began breathing the air of mortals. My ego was returning, and I was headed earthbound fast. The uneasy descent lasted around two months as my waning spiritual realization tauntingly lingered. As the spiritual portal continued to close, I rapidly lost touch with my soul. On that fateful day in December 1974, when I gave up believing in the reality of my own experience, my spirit began dying a slow death. To restate the words of poet Robert Frost, I thereupon chose the road *more* traveled by, which subsequently "made all the difference"[140] in my life.

During my spiritual awakening, my being had been rewired to withstand the energy of the Eternal. But when I lost contact with my spiritual essence, I was left hanging in midair—a stranger to both the divine and material worlds, not quite at home in either. I began wandering through an interior wilderness. What had been given freely, I now had to seek. Commencing in early 1975, I set out on a quest to recover my squandered treasure, a quest which continues to the present day. At that time, barely eighteen years old, I sought to reclaim my personal heaven, to reacquire what I had lost, and to consciously resurrect this unearthly experience that was gifted to me by God and once again establish it within my soul.

Afterthoughts

After this autumn 1974 narrative ended, I decompressed from my fallen mystical experience. I weathered many adjustments—and maladjustments—to life afterward, including facing my share of psychological and secular struggles. My spiritual experience forever affected and informed my life, both in terms of work and career, as well as relationships and lifestyle. I never "recovered" from my extramundane encounter. My experience had so profoundly conflicted with the prevailing view of reality that this discord created an undercurrent of alienation which underscored many of my ensuing undertakings in life. Amid this aftermath and fallout, however, I tried to remain true to the vision that was imparted to me during my First Awakening.

Starting in 1975, I would read accounts of analogous mystical experiences from different religious traditions, both Western and Eastern. This gradually allowed me to begin placing my own spiritual awakening in perspective. I realized that my experience was not unique; it was "nothing special"[141] as influential Sōtō Zen Master Shunryu Suzuki might have observed. It fell right within the bell curve of what many struggling mystics went through. Consequently, it was certainly nothing to boast about, especially because I could neither sustain my experience nor integrate it with my daily life. Instead, I lamented its loss, and I realized that a far more difficult journey would be needed to regain it.

I underwent many additional inner experiences, but those recounted here constitute the most significant ones during my spiritual awakening. I once met with Father Christopher and described a few seemingly unusual phenomena I then experienced, such as the sensation of walking on air, or feeling a continuous pronounced inner warmth in my upper torso. Father did not deny their validity, stating there are "esoteric lexicons" in most religious traditions that describe various "technologies of the soul." These lexicons and technologies help to map out and explain the interior spiritual terrain. They assist a person in navigating the varied experiences often encountered when unfolding these relatively uncommon states of consciousness.

In addition, the meditation technique I stumbled on differed from Father Christopher's method in that I concentrated on an object to still my wandering thoughts, typically a biblical passage or music, and I concurrently summoned up and utilized a massive amount of effort and willpower to forcefully control my mind. Father Christopher recommended the former—focusing on a home object—but he discouraged the latter. While both approaches require single-minded dedication and commitment, mine was a particularly arduous practice, which is why I believe Father didn't promote it.

Finally, I learned four principal lessons from my First Awakening. First, it affirmed for me the authenticity of spirituality and the validity of the mystical experience. Second, it proved to me that following the spiritual path and realizing God were the primary goals of life. Third, it taught me never to lose faith in the conviction of my own experience, regardless of what others think. And fourth, it revealed to me that anyone can realize the truths of spirituality if they want them badly enough; the spiritual path is never for an elite few.

~~~~~~~~~~~~~

During one of my early visits to see Father Christopher, I met with him privately and related the following. "Father, I underwent a spiritual experience more than fifteen years ago that transformed my life. It centered around Jesus. It was joyful beyond words. No one understood it, least of all me. All I wanted to do was to live perpetually in that state. But the world didn't support me and what I was going through, so I lost my faith and subsequently I lost my experience, which I've deeply mourned all these years. I've been trying ever since to recapture it."

Father immediately responded, "First of all, you never lost that experience. You were put in touch with your true spiritual nature. Don't ever doubt for a moment that it can be experienced again once you rid yourself of the layers which now cover it. More important, it sounds like you yourself caused it to end because you lost your faith. You looked to the world to validate what you were undergoing, which was a mistake of youth. Remember the wise words of the Psalmist, 'It is better to take refuge in God than to trust in people.'[142] When you try to please others, especially in matters of spirituality, you will never succeed. You must henceforth regain the conviction that your experience was genuine and ignore what the world thinks. You must fix your soul on God alone. Otherwise, this experience will elude you no matter how hard you try to re-establish it."

FIFTH VISIT (October 1991)

The Cosmic Mandala

I CONTINUED MY JOURNEY toward MacKerricher. The Fort Bragg–Willits Road is a scenic, twisting highway that passes through heavily wooded Jackson State Forest, where a mystical fog often envelopes the thick canopy. I've found it emancipating to meander through such a natural haven, especially when driving by myself. When traveling alone, I feel physically light and unfettered by the cares of life. I'm calm and content. I often feel the presence of God. At times I become rapt in a spontaneous, ebullient kind of joy. Spiritual practice seems effortless. I possess tremendous energy. There's nothing from which to escape, no tension to unwind. There's no grappling with personal demons. I am at peace. The budding writer in me—long dormant—emerges as well; my creativity is set free. The trick is to feel this way when I'm back in Ukiah.

As I drove farther along the northbound coastal road on my way to the campground, this tranquil mood soon came to an abrupt halt when yet another bout of self-doubt seized me, as I again wrestled with my thoughts. I was proud of what I was accomplishing in the world. All these various experiences—apartment living, relationships, earning money, dealing with people and situations—were helping to forge my character. But I again wondered, as I did at Hurkey Creek nearly three years earlier: Have these worldly achievements come at the cost of my soul? Why have my spiritual goals once again receded into the background? A decade ago, before my increasing involvement with the world, I was relatively satisfied with my spiritual lifestyle. But I caved in and began to adopt society's conditioning as the norm. Now, by default, I've joined the system, so I am forced to participate in a reality that is defined by others. By so doing, I have veered in a direction other than where my inner spiritual compass had pointed. But am I truly happy? Who am I kidding!

I settled in at MacKerricher and set up my tent. I spent much of the afternoon walking along the coastal shoreline, absorbing the wide expanse of the Pacific Ocean and inhaling the brisk salt-tinged air that wafted in on the westerly breeze. I lost myself in the roar of the roiling, tossing waves. I climbed an occasional rocky crag that jutted up from the sandy beach. I'd always felt at home in nature, more so than the world of man. Although I had not resolved any of my issues, the soothing experience of immersing myself in the natural world helped quell my conflicting thoughts. As famed peripatetic poet Robert William Service aptly reflected:

> It's the beauty that thrills me with wonder,
> It's the stillness that fills me with peace.[143]

After returning to my campsite, I ate my brown rice and Vege-Burger meal before jumping in my car and heading straight to Father's cabin.

There, Heather warmly greeted and hugged me. As I typically wore my emotions on my sleeve, Heather didn't need to rely on her highly developed sense of intuition to see that I was caught up in a heavy mood. She and I broke from the group and walked outside along the nearby gravel road. I told her that at one time in my life my spirit soared. I once dreamt noble dreams and felt the world was mine for the taking. But I had since become shackled to the world, oppressed by the weighty cares of life. My once three-dimensional Technicolor universe of endless possibilities had been reduced to a one-dimensional black-and-white tedium of never-ending obligations and dreary routines. The otherwise free-flowing stream of my life had become bottled-up and stagnant. I told her that Ukiah was not the ultimate destination for me. Despite its beautiful surroundings, as succinctly captured in the hauntingly evocative 1973 Doobie Brothers' song of the same name, the town had become for me more like a pit stop located at the crossroads of life, a cosmic outhouse of sorts, as I scornfully observed. I also expressed frustration at my inability to sustain a long-term romantic relationship. I called myself a fool, faulting myself for my own unhappy state.

Heather instantly responded by saying it wasn't foolishness on my part, just lack of experience coupled with a kind of naïveté. She maintained that I must continue to love, that I must try to heal from the wounds of my past. She said I should "love many, trust few, and paddle your own canoe," as a wise woman once told her. She mentioned that in many ways Ukiah had become a staging ground for me—a place where I was given the opportunity to develop skills, learn about the world, and mature emotionally. (Heather was correct. I forayed into the world somewhat raw, green, and unsophisticated. I possessed little ambition for worldly pursuits, and I altogether lacked street smarts. Indeed, in many ways I grew up in Ukiah.)

She further said that I cannot wait for something to happen on a grand scale which would alter my life, and that I must strive to excel in the small, simple things which occur every day. "You must try to see the perfection in all things," Heather sensibly counseled. "You must find happiness in the niche of life that's been carved for you."

~~~~~~~~~~~~~

We returned to the cabin just as Father Christopher appeared. He was looking jovial, but perhaps a bit lethargic. The regulars had all shown up. Brandon brought along a couple of his buddies from Humboldt State—Todd and Corey, both of whom I would only see at this one meeting. Father took his seat and began speaking with Erin, who was seated on the floor next to Marta. It was twilight, and the log cabin was lit by the peculiar indistinct glow that is given off by soft lights and flickering candles. Although he directed his words to Erin, he might as well have been speaking to me.

"You're missing the big picture, my daughter. Each person has extensive karmic relationships with other beings, which are destined. Not only with other beings, but with the geography, the climate, their home, their employment situation, and many other factors both seen and unseen. All these factors never stop interacting with one another. At all times they affect our lives; their influence is widespread and un-alterable. Your various responsibilities and the way you spend your free time—these are but tiny ingredients in the all-embracing karmic mechanism that ceaselessly turns."

Erin remarked, "So Father, you're saying everything's con-nected. I understand that. But why do so many random events occur, like people suddenly arriving in my life out of nowhere?"

"If an individual appears on the scene or an event materializes without prior notice and intervenes in your life, it is merely the kar-mic mechanism grinding its wheels so these events and people can intersect in certain places and times. We are simply awaiting our un-avoidable appointment with them as they parade across the invisible conveyor belt that is inescapably headed in our direction. There are literally infinite variables at work that produce any number of ap-parently random, out-of-the-blue events, which are in fact prearranged. This is what the Tibetan Buddhists refer to as the boundless sweeping cosmic mandala, which symbolizes the uni-verse moving through the time–space continuum. Propelled by forces and circumstances long ago set into motion, what we see and experience in our lives is a miniscule fraction of this all-encompass-ing universal mandala.

"This mandala represents the limitless interconnectedness among all things. It is synonymous with the Buddhist doctrine of de-pendent origination. Every one of the people and events within it are intimately linked: the good and the bad; the heroes and the villains; the famous and the forgotten; the powerful and the meek. For eons and eons, this intricate karmic web has moved dynamically through space and time. The Tibetans believe this mandala is bound together by an entwined network of karmic relationships among all things—

humans, animals, plants, insects, water, air, and so forth. These elements are likened to spokes on this gigantic cosmic wheel."

Father gazed across the room. This was the most abstract talk I'd ever heard him give. I felt the truth of what he was saying, even if some of it was over my head.

He continued, "The events that occur in the world do so because of circumstances long ago set into motion. The individuals who reach a position of prominence in any given era do so not because of what seems to be chance or accident, hard work, or skill, which is what we casually assume, but as a result of their previous karma. It is one's karma that imbues them with certain skills and talents and lands them at the right place at the right time. And so, karma is the primary factor that precedes any accomplishment in life. This also explains why we often see con artists and the untalented achieve fame and fortune. Sometimes skillful persons struggle endlessly and get nowhere, whereas less-accomplished, apparently undeserving souls seemingly without effort attain to riches and renown. Yet, we so readily become puffed up with pride, inflated with a sense of power and filled with self-importance, smugly convinced that we control our own destiny. This is a joke to more spiritually advanced beings. In the overall scheme of things, we humans are insignificant insofar as the sphere of our influence, from the vantage point of eternity, is infinitesimal.

"All events and circumstances, all people and living things, as well as the planet itself, and the wide-ranging and intertwined relationships among them, are constantly turning round on this grand mandala. It is so infinitely complex that free will is a moot point. Truly, there is very little we can do! According to the Tibetans, this immense mechanism originated from a beginningless past. Round and round the wheel revolves, spinning off accumulated karma and generating fresh karma. All material substances and living beings move continuously on this cosmic wheel—sometimes connecting, sometimes diverging, but all the while forever joined by the unseen adhesive of karma. It's quite useless to keep track of all these vast and complex relationships."

I asked a question, echoing the free will versus destiny theme of this and previous discussions. "But Father, are you saying that people who work hard to attain a goal should abandon their efforts; that they should accept whatever life has to offer without trying to better themselves or change their circumstances?"

Father replied, "People superficially think that they can accomplish this or change that. But, according to the theory of predetermination, the aspirations they seek merely lead them to a rendezvous with their fate, which they are helplessly destined to encounter. The very effort they expend to obtain their goals is preordained; the hard work they put out to achieve any objective is part and parcel of their apportioned path. The goals they do attain are in fact fixed in advance. They lie in wait to be delivered much in the same way a gift on layaway is waiting to be picked up. The desire to achieve a particular goal, the effort spent to reach it, and the attainment of the goal itself are all part of the endless loop of one's karma. From this perspective, all of life is a *fait accompli.*

"This is why, from a larger viewpoint, it is equally useless to plan. From God's perspective, your plans mean nothing. That is tantamount to counting chickens before they hatch. As Jesus advised, 'Do not worry about tomorrow.'[144] Lao Tzu similarly instructed, 'Simply act without planning, and all things will fall into place.'[145]

"Your plans, in reality, merely map out the predetermined terrain that inevitably awaits you. They will take place one way or another if intended; if not, they cannot occur no matter what steps you take to ensure their completion. Think of how a clockwork apparatus works, utilizing various gears and cogs that incessantly turn. It is only when the gears grind ahead to a new position that your current stockpile of karma becomes depleted and a whole new chapter begins. So, surrendering and comporting yourself to a graceful acquiescence of your apportioned slice of reality is the only alternative to a fret-filled life. It's a matter of humbling yourself to the Infinite. To put it in theological terms, someone else prefers that things go a certain way. That someone is God, whom the prophet Isaiah thus reverently describes:

> O Lord, you are our father!
> We are the clay and you are our potter.[146]

"Our lives are entirely in the hands of God."

~~~~~~~~~~~~

My earlier ruminations, peppered by uncertainty and angst, faded into meaningless obscurity when Father's words powerfully impinged on my soul, opening me up like a patient on an operating table, touching the deepest part of my being. I managed to remain as silent and expressionless as possible, fighting the surging feeling inside me and concealing my welling emotion before it overpowered me and surfaced. Then suddenly I recalled a dream I once had, which prominently featured a female Sufi teacher. In the dream, she was a medical doctor, diagnosing people's ailments while they lay on her clean, white examination table. She treated them and made them well.

In my dream, I was lying on her examination table. Then I got up and followed her through her home. She walked toward a room located deep inside her house. We passed through one room after another until we reached this inmost room. She went in, but I paused outside the door. All this time, she hadn't uttered a word. When she finally spoke, she talked very softly; her voice was almost inaudible. I asked her to repeat her words because I couldn't clearly hear her the first time. I never did make out what she was saying. I explained to her that sometimes my hearing wasn't too keen.

Then I entered the room, moving right up to her face until we stared at each other closeup. Her eyes were open wide and glazed, as if she were silently absorbed in God, communing in ecstasy. We did not speak. She continued gazing into my eyes, probing the essence of my being, piercing the very depths of my soul.

The dream ended. When I awoke, my soul was bathed in a sublime bliss. None of the cares of the world intruded. I felt as though I were floating on an ocean of inexhaustible peace. I later interpreted my dream to mean that God led me to the innermost realm of my being—my spirit. But I couldn't go inside, nor could I hear anything there. It was foreign to me because my current life prevented me from listening to my own soul. When I finally was able to enter— when I could break free and move past my worldly obligations— that's when God was able to transmit spiritual blessings into me and restore my spirit to wholeness ...

~~~~~~~~~~~~

Father Christopher's soft but richly expressive baritone voice broke my reverie. Looking over at Erin he said, "Do not bemoan your fate—which projects you can or cannot accomplish; which people suddenly or unexpectedly appear in your life; which events occur without warning; which situations unfold despite your best efforts to avert them. Rather, take care to ensure that your mind is not consumed by agendas and dominated by plans. Keep the aperture of your awareness wide open, and remain in a state of surrender and acceptance at all times. As you have perhaps discovered, when you resist your fate or lament your circumstances, the person who most suffers and undergoes mental anguish is you. Such reactions abruptly pull you away from your spiritual consciousness and reinforce the notion of the illusory ego. And this is the one trap that keeps holding you back."

Erin nodded introspectively.

Then Father addressed us all. "The idea that circumstances recur time and again until you master them is a simple explanation to describe a phenomenon that actually occurs because of another reason. While in fact similar people and situations can and do reappear in our lives, this phenomenon originates solely in the mind, just as the Yogachara school of Buddhism maintains in its doctrine of *vijñaptimātratā*, if I can recall the correct pronunciation.

"As we've previously discussed, the outer circumstances of life perfectly reflect one's karma, one's destiny. When the same mental and emotional patterns continually manifest in a person, they etch a groove in the mind—this becomes a personality trait. A personality trait is a fossilized pattern that is imprisoned by destiny. The personality trait will repeatedly assert itself until the spiritual consciousness is awakened and gains the upper hand. Then the personality trait loses its strength and becomes overshadowed by the spiritual consciousness, which is now in the ascendancy and shines ever more luminously than the now-diminishing trait.

"It is not outer circumstances, therefore, which trigger a series of lessons that one must master. Instead, it is a matter of elevating one's spiritual consciousness so it vibrates at a higher frequency and pulsates with a greater magnitude than one's destiny, which can revolve like an endless merry-go-round in a repetitive rut. The same applies to the personality traits that are embedded in one's mind. To raise the spiritual consciousness above the influence of one's destiny and one's personality traits produces inner freedom. The way to attain this state is twofold: not reacting to your destiny as it unfolds, and routinely meditating so that you continuously abide in your spiritual self.

"Once you outwit your karma, so to speak, by surmounting your reactions to it and by increasingly residing in your spiritual self, the outer circumstances of your life will begin to change. This outer change is an aftereffect of your inner shift. The revolving door of similar people, situations, and patterns that have been plaguing you ever since you began reacting to the particular sliver of karma that vibrated at the very same frequency as those things will start to disappear. Your ship will then be freed from its moorings so it can set sail to the new karmic adventures that await you."

Heather and I glanced at one another. Father was in a heightened state, inwardly immersed. His countenance seemed to radiate a soft, golden aura. His words were but an excuse for that which was being conveyed on far deeper levels, which all of us palpably felt.

Then Todd offered up his thoughts. "If what I understand you're saying is true, then there's no way to escape our fate. I can see how this sometimes happens, but I can also see that sometimes when I make a choice, I can change things. But if I still can't get away from a bad situation, I say to myself, 'Todd, my man, you didn't sign up for this. It's exit stage left before you can say Jackie Robinson!' But even that won't always work."

We all burst out laughing at Todd's down-to-earth humor and his sly play on the familiar "Jack Robinson" idiom in the context of his Black heritage.

Father said, "I might suggest that you *did* sign up for this and all the situations in your life. My son, these events are merely your destiny unfolding before your very eyes. Some of them are pleasant, while others are unpleasant. As Dorothy observes at the end of *The Wizard of Oz*, 'I remember that some of it wasn't very nice. But most of it was beautiful.'[147] We can likewise hope to say the same as the last reel of our life winds down. So, when the bad scenes do appear, try to remain as detached as possible. Try to stay calm as these storms pass by. By maintaining your peace of mind, you'll lessen their impact."

"Sure, I can try to do that," Todd said. "But if it still won't work, I can always ask the Good Witch of the North to wave her magic wand and whisk me away."

Father smiled. "In that case, don't forget your ruby slippers!"

Todd himself led the ensuing round of laughter.

Led by the Spirit

Father switched topics. "So, the main purpose in spiritual life is to awaken, then kindle your spiritual consciousness and not do anything that might extinguish it once it has awakened. Remember, a person's actions perfectly reflect the contents of their mind and their level of spiritual unfoldment. Actions are one's beliefs in practice. And so, relatedly, once one's spiritual consciousness has gained a strong foothold within, certain actions and behaviors will no longer manifest that would have manifested at levels where lower and more unevolved personality traits operate. They simply fall off. This is because the entire karmic field where they would have played themselves out has been altogether eclipsed on account of one's spirit now residing at higher levels of consciousness and more subtle states of being. At each new plateau, the grosser and more unevolved thoughts and behaviors drop off, and more refined and sublime ones take their place. In this manner, an aspirant also comes to embody more spiritually oriented and therefore more evolved ethical values."

Stuart raised a question. "Could you please clarify what you said? All religions have their version of the Ten Commandments. If undesirable actions simply drop off during a person's spiritual development, then why follow these rules in the first place?"

Father replied, "It is true that St. Paul taught, 'If you are guided by the Spirit, you are not under the law.'[148] However, this teaching can be grossly misunderstood. If you are genuinely guided by the Spirit, then you are not bound by the law precisely because all your actions will incorporate, embody, and be fully in accord with the law. A person will, in effect, become a living exemplar of the law.

"Ethical guidelines, although often somewhat arbitrary and subjective, are necessary. They provide an anchor, a context for one's spiritual practice. Without adhering to basic ethical principles, a

168

person is adrift on an anarchical ocean of relativistic beliefs, so life for them becomes a purposeless crapshoot, an unprincipled free-for-all. As long as one's sense of ego persists, adherence to ethical values is essential for spiritual progress.

"Even after realization, adhering to ethical standards provides an example for others to follow. Otherwise, a person may lapse into a de-lusory state wherein they believe, falsely, that God ordains everything they do, all the while dismissing the idea that their behavior matters in the slightest, which is similar to antinomianism. Or, equally odious, they may perpetuate the illusion that they are enlightened and can do whatever they please. Those who believe and promote such false-hoods—typically egomaniacal cult leaders and delusional fanatics— are prompted solely by their own desires, not God's will. Yet, if you observe them, their actions more often than not betray a state of *un*-enlightenment, not sainthood. This is because they are slaves to their ego, and beyond that, 'Their minds are occupied with the things of this world,'[149] as St. Paul shrewdly observed. Such a person is incapable of adopting a non-egocentric point of view precisely because of their massive ego and their deeply entrenched secular orientation.

"However, spiritual life is not about enhancing the ego, but dis-mantling it. Rather than receiving a divine sanction from God, the only being who confers on them the justification to act the way they do is themselves! Such is the tenacity of an unchecked, out-of-con-trol ego. The key lies in this New Testament verse from St. John: 'Whoever claims to abide in God ought to walk just as he [meaning Jesus] walked.'[150] In other words, a person must practice what they preach.[151] Seeking God does not mean abandoning one's ethical prin-ciples, or that anything goes."

Stuart followed up. "You said St. Paul taught that if you're led by the Spirit, you're not under the law. Wouldn't this also imply that a person can shirk responsibility for what they do and suffer no consequences?"

"That is another related trap of the ego," Father replied. "A per-son might think that because everything is ordained by fate or God's will, they are not accountable for their actions. This is pure non-sense! When one is enlightened, they will see firsthand that everything happens according to God's will. But short of that state, one must continually use their free will and best judgment in all circumstances. You are still very much responsible for your own actions. If you let go of the steering wheel while cruising on the freeway, will God take over and start driving your car? If you stop paying your taxes, will the IRS send the bill to Jesus? You cannot simply blame everything on God or fate, then wash your hands of all responsibility by relinquishing accountability for your own actions!

"In addition, ethics are important because they help an aspirant implement their spirituality. While it can be useful to discuss the workings of destiny and other heady issues on a purely intellectual level to aid in our understanding of these things, when the rubber hits the road, no such cerebral discussions will bring about God realization. You may memorize the collected works of St. Augustine, but that won't get you any closer to God. We must *practice* our spirituality by working diligently and by continually applying it in our daily lives." Father paused and playfully smiled. "We can then transcend all heady matters entirely and be granted a truly head*less* experience."

Father continued, "Ethical guidelines thus help to stabilize one's ever-growing state of spiritual attainment so there are no loopholes. They provide a valuable means of checks and balances to ensure a person doesn't slip into a delusional, ego-driven state. Because they are guidelines, they invest a person with inner conviction, which is an essential ally when navigating the spiritual quest."

Father briefly looked at each of us.

"When practicing ethics in your own life, try embracing a single uplifting motif as your guiding principle, such as 'I will love my neighbor as myself and regard their welfare as my own' or 'I resolve to practice unconditional forgiveness.' This will become your theme, the ideal you will follow and try to emulate. This approach is especially beneficial when shoring up areas in your character that you know are in need of improvement.

"For example, if you are quick to anger, practice forbearance. If you are impatient, make a special effort to be more accepting when undergoing delays. When someone offends you, instantly counteract their actions by mentally thinking, 'May God bless you!' in accord with Jesus' exalted instruction to 'Love your enemies, and pray for those who persecute you.'[152] This is also in keeping with St. Paul's noble-minded counsel: 'When we are reviled, we bless; when persecuted, we endure; when vilified, we respond courteously.'[153]

"Each morning when you awake, you can renew your commitment so your behavior reflects your ideal throughout the day. You thereby ingrain your motif until it becomes part of your nature, just as an athlete trains for an event until they know it by heart. If you suffer a setback or even backslide into your former bad habits, you can forcefully draw yourself back into alignment with your ideal, provided your intentions are pure and your commitment is uncompromising. This will help iron out all the patchy spots in your character. In these many ways, you will be striving to live a principled life. Your ethical practice thus goes hand in hand with your meditation routine to ensure that your behavior matches and manifests your inner realization.

"Bear in mind, however, that the fundamental trait which characterizes all ethical behavior is summed up in one word—*integrity*. As we read in Proverbs, 'The integrity of the upright shall guide them, but the unscrupulous are ruined by their own crookedness.'[154] If you live a principled life that is grounded in ethics, and if you are able to maintain your integrity continuously, and if you practice the Golden Rule under all circumstances and tell the truth at all times, you'll automatically be practicing the highest ethical codes."

Carla asked, "Father, I try to practice ethics in my own life—when I'm at school, with my friends, and so forth. How can a person know if they're succeeding?"

Father answered, "There is one simple test that indicates if you're mastering your ethical practices: how you behave in private. No truer indicator exists of one's character. If you appear as a soft-spoken, congenial saint in public but are a self-centered, insensitive ogre in private, what does that say about you? If I were evaluating an individual to determine whether they would be a worthy candidate for sainthood, the very first persons I would interview would be those with whom they lived. If they had been married, I'd initially speak with their spouse!

"The Bishop of Belley, a friend and disciple of St. Francis de Sales, spied through a hole he drilled in Francis' door so he could observe Francis in private, only to find he behaved the same alone as when he mingled with others." Father fetched a book from his library, then read the following passage that the Bishop wrote about Francis, " 'Well, I can truly say that whatever he did, whether he prayed, read, meditated, or wrote, in his lying down and in his rising up, at all times and in all circumstances, he was the same—calm, unaffected, simple—his outward demeanour corresponding with the interior beauty of his soul. Francis quite alone was the very same as Francis in company.'[155] Similarly, as a result of your continued practices, you will eventually smooth out all the behavioral wrinkles in your character. You will then become the same person round the clock, putting an end at last to all the vacillating emotions and unpredictable Jekyll and Hyde elements in your character that have prevented you from embodying an unshakable and consistent spiritual realization.

"However, when practicing moral virtues, never forget that you are not morally superior to anyone. To think so is nothing more than sanctimonious hypocrisy. You may in fact be morally superior to someone. But the moment this thought crosses your mind, you will have judged yourself as superior and the other person as inferior. At that very moment you become morally inferior to them. This is yet another trap of the ego.

"Does anyone have any more questions or comments?"

Corey asked, "You said earlier that God prefers things go a certain way. How can God prefer war, or murder, or natural disasters? Wouldn't God prefer for us to have peace and happiness?"

Father sighed. "I invariably get into trouble whenever I use a theological reference! You certainly make a valid point. This is why I typically prefer to use the impersonal terms 'karma' and 'destiny' to explain these things. Why blame God for the world's atrocities? The world is insane enough without attributing its insanity to God. As George Bernard Shaw wittily quipped, 'I don't know if there are men on the moon, but if there are they must be using the earth as their lunatic asylum.' Therefore, leave God out of the equation so you have an unsullied visualization of God as a loving, helpful Presence, not some sinister despot who maliciously gloats as he plots travails and conflicts for humanity. Let's ascribe such blame to Satan, not God."

Brandon chimed in, "Let's say a person constantly encounters obstacles that prevent him from getting ahead in life. How do we know if it's God or Satan that's causing them?"

Father replied, "The cause might be neither, but simply the workings of destiny."

"What if God and Satan are one and the same?"

"Then we'd all be in big trouble!"

~~~~~~~~~~~~

Clasping his hands, Father touched on another topic. "While the grand evolutionary movement impels us toward enlightenment, we must always make purposeful efforts to accelerate and advance our own progress toward this supreme goal. There are many stages and layers that one's consciousness must pass through, which the Sufis refer to as *veils*, until it sheds the last remaining vestige of duality. This occurs in the higher stages of union with God, where the seeds of one's ingrained traits are fried, forever rendered inert, having been burnt in the blazing fire of spiritual communion. The storehouse of karma becomes exhausted and emptied of its contents, nevermore to ripen within this realm of existence.

"A person then continues living in the world because of the momentum of the karma that carried them into this life. Their body and mind, including certain features of their personality and character, continue to function on account of their present destiny, which persists until death. The Hindus call this *prārabdha karma*. Then, at their passing, the inner binding mechanism that holds their personality together is blown wide asunder and can never again coalesce to form a human body—the ingredients simply no longer exist. According to the theory of reincarnation, the physical births have completed their cycles.

"Enlightened masters have only described a portion of these higher states of consciousness—the *samadhis* of Hinduism, the various advanced stages of contemplation in Catholicism, the *jhānas* of Theravada Buddhism, the *maqāmāt* of Sufism. Many of the saints, in their visions, tell of vast inner realms and universes that make this planet and its history appear as a fraction of an atom in a grain of sand when compared to the largest and most distant galaxy! As King Solomon marveled, 'Before you, the whole universe is like a grain of sand or a single drop of morning dew.'"[156]

All were affected by Father's comments. We were *experiencing* what he was teaching, assimilating his words on a deep inner level. He was enveloping us all in his vision, which was being conveyed like a pictogram, impressing images of an astounding, vast reality on to our minds.

"This is, alas, one of the lower realms." Father's dry humor broke the spell. Many acknowledging expressions could be seen.

"Look around at all the suffering, the hatred, the destruction. Look at people's motives and conduct. Many behave just like talking animals. In fact, many animals behave better than some humans. However, this is the place where a person can engage in spiritual practice, and by so doing, elevate their consciousness. This is what the Tibetans mean by saying that someone has gained a 'rare and precious human birth.' Accordingly, they caution us not to waste the opportunity for spiritual advancement in this life."

Corey asked another question, "I understand that Buddhists believe in reincarnation. So, couldn't someone evolve spiritually over the course of several lives?"

"What you say about reincarnation is true; however, any talk of future lives is pure speculation," Father said. "The Buddha once told a parable about a man's house burning down while his sons blithely played inside, oblivious to the approaching flames. The father persuaded his boys to evacuate, thus saving them. The lesson is that we need to wake up from our hypnotic preoccupation with worldly allurements and act quickly in *this* life to escape this realm of suffering, dissatisfaction, and delusion with the same sense of urgency as though our own home were on fire.

"Along with that, the opportunity to evolve is not wasted if one engages in spiritual practice *and* simultaneously views this earthly realm merely as a playground of destiny—a platform where we enact our desires and emotions, likes and dislikes. The body and mind are nothing more than focal points through which our destiny is played out. By embracing this perspective, one is less likely to get caught. Otherwise, you will become a prisoner—a trapped and bound soul, defined solely by your preferences and distastes, helplessly ushered along the house of mirrors that constitutes your little cage of life."

There was absolute silence in the room.

"Even relatively enlightened beings have their karmic baggage; no one is entirely free from their own past influences. But many advanced beings can transcend these limitations and not allow certain behaviors to manifest that might appear odd in the eyes of others. If not, this results in the quintessential eccentric or unorthodox saint, one who often tosses all social conventions to the wind: St. Francis of Assisi, Shirdi Sai Baba, St. Maria Magdalene de' Pazzi, or the Sufi mystic al-Hallaj.

"And there is a special class of beings, which the Hindus call an avatar, the Christians an incarnation of God, and the Mahayana Buddhists a bodhisattva…or, I should say, those who are considered fully illumined bodhisattvas by their having attained to Buddhahood, such as Avalokiteshvara and Tara. These highly evolved beings hold their karmic ingredients together with the glue of radiant love.

"The Mahayana Buddhists maintain that a bodhisattva's wholehearted wish to emanate boundless spiritual love and elevate others spiritually causes them to reappear in this lower planetary realm, whereas otherwise they would vanish upon physical dissolution. According to Hindu thought, derived from the Bhagavad Gita, God incarnates whenever unrighteousness abounds.[157] Christians hold their own view, 'For God so loved the world that he gave his only begotten Son, that whosoever believes in him shall not perish but shall have eternal life.'[158] However, regardless of these differing doctrinal approaches, suffice it to say that these benevolent beings—Jesus, Krishna, Buddha; Moses, Mohammad, Nanak, Lao Tzu; avatars, incarnations, great sages, saints, and bodhisattvas—are in many ways the spiritual caretakers of humankind."

Father peered outside into the darkness. Then he scanned across the room at those gathered, all the while beaming a sweet smile. He took a deep breath as he came down from his elevated state, then he reoriented himself before speaking. "These are some of the workings of this miraculous universe. Do not worry about the various tasks and projects in your life, what may or may not come about. Rather, focus your efforts on keeping your mind in a constant state of surrender. Recall what St. Paul taught, 'Do everything without complaining or arguing.'[159] Be patient, express gratitude, and radiate boundless joy. Meditate regularly to train your mind so it maintains a toehold in God while you are busy with your various activities. You will soon come to live wholly in the spirit even as your body goes through its karmic motions."

This seemed a fitting place for Father to conclude. He served up a large feast tonight, and we needed time to digest it all. Fortunately, he immediately led us into silent meditation, which allowed our bedazzled minds a chance to settle down. He prefaced our sitting by first stressing the importance of making use of devotion in our practices, which, he emphasized, can significantly aid an aspirant.

Father also reminded us not to entertain stray thoughts when meditating. "Remember, the purpose of meditation is to bring the mind to a halt. We don't sit in silence in order to replay our memories or to visualize how our various plans might pan out. Or to devise ways on how best to extract revenge on our enemies. We turn our attention inward and shut down the wandering mind. As Lao Tzu asserts:

> Shut the gateways of perception
> Seal the portals of desire
> Then you will know peace throughout your life.[160]

"We focus on the home object until the racing mind is brought under control. This can be done by an act of intention and applied persistence. And by constructively utilizing our free will to silence our lower emotions ..."

Nick, who was sitting quietly with Carla, suddenly interrupted. "Speaking of lower emotions, I can be a little intense at times."

Carla butted in. "He means hotheaded."

"It only happens on occasion," Nick explained.

"I think it's hardwired into his personality," Carla added.

Addressing Father, Nick asked, "So when I'm in an intense frame of mind, how can I use that intensity in my meditation practice?"

Carla, herself a buoyant, no-nonsense personality, implored, "Please, Father, anything that will help tone down his intensity or whatever he calls it!"

All of us laughed at The Nick and Carla Show.

Father, who was also amused, responded, "Very well. Those who possess both intensity and hotheadedness are certainly grist for the meditative mill. It's a matter of directing those and all emotions toward God. For individuals with emotional temperaments in particular, devotion coupled with meditation is an ideal path."

God Caresses Their Souls

Father expanded on this theme. "You may recall that most of the well-known Christian saints were devotees—lovers of God—including many of the spiritual giants: Teresa of Ávila, John of the Cross, Thomas à Kempis, Catherine of Genoa. The Jewish mystics are intensely devotional, as are the Sufis and many of the Hindu sects. Some Buddhist groups employ devotion, most notably the Mahayanists and Tibetans. Harnessing devotion to aid in your practice is like adding rocket fuel to the mix: it exponentially boosts your efforts. Using the mind alone is a fairly dry approach. Devotion lubricates the mechanical aspects of practice and helps one naturally and effortlessly reduce their worldly attachments. Because, when you're madly in love with God, all else pales into insignificance. To combine devotion with meditation is an excellent path, addressing the needs of both head and heart. Both go hand in hand, like two wings of a bird.

"Just as Patanjali developed a psychological science of God, so too the Vaishnavites of Bengal developed a devotional science of God. According to their teachings, there are four progressive stages of devotion: *bhakti*, devotional feelings; *bhava*, devotional ecstasy; *mahabhava*, intense devotional ecstasy; and *prema*, which is nondifferentiated ecstatic spiritual communion. This schema is extremely useful for placing the devotional experiences from mystics of any religious tradition into context. It shows us that the path of devotion progresses by degrees and is universal in its scope and applicability. All devotional mystics undergo the same or similar experiences, only those experiences are interpreted in the milieu of their religion, culture, language, and times.

"I should note," Father added, "that the three higher stages in the Vaishnavite model—*bhava*, *mahabhava*, and *prema*—and their equivalencies in other religious traditions, are exceedingly rare, especially *prema*, the highest state of ecstatic communion with God, which is typically only experienced by highly spiritually advanced beings. Even *bhava* and *mahabhava*—ecstasy and intense ecstasy—are atypical. God tends to be stingy when granting divine love, and he only bestows it on those who first give a hundred percent of their hearts to him. Even so, the nature and intensity of the spiritual intimacy experienced by devotees who unfold these sublime states of divine ecstatic love remains beyond the scope of comprehension by the ordinary mind. This divine love is not the same as ordinary human love.

"In addition, the blissful ecstasies generated when following a devotional path become a self-perpetuating pathway to God. A devotee needs no enticement to practice, because they become habituated to the nectarous outpourings of divine love and otherworldly joy that bathe their soul. The more they practice, the more they are imbued with this intoxicating love and joy, which soon becomes their second nature. It's worth noting that love and joy are topmost among St. Paul's 'fruit of the Spirit.' This affirms for them that they are on the right path. Further, these experiences of mystical inebriation deepen over time, transforming the devotee's personality by eclipsing their worldly self whenever they are absorbed in divine union. The otherwise unmalleable ego is altogether erased during the devotee's fervent devotional mergings with God.

"The only caveat here is that lesser evolved aspirants may use devotion as a means to generate a spurious ecstasy of sorts, to which they become addicted. One might say they get momentarily high, then come back down to their same ego-dominated state as before. Hence, they haven't advanced one iota. Such practitioners can ride an endless roller coaster of spiritual emotions without ever once controlling their mind and overhauling their inner nature. This then becomes no more than a cheap, low-grade titillation, mere self-gratification, and is to be shunned entirely because no real inner transformation takes place. St. John of the Cross refers to this as 'spiritual gluttony,'[161] while Theophan the Recluse calls it 'spiritual hedonism.'[162] The spiritual path is not for thrill seekers or the self-indulgent.

"Also, the Sufis distinguish between 'drunken' and 'sober' states of divine intoxication. Think of this figuratively as the ability to hold one's spiritual liquor. If you don't want to risk having your peers confine you to a psychiatric ward, you had best express your

178

devotional sentiments in private! Jesus prudently taught us to pray in secret.[163] Otherwise, you are merely fanning the flames of your ego. The quickest way to lose your spiritual gains is to display them in public.

"Now, the purpose of devotion is to strip away the layers of one's ego and thereby remove all sense of differentiation between the devotee and God. This is accomplished when the aspirant's soul merges with their Beloved during deep states of spiritual communion. In the Catholic tradition, this rare state is called the Prayer of Union, along with its subsequent advanced stages. This is called *fanā* in the Sufi tradition, and, as previously mentioned, *prema* in the Vaishnavite tradition. A passionate devotee becomes ecstatically embraced in devotional union with God. Their ego is completely transcended. This deep inner absorption produces a state of nondual consciousness, which is induced by means of devotional fervor and becomes intensified by the devotee's continued concentrated effusions of love toward their divine Beloved.

"In this state, the devotee's heart overflows with pulsating surges of this all-consuming love. They are infused with delicate, quavering dimensions of multifaceted bliss. The exquisite sensations of divine love are so intense they rip to shreds any sense of self. Mystics attempting to describe this love write of being immersed in undulating shivers of ecstatic horripilations, as God caresses their souls with unending deluges of sweet consolations."

Following a brief pause, Todd remarked with a straight face, "I don't mean to sound impolite, but this sounds to me like the sexual experience." Peals of laughter filled the room.

Father, smiling, responded. "Quite the contrary. The erotic sensation is a pale, poorly developed imitation of what are universally described by mystics as the ineffable blissful sensations that occur when the soul attains to union with God. I would estimate this spiritual ecstasy is ten times more sublime and potent than if corporeally fulfilled. At its peak of intensity, it might be called a spiritual climax, a climax of the soul, which all devotional mystics experience. This is far more subtle and all-encompassing than any physical climax because it originates in the spirit, not the body. The soul merges with God, and indescribable groundswells of ecstasy accompany this felicitous union. This in turn produces a torrential influx of smoldering waves of molten bliss. Inconceivable quantities of this bliss then flow from the soul and fill the mind and body, often congregating in the heart or head, totally enwrapping the devotee with incalculable infusions of ecstasy.

"This spiritual ecstasy belongs to an entirely different realm when compared to the physical sensation of lust. It does not originate from any physical source, nor is it characteristically produced through physical means, although certain of the Tantric and Southern Taoist schools use physical methods and specialized practices to produce it. But most commonly it is altogether an *interior* state, as mystics have attested to for centuries."

Some of the males who were in relationships especially perked their ears, paying close attention to Father's words. Tom and Stuart appeared to be vying with each other to voice the following question, which Tom ended up asking, "Father, is it possible for ordinary people to experience these states?"

"Of course! But these states are rare. It is simply impossible to enumerate the varied textures, contours, and multidimensional nuances of spiritual ecstasy. They imbue the ardent devotee with numerous subtle shadings of rapturous divine intoxication. These numinous, iridescent sensations of divine love palpably impinge on the devotee's soul. This occurs during deep devotional states, as interiorly experienced by devout mystics of all religious traditions. Read for example, the testimonials of Hugh of St. Victor, Angela of Foligno, Richard Rolle, Hadewijch, Blessed Jan van Ruysbroeck, Walter Hilton, and of course St. Teresa of Ávila and St. John of the Cross. Then venture into Orthodox Christian writings. Then the Jewish mystics. Then the Sufis. And so on. Because these sensations flow through the physical body, they could be construed as roughly equivalent to the physical sensation of eros. But this is a crude approximation which describes a phenomenon that actually originates from a divine and not a corporeal source. I might add—this all-permeating divine love is beautifully and allegorically depicted in the Song of Solomon, a poetic masterwork in the world's mystical canon."

Then Stuart, appearing puzzled, asked the inevitable corollary question, punctuated by a certain trepidation. "Father, you said this ecstasy differs from lust. Are you implying that sex must be given up in order to experience these states?"

Everyone broke into laughter, including Father. We now understood the underlying reason for these men's concerns!

Father responded, "It is true that the highest recorded mystical states are typically, but not exclusively, derived from celibate nuns and monks, especially in the Catholic tradition. But this certainly does not preclude married couples from experiencing these states."

Both men appeared significantly relieved.

"St. Paul recognized this dilemma when he gave the following advice: 'It is better to marry than to burn,'[164] that is, to burn with concupiscence. The key is moderation. And this requires practicing self-control, another of the 'fruit of the Spirit.'

"Celibacy in and of itself is a pointless act that will come back to bite the practitioner unless one element is present. That element is sublimation, known also as transmutation. The Hindus discuss this as do the Taoists and the Tibetan Buddhists. Without converting corporeal sensations of eros into spiritual sensations of hunger for God, the unappeased physical sensations will continue to seek an outlet. But, through an act of sustained resolve accompanied by the practice of self-restraint, these same physical sensations can be redirected to seek an *inlet*. That inlet is God residing internally, within one's spiritual heart. Once properly sublimated, these sensations are sublimely fulfilled whenever the mystic enters into union with God.

"While some Eastern religions use technical means to effect this transmutation, the Catholic mystics proceeded without any roadmap. However, because of their unshakable faith and fervent aspirations, they were able to find and pass through the 'narrow gate'[165]—the inner spiritual passageway—that leads to God. They then experienced the deepest mystical states of divine ecstasy and union. We are fortunate to possess many of their accounts, which clearly demonstrate the transformative effects wrought by this spiritual alchemy and the ensuing inner metamorphosis it produced in them.

"This transmutation occurs when the celibate practitioner performs one simple act: they sublimate the physical sensations of the erotic impulse into ones of transcendent spiritual ecstasy. While I believe that celibacy imparts a quantifiable increase in the magnitude of this ecstasy, one need not be celibate in order to experience these states.

"But even if not celibate, it is important for any practitioner to practice moderation in these matters as best they can, torturous as this may sound. This helps to bring about sublimation. If sublimation is successfully induced, a tangible inner shift occurs whereby the devotee's soul is drawn into a massive vortex of pure inebriating bliss, which is like no other. It simply deluges the graced aspirant, who is saturated with wave upon wave of intensified spiritual ecstasy and bliss. It's as if God's living ecstatic rapturous love becomes liquified and rains down particles of delightful bliss on the awestruck, speechless devotee. If devotional love is combined with sublimation, the effects are markedly increased. Further, if love and sublimation are conjoined with deep, unwavering concentration on God, the effects are multiplied even more, producing an amalgamated state of symphonious mystical intensity that defies description. As the mystic becomes more and more immersed in this state, they realize there is simply no end to God."

Pindrop silence permeated the room.

Father continued. "But even when produced through devotion alone, without the added effects of sublimation and concentration, this *ekstasis* is experienced as a palpable bliss, which fills one's spiritual heart. The spiritual heart becomes a receptacle for the gentle tremors of devotion, subtle and illimitable, and entirely nonphysical in origin. This joyous bliss completely blankets the mystic and overwhelms them with divine raptures no tongue can give voice to."

Upon standing, Father grabbed a few books from his remarkable library. Then, sitting back down, he read some passages. "Ruysbroeck writes of this state, 'This well-being melts the heart to such a degree, that the man cannot contain himself through the fulness of inward joy...From this rapturous delight springs spiritual inebriation...a man receives more sensible joy and sweetness than his heart can either contain or desire.'[166] These sensations then irradiate outward from the heart and spill over into the body. When mystics are absorbed in the most profound of devotional states, we sometimes read of them experiencing a kind of spontaneous polymorphic cellular ecstasy, whereby the surging bliss originating in their spiritual heart suffuses their entire being, flooding each part of their body with ethereal stirrings of unspeakable joy. These blissful sensations vary in degree, as each trembling influx produces sweet, ever-new permutations of ecstatic feelings that course and quiver through every fiber of their being."

Father read from another book. "St. John of the Cross also mentions this state: 'the unction of the Holy Spirit sometimes overflows into the body, and this is enjoyed by...all the members of the body...with a feeling of great delight...'[167]

"During the mystic's devotional session, these undulating sensations increase and become amplified over time, engulfing them with tremendous upsurges of bliss, impinging everywhere in a random, omnidirectional manner, spreading uncontainable divine elixir throughout their entire being. At the same time, their consciousness is increasingly immersed in this bliss until, like a house being flooded by a rising river overflowing its banks, it is at last inundated by the overwhelming bliss. Whatever fragments remain of their consciousness then melt away into nonduality, whereupon the aspirant is rendered incapable of differentiating between self and other than self. At this stage, the mystic becomes unaware of any physicality whatsoever; they are so completely enveloped by God that they are no longer conscious of their body. This is equivalent to the Prayer of Ecstatic Union, or Spiritual Betrothal, in the Catholic mystical tradition. St. Teresa of Ávila refers to this elevated state of consciousness as both the 'fourth water' and the 'sixth mansion.'

"The devotee is thereby infused with the blissful intoxicating raptures of spiritual union, which enfold them in the all-inclusive, loving embrace of God. Their very soul is saturated with God's essence in a kind of spiritual osmosis whereby the devotee absorbs the core of God's being, as it were. This divine infusion is transmitted to the devotee as a tangible inundation of unlimited love and pure unalloyed bliss. This exalted inner communion, wherein the essences of God and devotee seemingly intermingle, pervades the deepest recesses of the devotee's soul."

Father stopped to read from yet another book. "St. Teresa confirms this in her writings. 'This secret union takes place in the innermost centre of the soul where God Himself must dwell.'"[168]

"In this sublime union, we 'become partakers of the divine nature,'[169] as St. Peter jubilantly proclaims. We participate directly in the mystical experience because we are 'heirs of God and co-heirs with Christ,'[170] according to St. Paul. We realize in the center of our being that 'he who is united with the Lord becomes one spirit with him,'[171] as Paul narrates, because indeed, 'The kingdom of God is within you,' as Jesus plainly asserted."[172]

Father was in an inspired state. He continued, "St. Paul asks, almost incredulously, 'Do you not know that you are God's temple, and that the Spirit of God dwells within you?'[173] Paul further notes this takes place on a level that cannot even remotely be conceived, much less understood, by the secular mind: 'A worldly person denies spiritual matters and considers them foolishness. He cannot understand them, because they can only be discerned by a spiritual person.'[174]

"Just peruse some of the world's mystical literature and read for yourself the mystics' own words! They will ring unmistakably true in the heart of any genuine mystic."

Father paused. This momentary break gave us an all-too-brief opportunity to assimilate what he had shared with us.

After a few moments of silence, Heather asked, "Father, how can devotion bring about such a superhuman state?"

"Devotion can be likened to a pressure cooker," Father said. "The devotional mystic's intense yearning for God becomes concentrated during spiritual practice. Then, as these feelings increase, they become intensified even more in the crucible of divine love that is gathering within their spiritual heart. This creates a pressurized effect that builds ever-accumulating, congealed spiritual energy. As a result of the mystic's focused, sublime outpourings of devotion, which are now being heated under compression, so to speak, bliss is generated. Over the course of the devotee's practice session, their continuing expressions of love act as a bellows that fans this bliss, which increases in intensity, magnifying both in substance and scale. Then the sparks fly as this internal combustion expands outward from their spiritual heart, which can no longer contain the surging bliss, and so it overflows into their physical form. Thus, they feel an uprush of unimaginable waves of bliss coursing through their being. Think of a wildfire shooting out embers and firebrands, which kindle adjacent vegetation until an even greater conflagration ensues.

"Let's again hear from Ruysbroeck: 'From this sweetness there springs a well-being of the heart and of all the bodily powers, so that a man thinks himself to be inwardly enfolded in the divine embrace of love. This delight and this consolation are greater and more pleasant to the soul and the body than all the satisfactions of the earth, even though one man should enjoy them all together.'[175]

"Of course, these analogies amount to more informal and colorful explanations, whereas most Christian mystics quite rightly would simply attribute the phenomenon of ecstatic, devotional bliss to the mysterious workings of God's grace. But St. John of the Cross, as we read earlier, directly attributes these graces to the Holy Spirit. I couldn't agree more. These spiritual ecstasies are the tangible manifestation of the divine Presence in our beings.

"Still, some traditions posit more technical explanations, such as the esoteric Hindu Tantra texts, which refer to this spreading of spiritual bliss as the flowing of *sóma* or divine elixir. Certain Eastern religious traditions directly attribute this phenomenon to the awakening of the divine Presence, which they term *kundalini*. Tibetan Buddhism offers explanations as well.

"Some Hindu and Taoist traditions employ the conscious manipulation of internal energies and various practices to generate this bliss. These blissful inner states can thus be coaxed without using a devotional approach. But using mechanical techniques alone to induce these states often brings about a limited, one-dimensional realization which lacks the multifaceted, all-encompassing, expansive quality that an integral approach produces when devotion is incorporated.

"Yet, all this is for naught unless the character and habit patterns of the devotee are transformed. This is why most mature mystical approaches emphasize certain fundamentals, such as observing ethics and practicing universal love and compassion. This is also why devotion combined with meditation is such an ideal practice. A devotee need not worry about learning specialized methods or esoteric techniques. They will stumble on to this bliss, or rather, the bliss will find them. It is a byproduct of their devotion.

"In addition, I incorporate a custom from the Catholic tradition, whereby a Mass is dedicated to a certain person. This has a parallel in Tibetan Buddhism. It involves mentally offering the cauldron of divine love and bliss that is generated during one's practice session to all living beings everywhere. You thereby engage in an act of selfless love by altruistically divesting yourself of every spiritual blessing you've accumulated during your session by mentally giving it away to benefit others. In this manner, your spiritual practice becomes an ongoing ministry." Father's eyes twinkled. "So, if you really want to silence the cynics who criticize your meditation routine, just say to them, 'I meditate to help spiritually elevate the world and all beings in it, including you!'"

"Devotion thus opens up a whole other dimension of spirituality, heretofore unimagined. It smothers the wandering mind and thoroughly renews one's attitude. It dramatically transforms a stale, jaded outlook on life. As St. Paul declares, 'Be ye transformed by the renewal of your mind.'[176]

"In summary, devotion acts like a magnet, drawing forth indescribable divine consolations and blessings. The devotional mystics I mentioned write of being engulfed by inexpressible sweet graces and euphoric divine moods. They describe feelings of overwhelming ecstatic communion with God. Many recount states wherein they are enveloped by rippling paroxysms of shuddering joy for which no human dictionary has words. They develop such an intimacy with the Divine that they never feel alone, never lose their faith in God. God becomes as real for them as all of you sitting here before me. These mystics interact with God continuously on an intimate level we cannot now conceive. They experience a continuing expansion of divine love within their heart, the magnitude of which is simply unfathomable. It floods their being with undreamt of sweetness, tenderness, and unutterable joy. From there, it extends outward to encompass this vast universe and all beings within it.

"At the culmination of their ecstasy, they are plunged into a grand silence in which there is no sensation, no awareness. Their ego is entirely absent; their soul dissolves into the very fabric of God's infinite being. This fusion is the only consolation that can appease the insatiable hunger they feel for their divine Beloved.

Through repeated practice, this state of merging with God gradually stabilizes and becomes permanent, even when they are active. Thus, the devotional mystics get the best of both worlds: they commune with God in rapturous fervor, and they also dive into God's immeasurable nondual essence.

"I should mention, irrespective of which path one follows—whether devotional or meditative—this permanent, stabilized state is the final, post-illumination phase of enlightenment, which continues unabated whether one is active or inactive. This marks the completion of one's spiritual journey. In the language of Catholic mysticism, this extremely rare state is known as the Transforming Union or Spiritual Marriage, which follows the earlier stage of Spiritual Betrothal."

Father reopened his book by St. Teresa and read from a couple of pages: "St. Teresa writes, 'Spiritual betrothal is different ...'[177] She explains why: 'Separation is still possible ... This is not so in the spiritual marriage with our Lord, where the soul always remains in its centre with its God.'[178] In this state, which she refers to as the 'seventh mansion,' Teresa unambiguously asserts, 'The soul ... is made one with God.'[179]

"But this nondual state is universal. In Sufism, it is known as *fanā al-fanā* or *baqā*. In Theravada Buddhism, it is called *nibbāna*; in Zen, *nirvāṇa*. In the Tibetan Buddhist tradition of Dzogchen, it is called *rigpa*. In Hinduism, it is referred to as *jivanmukta* or *kaivalya* or *turiyatita*. The Hindu saints Ramakrishna and Ramana Maharshi discussed this state. Ramakrishna called it *vijñāna*, while Ramana Maharshi termed it *sahaja samadhi*. And so, this state is universally recognized as the culmination of the mystical path, whereby the realized aspirant carries God with them at all times. Or, more accurately, God carries the aspirant.

"Moreover," Father concluded, looking over at Carla, "those with a component of intensity in their character become softened by the balm of devotion." Father's lighthearted comment provoked laughter, which helped bring the discussion back down to earth. "Devotion," Father added, "will sprinkle an effusion of charm over the most intense personality!"

Carla declared, "Now I've got the formula!"

The Best Time to Practice

Following a short pause, Brandon asked, "Why do I sometimes get sleepy during meditation?"

"First," Father asked Brandon rhetorically, "are you getting enough sleep? If what I've heard about the late-night goings-on at the campus dormitories are true, that may be a contributing factor!" Brandon, Todd, and Corey all coyishly grinned.

"But there is nearly always a larger, more significant reason. When you meditate, you are swimming against the evolutionary tide. The tendency of the mind is to focus outwardly. Just as a child is mesmerized when playing with its toys, the mind similarly craves to be entertained and occupied by an incessant stream of thoughts, emotions, and external objects. When you meditate you reverse this outward tendency, which goes against the mind's natural inclination. This can result in fatigue or sleepiness, especially at the beginning of one's spiritual quest, because it takes a great deal of energy first to turn your mind inward, then to concentrate it until it becomes completely devoid of thoughts.

"Just try visualizing an apple to the exclusion of all else. Everyone please try this for a minute."

We all attempted this for around a minute.

"How many were able to hold the image of an apple in their mind's eye without one single interruption?"

No one responded.

"When you muster up the energy and apply the resolve to walk the spiritual path, you are fighting an army of distractions and obstacles, which are very real from a relative standpoint. It's difficult enough to meditate without disruptions, let alone practice conscientiously and attentively in the workplace, at home, or while out and about. And yet you must do this. As Jesus instructed, 'Be ever vigilant at all times.'[180] And so, you're facing any number of challenges that you must surmount, both inner and outer, such as inertia, lower emotions, intruding images of the past, envisioned scenarios of the future, fatigue from overwork, ridicule from so-called friends, and interruptions from family members. These disturbances all drain you. On top of that, pile on the demands of your job and the routines of daily life. In addition, certain medical conditions, long-term illnesses, and even dietary deficiencies can adversely affect one's ability to practice effectively.

"Beyond that, we haven't touched on the role your psychological state plays. Do you have a positive or negative outlook? Are you a victim of unpredictable moods and baseless anxieties? Is your mind relatively free from inner congestion, or is it a quagmire of wandering thoughts and uncontrolled emotions? All these factors deplete your energy. Yet you must somehow find the strength to overcome them. Unquestionably, it is far easier to remain complacent than to fight against these seemingly all-too-real obstacles that confront us at every turn when we engage in the process of liberating ourselves.

"And so, back to your question. Right now, your meditation muscles are flabby. When you first begin an exercise regimen, you feel tired afterward and your muscles are sore. Likewise, when you begin to reverse the outward focus of your mind and start to chisel away at these many inner obstructions, this puts a strain on your body and mind, which are geared toward normal worldly functioning. Because you're going against the grain, this very exertion can cause fatigue and produce sleepiness. You are acclimating to increasingly subtle spiritual realities, which must take root inside you. But, as you build up your endurance and your inner circuitry becomes rewired to accommodate these newfound spiritual states, the tendency to be overcome by drowsiness lessens."

Changing topics, Nick volunteered the following. "Yesterday the driver who was stopped in back of me kept honking at me to turn at a stop sign. But I was stuck. There was nowhere to go! There was too much oncoming traffic, which he couldn't see. I lost my patience and turned around and yelled at him."

"What he means is that he swore at him," Carla revealed.

Nick added, "I felt bad after that, like all my practice this past week went down the drain. It really bothered me."

Father said, smiling, "Remember, the whole effort in spiritual life is anchoring your being firmly in the divine Presence while at the same time not reacting to external events. These two actions must occur simultaneously. Without being pulled in all directions by the constant tug of outer events, your attention can be trained to remain grounded in God within. Otherwise, it becomes an unwitting partner to your mind's constant preoccupation with entertaining this or that external object. Your soul thus abdicates its sovereignty by kowtowing to whichever direction your mind is drawn. Once you capitulate to an external event, whatever it may be, including angry drivers, you fall prey to a thousand emotional reactions, because the once-impregnable fortress surrounding your soul has been compromised. Your mind then becomes vulnerable to repeated hijackings by your prickly emotions. This turns into a domino effect. When this occurs, you become caught in the quicksand of your own emotional debris, and down you go!

"Your practice must utilize such single-minded focus that you are fully immune to outer bombardments. You must defend your inner citadel by constantly guarding against the weak mind. You must deftly protect your soul from all intrusions. At present, you react with elation when you get your way, and you throw tantrums when you are thwarted. But we must not register, not even once allow outer events to create an imprint on the mind that would cause it to react. It is essential to train your mind to ruthlessly expel, without hesitation, all thoughts and emotions that would usurp the connection with your spiritual self that you are working so hard to establish."

Corey asked one last question, "So Father, when is the best time to practice spirituality?"

"Right now!"

Father then drew the discussion to a close. "All right," he said. "Let us pray, as St. Paul prayed, that we are filled 'with every spiritual blessing in the heavenly realms,'[181] so that we may focus on God alone as we sit in silence."

The meditation that night was sublime and noticeably powerful. A number of those present appeared intoxicated afterward, as if reeling about until they re-established their bearings. Few spoke as we all dispersed from the gathering and went our separate ways.

After adjourning, I headed back to nearby MacKerricher, where I quickly dove into my tent and allowed the darkness and the crisp night air to engulf me, to quiet my mind, and to heal my restive soul.

Autumnal Introspections

In Ukiah, I received an assignment to write a travel story about points of interest in southcentral Sonoma County. I began researching the area, and I phoned ahead to arrange for a visit. On a Friday morning in late October, I drove with my assignment editor Jennifer, who was happily married to Phil, her apartment-manager husband. Jennifer accompanied me so she could take photos, write her own editorial overview, and drum up some advertising. We traveled to Santa Rosa, where we had booked two separate rooms at one of the local hotels. We spent the rest of that day and most of the next day touring Jack London State Historic Park, Sonoma State Historic Park, the charming town of Healdsburg, and Sonoma Antique Apple Nursery, which was holding its annual apple-tasting open house that weekend. Then we explored the Luther Burbank Home, where we were shown many of the botanical wonders that Burbank miraculously created. Jennifer and I shared a warm, friendly camaraderie, and I was never viewed as a threat to her marriage. She was like a sister to me, and she proved a solid friend for the time I knew her.

When Gail and I broke up some weeks later—relationships undertaken at that time in my life often carried with them a certain ill-fated inevitability—I phoned Jennifer that night and spoke with her for an hour. She was especially consoling and sympathetic. Along with news of the breakup, I shared with her several happy recollections, such as my boyhood penchant for gazing at the stars for hours on end, and the complete sense of freedom I experienced when viewing stars while camping—pointing out constellations; looking for shooting stars—as when a friend and I stayed at Kennedy Meadows Campground (elev. 6,200 feet) in the southeastern Sierra Nevada during the time of the waxing crescent moon in December 1973, just after Christmas. Or the unparalleled experience of becoming part of a never-ending brilliant dome of twinkling starlight while cruising out at sea on a moonless night. I'd lose myself in the stars.

During the middle of that night, I had an exceptionally lucid dream. Jennifer, appearing in her street clothes, sat on the side of my bed, gently stroking my forehead. This was so intense as to be real; she *was* there. I awoke and glanced over at her, but all of a sudden, she was gone. I looked around the room, but she was nowhere to be seen. I got up and walked into the living room of my apartment calling her name. Suddenly, it dawned on me that I had awoken from a dream and she in fact was not present. At least physically. She was there in spirit.

A week later, I told her about my dream. When I did, she told me she got goose pimples. She said she had prayed for me that very same night, sending reassuring thoughts to me after my breakup. Then she added something that caused me to get goose pimples. Whenever she comforted her children, she gently stroked them on the forehead, exactly as I had described in my dream.

~~~~~~~~~~~~~

Mentioning Kennedy Meadows to Jennifer resurrected a flood of memories from when I camped and backpacked in my mid-teens. Roaming around in nature provided solace to my young soul. My first hiking trip took place in nearby Angeles National Forest, where I accompanied several diehards from my high-school hiking club. Subsequently, and especially after I acquired my first automobile around February 1973, a used delta-green 1969 VW van, I routinely took camping excursions with likeminded friends. We most frequently traveled from our homes in West Los Angeles to either side of the southern Sierra Nevada mountain range.

On the Sierra's western slope, we stayed at assorted campsites and hiked different trails along the Kaweah River watershed inside spectacular Sequoia National Park, such as the boulder-laden Middle Fork tributary and the fancifully named Marble Fork offshoot. We undertook similar jaunts into the Eastern Sierra, most often along the expanse of gentle terrain between the Chimney Creek backcountry and the tranquil Kennedy Meadows tableland that rests on the Kern Plateau then skirts northward, straddling the South Fork of the Kern River until it reaches the understated majesty of Monache Meadows.

We also trekked locally to the outlying mountainous regions near Los Angeles: scenic locations inside the San Gorgonio and San Jacinto wildernesses; trailheads and campsites along Angeles Crest Highway; and the peaceful, pastoral Sespe Creek and picturesque

Mount Pinos areas in Los Padres National Forest. In addition, I hiked in my own backyard, figuratively speaking, traipsing through the Santa Monica Mountains, following paths that led through Temescal Canyon, Rivas Canyon, and Will Rogers State Historic Park. I and various members of our loose-knit circle of friends would sometimes drive up the coast and cavort innocently on Zuma and Leo Carrillo beaches. I felt particularly at home in nature, and these many experiences of nature's impressive grandeur deeply affected me. They enabled me to encounter heretofore unknown wonders of the natural world. For a young person raised in the city, it felt as if I were stepping out of a bad dream and walking straight into heaven when leaving the strangulating confines of the megalopolis and visiting these astonishing places where nature reigned supreme.

An equally influential event occurred around seventh or eighth grade when I came across two Signet Classics paperbacks: *Selected Writings of Ralph Waldo Emerson* and *Walden*. Both made a profound impact, and the ideas expressed in Emerson's essay "Self-Reliance" and in Henry David Thoreau's *Walden* fundamentally changed my outlook on life by convincingly sanctioning what was already percolating inside my impressionable, individualist young mind. Add to the mix my high-school discovery of John Muir's *The Yosemite* and *The Mountains of California,* and the peerless, transformational ideas from this towering trio of naturalists and iconoclastic philosophers implanted in me a seminal, radical vision of life. The three became role models—heroes—and theirs was a clarion call that resonated to the core of my soul.

But now, caught in the grip of my dithering autumnal introspections of 1991, I could no longer conjure up the innocent magic of my early hiking trips. All I could visualize were grayed-out, one-dimensional cardboard images flittering across my listless mind. No matter how hard I tried, I could not animate these ghosts from my past. The whir and bustle of laughter and play, of exploration and adventure, of imagination and idealism, receded into feebly grasped, ashen mirages. Nor could I breathe life into the booming mandates of Emerson, Thoreau, and Muir. Their sublime edicts on how to live life nobly were now muffled into a faint whisper, archived in a dusty inner file, as the stark reality and frenetic obligations of daily life overshadowed their once mighty influence. The encroaching sense of my own mortality further fueled the flames of my on-again off-again existential crisis. I felt powerless to cast off the worldly overlays I had accumulated in life. Even my First Awakening experience was void of vibrancy and substance; it seemed a distant, hazily recalled memory, as though belonging to someone else. Whatever insights sustained me during that time had faded away.

All the uplifting experiences from my past that once buoyed me now appeared vacuous and barren; all the people with whom I once mingled seemed as if hollow apparitions. Like sand running through my open fingers, I futilely clutched at my vanishing personal history, but stood by helplessly as nothing caught hold. And so, confronted with a fading past, a tenuous present, and an uncertain future, and especially despairing of my chronic inability to find a way to integrate the spiritual and secular aspects of my life, I lingered on dispiritedly in October 1991, like a tormented specter who is similarly helplessly "doomed to wander through the world and witness what it cannot share, but might have shared on earth ..."[182] No matter how hard I tried, I could not resuscitate my *joie de vivre*. No matter how hard I tried, I could not resurrect my former spiritual vision of life. No matter how hard I tried, I could not perform CPR on my own corpse.

SIXTH VISIT (January 1992)

As Within, So Without

IT HAD BEEN NINETEEN MONTHS since I first met Father Christopher. When I initially visited him in mid-1990, he was still fairly robust. But since that time, and especially noticeable on this early January 1992 visit, he had declined. He now seemed older, more feeble. His once firm and resonant voice had weakened. His gait was slower, more deliberate. The glint in his eyes, however, was as strong as ever. But his vital energy had waned.

After traveling to Heather's earlier that day, she and I drove to Mendocino Headlands State Park day-use area on the western outskirts of Mendocino, where we hiked along the craggy cliffs situated above the ocean, which was crashing and churning below. The weather was chilly and threatening to rain. Afterward, amid occasional spits of light rain, we zigzagged through the outdoor and indoor exhibits at nearby Mendocino Art Center, which featured a gift shop where I bought a decorative ceramic tile by one of the local

195

artists, titled *Presbyterian Church.* Heather purchased a John William Waterhouse poster she had been admiring, which would perfectly highlight one of her walls. This artwork would complement several framed posters that already adorned her simple home. But the one I always recall, quoting Khalil Gibran, was set against a sunset–ocean background: "We choose our joys and sorrows long before we experience them."

I assisted Heather as she prepared a simple dinner: baked potatoes, a lentil dish, wheat rolls, and salad. Soon after, she drove us to Father's cabin in a gentle rain. All the regular attendees had gathered in the crowded front room, including two more of Brandon's friends, newcomers Laurie and Kurt, who were a couple, and whom Father warmly greeted. As with Todd and Corey, I would only see them at this one meeting. Jason and Stacy, now engaged, also showed up. They treated each other affectionately. They subsequently tied the knot and have remained happily married to this day. Father, however, appeared tired. His face seemed to droop. He wore a muted gold scarf, wrapped on top of a dark-brown turtleneck sweater, and beige trousers. He took his seat, then began speaking, although at a slower pace than usual.

~~~~~~~~~~~~~

"It's a beautiful winter evening. I'm happy to see you all. In fact," he said, diving right into his topic, "every time we see each other we engage in Vedanta philosophy. There is a concept in Vedanta known as *drishti srishti,* which means 'the world is as we see it.' That is to say, we interpret the objects we perceive according to our own inner state. 'Nonsense!' you may protest, 'The universe and all its objects exist independent of me and my interpretation of them.' But *drishti srishti* is a statement of relativity. We perceive what we are. Or, to be more exact, our interpretation of what we perceive reflects our level of spiritual evolution. If we are in a dualistic mindset, we interpret the objects we perceive as existing apart from us. But from a nondual perspective, we interpret the universe and everything in it as a vast, singular Being. Objects, including us, appear as images arising out of this infinite, omnipresent Being. So, from this nondual vantage point, when I see you, what I'm actually seeing is me. Or more precisely, the spiritual essence in my being is perceiving the same spiritual essence in your being. And so, the world is but a mirror of our own inner state."

Kurt interrupted. "Could you please back up a bit? You've lost me."

"Of course. I sometimes get ahead of myself because the aspirants here are at different levels of understanding. Some are more familiar with these concepts, while others may not have much of a clue about what we're discussing, which is quite understandable."

Then Father addressed everyone. "As some of you know, I was intellectually struck by several explanations of reality that originated in the Middle East, the Far East, and India, such as the theory of karma, and *drishti srishti*. I introduced and incorporated a handful of these philosophical concepts into my comparative religion classes. I found these ideas provided a well-developed and comprehensive, yet simple and plausible framework that describes many philosophical and psychological phenomena. Some of these ideas are extremely sophisticated, more so than Western explanations.

"Even though I consider myself a lifelong devotee of Christ and a dedicated explorer of Christian mysticism, many lightbulbs went off when I first discovered the Bhagavad Gita and the Yogasūtra, both of which I found I could read alongside the New Testament without conflict. It was Patanjali, to whom the Yogasūtra is attributed, who brilliantly put forth the idea that the state of unitive consciousness takes place once all the contents of the mind have been emptied." (*The state of Yoga occurs when all mental vacillations cease*, Yogasūtra 1:2.) "This has become a cornerstone of my thought, along with certain key concepts I adopted from different religious traditions.

"Returning to our previous subject, the world mirrors your inner state. The beauty you see in others or in objects triggers the part within you that interprets things as beautiful. Conversely, the ugliness you see in others or in objects triggers the part within you that interprets things as ugly. In addition, individuals may collectively agree on a particular definition of beauty or ugliness. Both beauty and ugliness, however, reside squarely in the mind of the beholder. How you interpret what you perceive precisely reflects what exists inside you. Whether the glass appears half empty or half full depends entirely on your inner state. 'As within, so without.'

"Any emotion, any feeling, any reaction of any kind that is provoked by your interaction with the world in reality exists within you, not in the object you perceive. This should be self-evident. In this sense, nothing exists independent of your mind. While objects may exist independent of more than one mind, like that table or this chair, which we all see"—Father pointed to both pieces of furniture— "everything you perceive is dependent on *your* mind. And so, each feeling, each emotion, and each reaction that occurs to you resides solely within your mind—they never originate or exist in any external object or event, which are entirely neutral. It is we who anthropomorphize these objects and events by imbuing them with emotion and meaning. However, whatever feelings they provoke or reactions they engender exist solely in your own mind.

"You thus project your inner nature on to outer reality. You paint over reality with projections of your hopes and expectations. But these are projections that you and you alone assign to outside objects and people. They exist nowhere except—where?"

Liz answered, "In your own mind."

"Exactly. When you lend credence to these projections, you animate them. By animating them, you give them power, which only reinforces their control over you. Your emotional reactions thus constantly assail your soul, overpowering it and pummeling it into a secondary, subordinate role. When they exert such control over you, outer events come to govern your mind at the expense of your soul, your spiritual self, which then recedes into the background, having been effectively usurped by the dominant, unchecked mind."

I could tell this would be another evening when we wouldn't be discussing this week's *National Enquirer*. Meanwhile, the now-moderate rainfall pitter-pattered across the living-room windows, providing a variable rhythmic backdrop to Father's somewhat strained voice. Aside from this sound, there is dead silence in the room.

"This is the only purpose that outer phenomena serve to the spiritual aspirant: they reveal to us our own state of mind. They clearly mirror our own attachments and aversions. They further indicate which emotions, especially negative emotions, we need to overcome. Our reactions are the clue; they act like a Rorschach test of the mind. They flawlessly reflect back our own mental state. And the truth is, so long as one continues to experience emotional reactions, undergo mood swings, and be affected by attachments and aversions, one is still a beginner in spiritual life."

Some expressed a defeated look.

"Not reacting is a preliminary stage of spiritual practice. Our moods and emotional reactions must not rule our minds. Until this is mastered, one cannot make more profound inner progress, such as stabilizing the deep interior states of consciousness. As is counseled in Second Timothy, 'Be calm in all circumstances.'[183] You simply cannot call yourself advanced as long as these emotions and associated reactions impinge on your mind and you cooperate by responding to them. By responding, you trigger a whole domino effect, knocking you down each time you succumb to them. It then becomes increasingly difficult to surmount this impasse. Whereas with continued persistence, you'll begin to attain mastery over your emotions. With time, the tendency not to react will become your second nature.

"The fact is, you must attain a state wherein not one single so-called external event causes you to react one iota whatsoever. You must remain unruffled and maintain your inner poise, centered day and night in your spiritual self—and God within you—regardless of what outer conditions prevail.

"When practicing, especially at the outset of your spiritual journey, it is important you take special care not to trigger those areas within you that you know will unnerve you. If you have a known propensity that causes you to lose your poise when you're subjected to a given situation, you must be especially vigilant not to activate it. If you know that shopping in a crowded supermarket taxes your patience, then go at a time when fewer people are around. If a barking dog annoys you, use earplugs."

Father, smiling, asked Carla, "What do you call these triggers?"

Carla laughed. "Our button-pushers."

"And so," Father continued, "your vision must turn inward and remain immovably fixed on God at all times. By continually practicing in this manner, you'll reach a state wherein not so much as a flutter of emotion will topple your inner composure. Nothing will faze you, whether you gain or lose, succeed or fail; whether you are healthy or ill, rich or poor. Such trifles as outer conditions will pass unnoticed in this unwavering state."

Laurie, who I learned was an avid Trekker, asked, "Are you saying we must become emotionless and live like Mr. Spock?"

Father replied, "No! Live like Captain Kirk, but remain emotionally detached like Mr. Spock." Laurie and everyone laughed.

Laurie added, "But I enjoy emotions and memories and the experiences of my life."

"I'll bet you enjoy only *selected* emotions and memories. Others cause you to wince."

Laurie remained silent.

"You see, we normally try to set the tone of our incoming experiences, seeking out the good while avoiding the bad. Which is basically not possible. Try as we may, we cannot screen the world according to our preferences or make it conform to our wishes. But when you rise above the whirlpool of all emotions and memories, be they good or bad, you will experience a sustained joy that transcends both.

"The same is true of our past. Just as an old jalopy spews out plumes of exhaust, so too are the images from our past and their associated emotions the sputterings given off by a congested mind. St. John of the Cross tells us that the memory must be annihilated for the soul to attain union with God.[184] We haven't an inkling in our present state what it's like to experience life with a fully uncluttered mind. Emotions and memories obstruct the mind with endless reels of inner films that obscure the perception of the soul with images and sounds which no longer exist. The nagging chatterbox that lives inside our head simply won't shut up. All this debris muddies the mind. But through ongoing practice, these same emotions, memories, and our noisy, ego-based internal voice eventually subside into a reverberating silence. The mind's endless commotion is finally quieted. The 'you' that you think you are will fade into nothingness. You will gradually grow accustomed to the absence of 'you.'"

Life Just Unfolds for the Illumined Sage

Kurt asked, "Then Father, how are we to live without emotions and memories?"

"In essence," Father said, "this means not being swayed by our emotions, and remaining unaffected by our memories. An aspirant must view so-called objective reality with complete detachment. There must not be so much as the slightest ripple of emotional reactions to outer events. But this does not mean living like a lump of clay! A person can be quite vivacious and engaged, yet utterly detached." Father slowed his cadence. "Anger, irritability, jealousy, resentment, frustration; fear, embarrassment, regret; despondency; envy, pride, arrogance; spitefulness and vengeance; clinging and covetousness: all are cesspools of lower emotions that keep the mind bound in time and space. Once the mind is bound, the karmic mechanism comes into play, operating full force, continuing the repeated cycle of cause and effect, cause and effect." Father moved his left index finger from left to right. "The seed and its eventual fruit. It matters not what the outer situation is. If it is met with emotional reactions of any kind, including positive emotions, karma is created and you become stuck."

Laurie observed, "That would be hard for me to do, not reacting at all. I find some people or situations can be intimidating, so I experience fear or whatever. I try to avoid confrontations; it's just not my nature."

"For those who are extremely sensitive, this state of imperturbability can be difficult to master," Father acknowledged. "If you find yourself in uncomfortable situations, feelings of apprehension or uncertainty may very well overwhelm you. This is normal and natural. So don't expect results overnight. Not reacting at all is the culmination of one's initial stage of practice. We can do our best if we try each and every day. You'll find you are making progress in spite of yourself. As Lao Tzu counsels, 'The journey of a thousand miles begins with a single step.'[185] Thus, it behooves us to take his cue and proceed, like astronaut Neil Armstrong, 'one small step' at a time along our spiritual path."

Laurie followed up, "What if some situations really bother a person or make them ill? Some people can't cope with stress as well as others."

Father responded with a look of utter concern. "If it's that bad and producing adverse health effects, then you must find a way to

201

remove yourself from that situation. First and foremost, these are practical teachings, so your health and wellbeing take precedence over everything else. Practice as best you can, but don't subject yourself to an unrelentingly stressful situation if at all possible. Spiritual training is not an endurance test. As Jesus said, you must never sacrifice your soul for the sake of the world.[186] If any circumstance in your life is taking a physical toll, you need to address the underlying cause while trying your best in the meantime to maintain your composure, no matter how oppressive or challenging the situation."

While presenting goals and teachings that can be practiced under any circumstances, Father never advocated that we engage in herculean stoicism, undergo mortifications, or subject ourselves to situations of mistreatment or undue stress just to prove a spiritual point.

"So," Father emphasized, returning to his earlier theme, "every moment a person is buffeted by an enormous amount of stimuli, both inner and outer. We are continually inundated by thoughts, feelings, concepts, and images from the inner world; our mental constructs of our own life-experiences along the continuum of time; and projections of these constructs on to both the past and future. The same is true of the outer world as perceived by the senses and interpreted by the mind. We think we experience all this with clarity, that we are stable captains at the helm of our boat of life. But again, we have deluded ourselves! We skew these data, distorting them according to our various moods and subconscious promptings. How often do we revise the past so we can recast ourselves in a more flattering light? Or gloss over our own hypocrisies? Or project qualities on to others that don't actually exist? In these and similar ways, we selectively filter and interpret this barrage of information, making it correspond to our beliefs, our worldview, our self-image, and the persona we want others to see. Thus, we rewrite reality in any number of ways.

"But all these stimuli are wholly neutral in themselves. It's only when a person makes the initial mistake of paying attention to them, thereby imbuing them with life and giving them credence, that they get pulled away from their spiritual self and thrust into the world of duality, replete with emotionally charged reactions. This is where the trouble begins. We project our inner makeup on to a neutral universe. Returning to the Vedantic concept of *drishti srishti,* we perceive what we are. We are conditioned by tradition and live according to expectations that are forged by habit and conformity to the world of humans. Our behavior is largely based on Pavlovian impulses and unconscious kneejerk reactions. We're really trapped on a hamster wheel.

"And the answers are given in the sacred books: Do your duties without attachment, aversion, and expectations. Do not seek emotional rewards or hidden objectives from your work. As St. Paul asserts, 'Whatever you do, do it all for the glory of God.'[187]

"Moreover, do not differentiate between activities, some seemingly more favorable than others. And never project yourself away from the present moment. Jonathan Swift keenly observed, 'Very few men, properly speaking, live at present, but are providing to live another time.'[188] Nor should you dwell in the artificial world of concepts and mental constructs. Most important, stay centered in the heart, focused in the here and now, bubbling over with love, fully content, lacking nothing.

"We may benefit from the example of Paul of Tarsus: 'I have learned to be content regardless of whatever circumstances I find myself. I know how to live in both poverty and abundance. In any and every situation I have learned the secret of contentment, whether I am full or hungry, have plenty or nothing. For it is Christ who gives me the strength to face anything.'[189]

"It is the demons of the mind—these wretched moods and emotions—that sway you to and fro, pulling you away from a loving base in your soul. Subdue these demons by refusing to cooperate with them. Stop dancing to their tune!"

Father's forceful words reminded me of a terrifying dream I once had. In the dream, I was held in the grip of some powerful force, which bore down on my chest with a crushing weight. I lay immobilized. I felt such tremendous pressure in my heart that I feared it might explode. No matter how hard I struggled to break free, I could not escape. Then a vision appeared of a demon resembling Pazuzu, the diabolical figure from the 1973 horror film *The Exorcist.* It was positioned directly above me, staring straight down at me. I yelled at the hellish entity, "You're the last one! Go away!" But the demon sneered back, "There is a million of me."

Father further observed, "With continued practice, you will have glimpses of the state of imperturbable joy and unbroken peace that awaits you. You must home in on that alone, setting your compass for that direction only, ignoring all else which distracts you from that goal. So, note the world, but don't buy into it. You're merely being seduced by an illusion. Do the work that presents itself before you. Don't distinguish between desirable and undesirable activities. React to nothing. Try to spiritualize all you perceive. Become a servant of joy!"

Bill asked, "How can a person work without an objective?"

Father replied, "To begin with, you already know what your objective is when you commence a particular activity. Let's say you set out from Spokane and drive to Tulsa for your family reunion. It's human nature for the mind to anticipate the future and feel an undercurrent of excitement about your upcoming blessed event, unless, of course, too many obnoxious relatives plan to attend. But, as a spiritual aspirant, you try not to ruminate over what lies ahead. With your travel objective in mind, you remain calm, and you don't become riled if something crops up to spoil your designs. You simply proceed to execute the plan at hand, retaining your poise and remaining immovably grounded in your spiritual self. Before you know it, you'll arrive at your destination, and your objective will be achieved effortlessly, as a matter of course. Then you can settle in at poolside and catch up with Aunt Mildred and Cousin Rufus. So you see, all these changing circumstances never affected the real you. Your body and mind moved through time and space, but the real you never once traveled.

"However, there is an alternative to living a goal-oriented life:

> Others have a well-defined purpose
> I alone drift about aimlessly;
> At all times, the Tao sustains me.[190]

"These words of Lao Tzu perfectly epitomize the state of enlightenment where life just unfolds for the illumined sage. Such a person never strays from their spiritual self. They are continuously anchored in God, in whom they 'live and move and have their being.'[191] They may seem to be present, but all the while nobody's home."

Stuart noted, "But most of the time we don't know the outcome of a situation. That can be unsettling, especially if there's a chance it might end up badly."

Father smiled. "This is where faith comes in. Sometimes God shows us the way a little at a time instead of revealing the whole plan all at once. This can be frustrating, because we want to know the result. We want a sneak preview of the ending. But God requires us to have faith without always knowing the finale. King Solomon pondered this mystery:

> Who among humans can know the intentions of God?
> Who can comprehend God's will?
> For the thoughts of mortals are tenuous
> And their plans are fraught with uncertainty.[192]

"And so, to again cite the Hebrew Bible, 'Trust in the Lord with all your heart,'[193] as the Book of Proverbs instructs. Therefore, take a leap of faith into unfamiliar waters. You must bravely take that leap in all your doings, which unfold for whatever purpose according to your destiny. Strive to possess that unshakable faith, knowing that God is situated nearer to you than your own heartbeat throughout each moment of every activity you undertake every day in your life."

More Exchanges With Laurie and Kurt

Kurt spoke up. "Could you please clarify what you said earlier about outer events appearing like a mirage or a parade."

"Yes, my son, I'll try." Father never tired of revisiting a topic. "What we experience in the world, in this relative sphere of existence, are mere shadows—an infinite number of ghostly images parading kaleidoscopically before the mind and senses. But the mind, the senses, and the apparent external world—anything that is an object to the 'I'—are completely interrelated. They are inextricably intertwined.

"Do any of you recall our discussion of *triputi*?" A few of us nodded. "*Triputi* is a Hindu concept which maintains that the ego consists of three interconnected elements: the subject, the object, and the process that links the two. For example, when I look at that lamp, there are three components involved: me, the lamp, and the connection that is established between me and the lamp when I look at it. This threefold process of perception is completely interrelated. It occurs every instant in our waking lives. This process marks the very genesis of duality, because one's 'I' always engages with a different object, which it perceives as separate and distinct from it.

"Our 'I' thus constantly changes as the mind moves from one object to another, perceiving this or that thing, always in relation to itself. It never breaks free from these constrictive boundaries to encounter the boundless spiritual self. The sensation we experience inside our heads as 'I' is merely our deeply entrenched personality traits interacting with and emotionally reacting to various situations. But this same 'I' is pried loose every time we displace it during deep meditation. Because of this inconsistency, the 'I' is unstable and volatile, forever changing and changeable. And so, every aspect of our relative identity—our ego—is transitory; the idea that our 'I' is permanent is but an illusion, as Buddha pointed out.

"In this manner, the web of duality blankets us all with the thick covering of *maya*, of delusion. Hence, there is division, not unity. Two, not one. Our perception is nothing more than a concatenation of ephemeral events. It is a round-the-clock, ever-changing series of passing encounters—a fleeting, dreamlike succession of mirages, similar to a series of illusions performed by a magician. Therefore, in this relative world, there is no constant other than change. As St. James writes in his magnificent Epistle, which I recently reread, 'Your life is nothing more than a mist that appears for a short while and then passes away.'"[194]

Kurt then asked, "Okay, so what is the purpose of life if everything is an illusion?"

"First of all, the seeming appearances we perceive are in reality playing themselves out on a very subtle level. This is the most refined and nearly undetectable realm where the mechanism of karma originates and operates. It is entirely nonphysical. Second, and relatedly, this physical world is merely a fabricated projection wherein destiny unfolds. Our life can thus be likened to a translucent image of no more substance than a silhouette moving through space and time through which destiny is discharged on this planetary sphere.

"As we've often discussed, when we react to our karma, even more karma is created. It's like chopping off the head of the Hydra: two heads grow in place of the first. So you see, at all levels karma mercilessly moves one 'round and round, as if on a wheel,'[195] as the Bhagavad Gita explains. But we can use our free will to help liberate ourselves, which is the purpose of life, by forcefully intervening and disrupting the normal workings of the mind. This is, of course, what we attempt to do in meditation. Meditation is simply an exercise in deconditioning. We reverse the outward flow of the mind and turn it inward, so it first recognizes then gradually adheres to the spiritual self within."

Kurt, dressed in a white T-shirt, open gray chamois shirt, jeans, and black watch cap, which he never removed, sought clarification. "I've read about karma, or destiny as you sometimes say. But how does it relate to free will? I thought that destiny and free will were opposite doctrines."

Father had become energized during his talk, seemingly rejuvenated from conversing on his favorite topics, no doubt motivated by his ingrained teaching instinct. He now spoke more dynamically; his entire demeanor was more animated.

"I'm very happy you asked," he replied. For those who are new, I'll briefly touch on the Hindu concept of karma, which parallels the law of cause and effect. It's similar to what St. Paul stated: 'Whatever you sow, that you will reap.'[196] Karma and its related concept, destiny, are driven and perpetuated by attachment and aversion. At lower levels of life, karma is programmed as unconscious impulse or instinct. At higher levels, it is bound up with free will, meaning that our choices both lead us to our appointed karmic destinations, and in a vicious circle, they create fresh karma.

"Free will—the sense of volitional choice—is one of the principal characteristics that separates the relatively unconscious forms of life from the more conscious ones. Free will is one tool that can help unshackle a person from being victimized by their karma."

I was reminded of a passage from Dickens' *A Christmas Carol*. "Men's courses will foreshadow certain ends, to which, if persevered in, they must lead," said Scrooge. "But if the courses be departed from, the ends will change."[197]

Father continued, "Let's suppose the mind is segregated into two parts—the lower mind and the higher mind. By harnessing one's free will and focusing on the higher mind, which is illuminated by spiritual clarity, a person can counteract the ceaseless cavalcade of emotions and the karmic rubble that lurks in the lower mind. It is 'raising the lower self by the Supreme Self,'[198] as the Gita proclaims. The lower mind—imprisoned by time and space, shrouded within the confines of duality, gripped by attachment and aversion, and constantly swayed by negative emotions—can never accomplish this task. If so attempted, it only compounds the exact same situation. This would be tantamount to using poison to remedy a condition of being poisoned, and I don't mean medicinally!

"But the higher mind, ignited by the impetus of one's free will, is the fulcrum that can catapult one into the realm of the spiritual self. It is a matter of making a determined effort and forging through the many layers of mental sediment and emotional resistance that are lodged between the lower mind and the spiritual self. This is the journey through the shrouds that cover the soul—the *veils* of the Sufis, the *sheaths* of Vedanta. From the thickest shroud to the most ethereal veil, the spiritual self becomes incrementally divested of its shackles and chains."

Kurt again jumped in. "But how can the mind be used to find the spiritual self? I thought you said we had to rise above the mind."

Father clearly enjoyed the exchange, as did the rest of us, who, unless we asked questions, had more or less become accustomed to sitting motionless like petrified logs while listening to Father's discourses, as we were intently focused on absorbing his teachings.

"That, my son, is a question that begs to be asked! You see, free will is a facet of the mind. It can be harnessed to facilitate spiritual growth. At each progressive stage of spiritual evolution, the free will, fueled by the heart's desire for God, pierces through the knotty mental and emotional matter, which acts like a massive barrier. By so doing, it can help the aspirant reside at more advanced plateaus. The Sufis call these plateaus *stations*. The free will hoists the aspirant ever upward where they can dwell at increasingly higher plateaus, which are subtler and therefore more evolved spiritual planes of existence, until it disconnects entirely from any association with the lower levels.

"It's like climbers ascending Mount Everest. They make some progress, then stop to set up base camp before proceeding farther. This allows them time to acclimate. From there, they make another ascent, set up another base camp, and so on, until they reach the peak, where their base camp is no longer needed. Similarly, the spiritually motivated free will drives the aspirant progressively upward, step by step, until it ascends to their spiritual self, the innermost essence of their being. There it resides in the very heart of God. At that stage, having accomplished its task of successfully guiding the aspirant to the very summit of spirituality, the free will can now be dissolved into the measureless expanse of infinite Spirit. This marks the state of liberation.

"But remember, by using this same comparison, as the ego ascends the spiritual mountain, it cannot survive in that thin air. However, the soul can and especially does thrive at this altitude. Thus, as the ego fades out of existence, the spiritual self takes its place. Don't ever think that the 'you,' which you've come to know and love, will make it to the top! In the highly rarefied atmosphere of God, the ego faces its own demise so the soul alone can live.

"So, we see how the higher mind, coupled with one's free will, can be used to elevate the bound soul to the pinnacle of spiritual development. Once its mission is complete, the mind and its components can be left behind, just as different stages of a rocket are jettisoned once they've served their purpose. The mind is used therefore to find the spiritual self, then it is transcended.

"Once freed from the binding influence of the lower levels of the mind, the spiritual self then discovers itself mirrored in the essence of all outer phenomena. The light of consciousness shines through the relativistic deception, which is this phantasmagoric material world. The soul is no longer veiled in ignorance. It attains to God and beholds God in all things, as the Gita asserts.[199] All superficial distinctions disappear, as the underlying essence of everything is recognized as a singular undifferentiated unity. God is found to be existing everywhere at all times, infusing all things, infinitely boundless, divided by nothing, forever undefined. Or, as is poetically illustrated in one of my favorite biblical passages, 'If I ascend to heaven, you are there. If I make my bed in hell, you are there also.'[200]

"But, unless the seeds of karma are fully burnt, the cyclic mechanism of cause and effect has not been destroyed. The state wherein this occurs is *samadhi*, or *fanā*, or *spiritual marriage*, or *nirvāṇa*—pick your religion—which burns up one's entire repository of karma. This causes the death, final and absolute, of any residual karmic seeds that would otherwise sprout up and grow in the future. When there is no storehouse of karma, a person is free."

Laurie quizzically asked, "Could you please explain more about these states?"

Father hesitated. "It's very difficult, because they are literally beyond explanation. They transcend intellectual understanding. Even to define them compromises them. This is where one encounters the unbounded, infinite 'peace of God, which surpasses all understanding,'[201] as Paul so elegantly describes."

Then Father gathered his thoughts. "Try to envision a state of meditation so deep that your awareness becomes subsumed in a vortex of pure nothingness swirling in a variegated blanket of ever-changing bliss."

Many appeared captivated by Father's colorful description.

"But 'you' are not aware of this; 'you' have been so completely consumed by the divine Presence that 'you' have been exterminated, so to speak. There is no one left to observe or communicate this experience, which can neither be differentiated nor objectified. Ramakrishna used a very apt analogy to describe this indescribable state: 'Once a doll made of salt went to the ocean to measure its depth. It wished to tell others how deep the ocean was. But no sooner had it plunged into the ocean than it melted away and became one with it. No one remained to convey any information.'[202] This is an extremely heightened, intensified state of consciousness. I'm not talking about falling asleep!

"This realization most commonly occurs at a mature stage of one's spiritual practice after much preliminary purification. The mind has been cleansed of most of its inner debris and is perched alongside the vast abyss of God. The body and nervous system have been prepared, by routine meditation, to sustain deep states of concentration. Then God, as it were, pulls the aspirant's dualistic mind into his very essence, for a time obliterating whatever remnants exist of their already attenuated ego. Breathing virtually stops; in the most intense instances, the vital energy is involuntarily withdrawn from the body. The last remaining flicker of self-consciousness is doused. The body remains still, suspended for timeless moments while the aspirant's soul is plunged into the Infinite. This sublime state is wholly ineffable. It cannot be attained through one's own efforts; it is strictly conferred by divine grace. The aspirant is mystically escorted into the very marrow of God's being."

Father briefly paused. Absolute silence filled the room.

"This rare state of consciousness, wherein the body is rendered immobile while the soul is immersed in nondual awareness and all sense of one's 'I' vanishes, is described in various spiritual traditions. In Yoga nomenclature, it is known as *nirvikalpa samadhi*, or 'unwavering absorption.' In Theravada Buddhism, it is analogous to *nirodha samāpatti*, or 'the attainment of extinction.' In Taoism, it has been called *ju ting*. In the Catholic mystical tradition, it is similar to an elevated stage of the Prayer of Ecstatic Union, or Spiritual Betrothal, and it especially refers to the raptures experienced in this state. As St. Teresa writes, 'Rapture ... stops the breathing, and one can neither speak nor open the eyes.'[203] In Sufism, it is called *fanā* or 'annihilation.'

"Extraordinary as it is, the condition of illumination produced by this stationary bodily state still marks the penultimate juncture on one's spiritual journey. Beyond this is the post-illumination phase, wherein the realized aspirant continues to live and act in the world, retaining an unbroken connection with their spiritual self while also perceiving God in all things. They experience an uninterrupted state of inner joy, and a delightful, expansive state of contentment that continually wells up from within and cannot be compared to anything of this world. This state of continuous enlightenment remains undiminished until their passing. It's the ability to experience this state while one functions in normal waking consciousness that marks the true line of demarcation between partial and full enlightenment."

Laurie commented, with knitted eyebrows, "I'm sorry Father, but this makes little sense to me." All of us smiled in sympathy. Laurie no doubt voiced what many of us felt.

Father smiled as well, then once more focused his attention before speaking, unfazed by Laurie's plight. "A fully illumined saint experiences the world as a kind of translucency whereby the light of God shines through all perceived images. These images appear as unreal as a dream, consisting of impressionistic swirls and washes, which undulate in surreal wavelike motions, similar to a semi-transparent sheet slowly flapping in the breeze. These images are devoid of substance.

"Again, to analogize an enlightened mystic's experience, it's as though they were walking on a gossamer cloud and everything they saw and touched were as insubstantial as a film image projected in a movie theater. Such realized souls vaguely perceive the forms and structures around them. Even so, these objects appear to pulsate between varying degrees of solidity and immateriality. Their X-ray-like perception drills a hole right through the apparent rigidity of three-dimensional reality, revealing a permeability underlying all matter that allows God to poke through, like prairie dogs popping up from their numerous mounds in a desert landscape.

"Much in the same way that water cascades over a waterfall, these enlightened beings behold reality as if it were perpetually cascading into oblivion. To use more abstract terminology, one might say these enlightened beings constantly experience a desolidification of the physical universe as it continually fragmentizes and disintegrates into the abyss of nonexistence, so that the external world for them lacks all spatial, temporal, and dimensional contexts, meaning that space and time and form per se don't exist for them. All such references cease. Thus stripped of the illusory garment that this world represents, all they perceive and encounter is God, the substratal Reality. Their body automatically discharges its destiny while at the same time their soul is thoroughly absorbed in God. At that wondrous stage, 'When God is revealed, we shall be like him, for we shall see him as he truly is,'[204] as the Beloved Disciple declares.

"However, these are but roughhewn analogies, poor approximations that do not even come close to describing the actual mystical experience as undergone by countless saints. These descriptions entirely fail to capture what can never be captured in words: the living, soaring experience itself, which is as elusive as a fleeting emotion and as powerfully evocative as a van Gogh painting. At the very center of this experience is the here-and-now, closer-than-close, palpable, subjective *feeling* of enlightenment, which can never be described."

Laurie now seemed altogether perplexed, as did several of us. Then again, Father was trying to explain the unexplainable.

Then Laurie asked the $64,000 question, "Father Christopher, have you experienced these states?"

Father instantly replied, "My daughter, I, too, like many seekers, aspire to experience these remarkable states of consciousness." Then he fell silent. Much to our disappointment, Father's answer adroitly dodged Laurie's forthright question. This was something we were all dying to know, but Father's response that day was as close as we ever came, for it was as much as he ever directly revealed.

An Endless Interconnected Ocean of Illusion

Tom inquired, "How can we work in the world when experiencing these states? My job as a data analyst requires me to strategize and plan in great detail, then anticipate a variety of contingencies. I must constantly think and evaluate."

"Well," Father responded, "the short answer is you can't. That's why we meditate—to isolate those times when we completely disengage the mind.

"In the deeper stages of contemplation, the mental faculties are fully suspended and the ego is effaced. For example, in the Prayer of Union, as it is known in the Catholic tradition, the soul is totally interiorly absorbed in God. This state only occurs when you sit quietly in meditation. However, when you resume your work afterward, you carry the imprint of that experience with you.

"The Blessed Jan van Ruysbroeck, one of the greatest of Christian mystics, precisely explains this vacillation between the times when we 'stand idle' during deep meditation and the times when we come out of meditation and 'fall back into reason.'"

Father rose and picked out a book, then sat back down. "I'll read the passage:

We feel ourselves to be one *with* God; for, through the transformation in God, we feel ourselves to be swallowed up in the fathomless abyss of our eternal blessedness, wherein we can nevermore find any distinction between ourselves and God. And this is our highest feeling, which we cannot experience in any other way than in the immersion in love. And therefore, so soon as we are uplifted and drawn into our highest feeling, all our powers stand idle in an essential fruition; but our powers do not pass away into nothingness, for then we should lose our created being. And as long as we stand idle, with an inclined spirit, and with open eyes, but without reflection, so long we can contemplate and have fruition. But, at the very moment in which we seek to prove and to comprehend what it is that we feel, we fall back into reason, and there we find a distinction and an otherness between ourselves and God, and find God outside ourselves in incomprehensibility.[205]

"In other words, the spiritually mature soul fluctuates between states of nonduality and duality, inactivity and activity, as it teeters between the worlds of spirit and matter. As Ruysbroeck observed, some semblance of the ego returns after the mystical state of divine union, but it is akin to the sensation an amputee experiences of a phantom limb. It is simply a vestigial remnant of the false identity that once occupied the throne of one's being. But at that stage, the ego is vastly diluted, having been thoroughly defanged, as it were, of any substantive reality. It has, for all intents and purposes, been effectively dispatched to the crematorium. I might add that Ruysbroeck was fortunate to have passed away before the Inquisition swept through the Netherlands region. I suspect his words, 'we can nevermore find any distinction between ourselves and God' might have considerably heated things up for him."

~~~~~~~~~~~~

Father returned to his earlier theme. "Remember, each of us has two selves—our secular self and our spiritual self. One of the Upanishads beautifully describes these two selves: 'Like two birds of golden plumage, inseparable companions, the individual self and the immortal Self are perched on the branches of the selfsame tree. The former tastes of the sweet and bitter fruits of the tree; the latter, tasting of neither, calmly observes.'[206]

"Our secular self, consisting of body and mind, continuously interacts with the world, experiencing its triumphs and disillusionments. Our spiritual self remains aloof from all this. When we engage in the world, we utilize our secular self; when we meditate, we utilize our spiritual self. So, when working in the world, allow your secular self to go through the motions, only remain as detached as possible while it does. Then in meditation, become wholly immersed in your spiritual self.

"In the deep meditative state, the mind cannot function. All its spinning thoughts and whirling emotions are brought under control. Once this state of inner calmness is attained, the workings of the mind and ego are suspended—held in abeyance—for a protracted period. But some of what you experience while meditating will begin to adhere and will start to pervade your waking consciousness. With increasing realization, this immensely calm and joyful state will progressively carry over into your everyday activities. You will then begin to palpably feel the living presence of God on a continual basis. Initially, it will flash in and out of your consciousness as you go through your day. Later, this will occur more frequently and remain for longer periods.

"When this happens, you will have finally tipped the scales toward making some headway on your spiritual journey. You'll be able to leave behind much of the blind struggle from your initial practice phase. You'll now have a tangible experience of your spiritual self, your soul, which you'll begin to feel continuously. This will act like a luminous beacon in the night. Instead of being governed by your ego, you'll come to identify with a new point of reference inside you—your spiritual self.

"Because of this, your spiritual efforts henceforth will, by and large, become easier, as this firsthand knowledge will take much of the guesswork out of your strivings. You will become so enwrapped in the living experience of your own soul that you'll instinctively strive to retain this experience no matter what occurs in your life. You'll intuitively work to unfold even more of it. You'll ultimately be able to maintain this connection at all times, without break, whether you're sitting in meditation or engaged in activity. The Bhagavad Gita mentions this state: 'Even while performing work, the enlightened person maintains the state of Union.'[207] It will never diminish no matter what you do."

Father's emphatic, authoritative words affected me on the deepest of levels. Although he had previously spoken about merging one's spiritual and secular selves, on this night it particularly hit home.

"When you come to notice little difference between the times when you're deeply absorbed in meditation and the times when you resume your activities, you will have made some progress. You'll be so engrossed in God that the external world won't matter; you'll barely even perceive it as having a solid existence. At first, this will seem strangely unreal to you, but you'll soon grow accustomed to it. Then both you and your work will be totally transformed. You will realize that you—the real you—are not your ego or your body. And you will realize it's not actually 'you' who is performing your work. You'll see it's merely an assemblage of molecules—your body—that works, while the real you—your soul—is consumed in waves of luminescent bliss."

Erin posed an issue. "You spoke earlier about being sensitive. Sometimes after meditation I can't cope with the world. Every little thing seems to bother me."

Father responded, "What you describe is quite normal, especially at the beginning stages of one's spiritual journey, but it can be disconcerting. During meditation, especially deep meditation, you are wide open and vulnerable. Your guards are down; your ego's defenses are rendered inoperable. Afterward, if you are suddenly thrust back into the commotion and kerfuffle of daily life and you are confronted with worldly matters, it can be abrasive, like fingernails on a chalkboard. This is why there are monasteries and nunneries! God accommodates those with sensitive temperaments far better than the world can. Recall the New Testament story of Mary and Martha.[208] Jesus commended Mary for her single-minded devotion, even though Martha was stranded without Mary's help while making all of the Lord's dinner preparations.

"Early on, a young man—Raymond—came here. Almost nobody here today would remember him. He had a very fragile temperament and was readily crushed under by the weight of the world. However, he had a deep love of God, which he concealed. I recommended that he consider a trial run at a monastery. This is why none of you see him here to this day!

"But for those of us living in the world who cannot retreat within the walls of a hermitage, it is critically important to avoid negative influences in general: people who drag you down, and activities that pull you away from your spiritual orientation. You know who these people are and what these activities are—at work and school, at home, in your various spheres of life. They are nothing more than disruptive instigators that will seemingly imperceptibly, and many times blatantly, drag you away from your spiritual practices. It's best to steer clear of such persons and activities—they are regressive influences whose only purpose is to lead you away from God.

"So," Father continued, addressing Erin, "don't be hard on yourself if you are ultrasensitive following your meditation session. That means you've accomplished your goal."

Erin nodded.

"When acclimating back into the world, you must try to insulate yourself as best as possible from worldly influences so you can preserve the mood of inner silence that you cultivated during your meditation session. In the overall scheme of things, it is far more important to protect your spiritual mood than expend it on worldly affairs. As Jesus asked, 'For what will it profit a person to gain the whole world but lose their own soul?'[209]

"Speaking of hermitages, it can be beneficial to attend a spiritual retreat or spend a day at a monastic center every so often. This helps a person shake off worldly associations and reprioritize and re-establish their spiritual focus. The residents there have a common goal, so you can immerse yourself in that powerful spiritual atmosphere, which reinforces your own practice."

Father resumed his previous topic. "What the normal dualistic mind perceives appears to an advanced aspirant as an endless interconnected ocean of illusion. It matters not what practices a spiritual aspirant may undertake, the dogma they adopt, or the interior raptures and graces that are bestowed on them. All these are karmic in nature; they operate in the realm of duality. For example, a person's beliefs form a structure, a context, for their spiritual growth. But all beliefs, all ideologies, and one's entire worldview are eventually transcended in the nondual experience of God. These are but concepts, and while most realized souls maintain their professed faith after realization, concepts per se will ensnare you if you cling to them.

"From a higher perspective, regardless of whether or not religious adherents call themselves Hindus, Buddhists, Jews, Christians, Muslims, Sikhs, Jains, or Taoists, if the mechanism of duality continues to operate within them, they remain bound. Their spiritual self has not been emancipated from the thick, encrusted layer of emotions that are entrenched in the dualistic mind. This is exactly why, as St. Paul enjoined, 'We look not on what is seen, but on what is unseen; because what is seen is temporary, but what is unseen is eternal.'[210] We must rise above duality and soar with the angels."

Kurt countered, "Okay, what if a person is not religious? What if they have no religious beliefs at all; for instance, what if they are an atheist? Then they'll never achieve spiritual liberation. So none of this really pertains to them."

"On the contrary," Father said, "atheists walk hand in hand with their theistic counterparts far more closely than they might imagine. Whether people label themselves theist, atheist, monotheist, pantheist, or polytheist, if they but strip themselves of all labels, what remains is the subject—the essence of their being. In that subject lies the kernel of truth about existence, because the basis of the subject is consciousness, which is the primary nonphysical attribute of all human beings and animals.

"The fact of consciousness is self-evident; it is scientifically, empirically proven. If the atheist and their theistic counterpart each admit to possessing consciousness, which should not be difficult, they then acknowledge the underlying meeting ground common to them both. This is tantamount to *atheistic theism*—both labels cancel themselves out in the commonality of consciousness. A person could arrive at a form of liberation apart from any religious association whatsoever simply by eliminating all the elements in their consciousness—emotional reactions, mental images, thoughts, feelings, their sense of ego, and so forth. This was, in substance, the ingenious insight of Patanjali, who stated in purely psychological terms, minus any religious overlay, that the state of unitive consciousness occurs when the contents of the mind are emptied.[211] By so doing, they do not have to adopt exotic names, wear specialized attire, or proclaim themselves affiliated with this or that sectarian religious group.

"After all, if one's faith is rooted in a path that leads to full-blown illumination, what's there to fault? A nontheistic practitioner might be more spiritually advanced than a so-called spiritual adherent who merely adopts reams of meandering Rube Goldbergesque beliefs or parrots some nonsensical 'metaphysical' gibberish, but who lacks such realization.

"The essence of any religious or nonreligious path is that it must bring about a wholesale transformation of one's character and un-veil one's spiritual core, regardless of what that core is called. Consciousness has no church, no synagogue, no catechism, no place of pilgrimage. God is a name that is synonymous with the ultimate reality. But a rose by any other name ...

"One can be an artist, an athlete, a poet, or a mathematician—well, maybe not a lawyer or a stockbroker, and certainly not a politician—and undergo fundamentally liberating experiences in consciousness without being the least bit religious. Provided, of course, they fervently strove for liberation and engaged in routine practice. And, as Moses, Buddha, and Patanjali each stipulated, they must follow a code of ethics. No seekers, whether atheist or religious, can fool themselves into simply imagining they are enlightened; all must work for liberation and practice certain fundamentals, such as abiding by an ethical code and living a principled life. But for the atheist, their strivings need not be theistically oriented."

Brandon, with an impish look on his face, interrupted Father's talk, "What about surfers?" he asked.

Father, smiling, responded. "Surfers especially can ride the end-less, perfect wave straight to God." Brandon and everyone laughed.

"So," Father continued, "a person needn't profess a religious as-sociation to attain freedom from duality. This nontheistic approach is a legitimate path to the ultimate reality. Bear in mind, this doesn't grant theistic proponents the right to pejoratively brand such per-sons as quote–unquote 'atheists' with negative connotations. The original Theravada school of Buddhism is entirely nontheistic, and no Buddhist believes in the concept of a creator deity. You can't disparagingly label tens of millions of Buddhist practitioners 'atheists' and fault them accordingly! To single out nontheistic paths and summarily condemn them is religious bigotry at its very worst.

"While, in my opinion, a nontheistic path lacks the added dimension that devotion imparts, I firmly believe that anyone can unfold enlightenment in most any context, even if that context excludes formal religious affiliation. The experience of the ultimate reality is too limitless to be constrained by any definition and too vast to be confined by any specific house of worship. No religion has a monopoly on or an exclusive access to interior mystical states. While there are a handful of primary mystical paths, in theory there are as many paths as there are humans, including the nontheistic path. But walking this pathless path can be challenging, because most all those who specialize in the mystical arena of life are historically found within formal religions, which is where they have left practical roadmaps for others to follow."

The Lord of Time

Kurt was now silenced. He sat entranced, intensely absorbed, with his clutched right hand resting at his bearded chin, like Rodin's *The Thinker*. Laurie continued to appear baffled, which was "quite understandable" to use Father's words. Granted, it took some getting used to his abstract level of discourse when he was really on. While some teachers refrain from sharing more advanced knowledge with newcomers, Father never did. Nor did he judge others based on their spiritual aptitude or religious background. He always welcomed everyone into his fold.

As with his discussion on atheism, we never heard Father propound any form of sectarianism, any exclusive path to the Divine. He accepted all paths as legitimate means to the ultimate Reality. So, for beginners in particular who might be looking for easy answers, or for certain persons who were unaccustomed to eclectic teachings and were seeking a more dogmatic path, Father's analytical approach and his nonsectarian, interfaith perspective could be difficult to comprehend, if not downright perplexing. It was the overarching significance of his message that had the most bearing, even if only tidbits could be digested.

"This then," Father proposed, "is the single most important criterion of spiritual advancement. In fact, it is the only characteristic that matters at all: the mind must be freed from the realm of duality. Nothing else matters, nothing else counts, as a waggish Bodhidharma once told a stunned emperor. I'll tell you the story.

"Bodhidharma, the First Chinese Patriarch of Zen, was invited to Emperor Wu's court. The monarch was filled with pride. He hankered for recognition and spiritual reward for having performed numerous good deeds and for his charitable sponsorship of Buddhism. But Bodhidharma was not impressed in the slightest. When the emperor asked him what merit he had accrued for his support of Buddhism, Bodhidharma simply replied, 'None whatsoever!' to the astonished emperor's chagrin. Bodhidharma's terse reprimand conveyed to the emperor in no uncertain terms that all such acts were irrelevant, especially when ego-driven. The emperor had completely missed the point of spiritual practice, which is to rise above the ego. And this was the lesson that Bodhidharma so pointedly brought home.

"On this relative, worldly level, it is essential that the dualistic mind undergoes spiritual practices, advances in acquiring noble traits, and divests itself of unproductive and unethical behavior patterns. This gradually frees it from dwelling in its habitualized dualistic mindset. Then the fire of concentrated spiritual practice propels it upward, entirely out of the sphere of worldly associations, toward the spiritual self. And so, a person walking the spiritual path must employ all psychophysical means that are given to beings. It must encompass, as Sri Aurobindo wrote, an integral yoga.

"Along with having a basic intellectual understanding of the path, one must live in the heart. It is this *bhakti*, this all-embracing divine love—which forms the very core of Jesus' teachings, and which the Tibetans call *bodhichitta*—that fuels one's entire spiritual practice. 'Love the Lord your God with all your heart, and with all your soul, and with all your mind, and with all your strength'[212] and 'Love your neighbor as yourself.'[213] This deep yearning for God and selfless love for others are the secrets to success in spiritual life. This joyous love is all-encompassing, all-absorbing—so powerful and overwhelming it can actually ache when enfolding one in its sublime, enchanting embrace. It is this visceral craving that quickly gets one to God: raw, driving emotion stripped of all self-consciousness, conjoined with focused, passionate, devotional longing. One's entire being—each cell, every pore—cries out and strains in a voracious hunger for naught but God. It is naked, heartfelt pining of an unimagined degree, as if the devotee were craning outside their skin to grab hold of their seemingly unreachable God. As we read in the Book of Job:

> I will see God with my very own eyes!
> My heart is consumed with indescribable yearning![214]

"Such spiritual yearning readily transports one's soul directly to God."

Father retrieved another book from his library. "Or, as is wonderfully and humorously expressed in this account written about the Italian Catholic mystic St. Maria Magdalene de' Pazzi: 'She ran through the convent as if crazed with love, and cried in a loud voice: "Love, love, love!" And since she could not endure this conflagration of love, she said: "O Lord! No more love, no more love!" ' "[215] Father recited the conclusion from memory: "Turning to the nuns who followed her, she said, 'Do you not know, my dear sisters, that my Jesus is nothing but love? Yes, he is mad with love.'[216]

"An ardent devotee truly feels that if all the divine love felt by all the devotional mystics of all time were combined, it wouldn't come close to matching the intensity and breadth of the love they feel toward their divine Beloved. If this same love were congealed into a single drop of water, which represents the magnitude of the love they feel toward their Beloved, such a devotee would feel that all the love contained in this tiny drop was more immense than all the water in all the oceans combined. Thus, love is the main ingredient without which spiritual practice is often just unrewarding struggle. Driven by one's intense longing, the spiritual doorway readily opens when accompanied by impassioned divine love. This incessant groaning for the Beloved must be an all-consuming act that seizes one on a primal level.

"Are there any questions?" Father asked. No one came forward, so he continued.

"Fervent aspirations, the unshakable determination to progress, and putting forth unmitigated efforts—all belong to the realm of spiritual striving; all are essential components of an aspirant's practice. Together with these, the higher emotions of selfless love and compassion combined with deeply rooted faith help steer one toward God. Not blind faith or fanaticism, mind you, but a ringing conviction that declares from the depths of one's being, 'Yes, this *can* be attained"—Father shook his fist—"and with God's help, I *will* attain it!' As St. James resoundingly proclaims, 'Draw near to God and he will draw near to you.'[217]

"Prayerful intentions and an attitude of reverence are higher spiritual emotions, which are found in a yearning heart. Ramakrishna, whom we mentioned earlier, said the spiritual path consists of *bhakti* tempered with *jñāna*—one-pointed devotion coupled with firsthand knowledge of God. Without this devotion—wholehearted love for one's chosen form of God, and unlimited, unconditional love toward others—one achieves a dry, one-dimensional, partial understanding, which is not, I repeat, not the full-blown illumination that is the classic indicator of all mature spiritual realizations. The ultimate state is one that both encompasses and transcends everything known and knowable in one searing, experiential, integral, and transformative realization, embracing and permeating body, mind, heart, and soul."

My God! I was fired up and spaced out. A pulsating, surging epiphany inwardly engulfed me. I felt that, for a moment, the thick covering of delusion was peeled back, and I was granted a glimpse into the inner workings of the universe. This man seemed to have access to the cosmic blueprint. He was like the Lord of Time, perched atop a commanding view of existence, revealing to us its secrets. He shared with us his insights, born of revelation and experience.

~~~~~~~~~~~~~

Kurt once again piped up. "Father, aren't you a guru of some sort?"

Father laughed. "Not if I can help it! Jesus taught, 'Whoever among you would lead must first become the servant of all.'[218] This is the attitude I try to uphold. I'm just an ordinary soul walking the path like all of you."

"But you instruct like a guru."

"You know, I once opened a fortune cookie that read, 'We learn most when we are teaching.' That tallies exactly with my approach. I consider myself a perpetual pupil of the Divine."

"Don't you charge money for your time?"

Father's expression became serious; he was at a loss for words. Ginny intervened, "Father never asks for nor accepts money for his time."

Then Father spoke. "My son, there is no greater abomination in heaven or on earth than a so-called spiritual teacher who exploits their charges for money, for sex, or to acquire power or fame. I will spare no effort in denouncing such 'teachers,' for they are like vampires, targeting then feeding on vulnerable souls for their own petty gain, which is utterly despicable.

"I met and studied with some exalted spiritual teachers, many of whom were completely unknown. Do you think these individuals possessed MBA degrees? Did they wage advertising campaigns to attract disciples? Did they set up huge organizations to sell the product of spirituality? Much of what is bandied about as spirituality is pure corruption. Many so-called spiritual teachers are charlatans through and through. St. Paul rightly said of them, 'They traded the truth of God for a lie.'[219] They've never tasted the Divine, and they've become addicted to material goods and adulation from the gullible. The wiliest among them present themselves as if they were enlightened. This is sheer duplicity. Furthermore, they engage in shameless self-promotion. They want to make their ill-gotten living by marketing the commodity of God and duping the masses into believing they themselves are spiritually illumined. This is outright fraud, and these swindlers are nothing but crooks."

Complete silence pervaded the cabin.

"But the true spiritual giants want nothing from you. It's hard to conceive, but they have no ego." Father's cadence slowed; his voice softened. "They simply *radiate the light of God.* I have seen this myself." Father, gripped by spiritual fervor, paused to wipe away a single tear that ran down his cheek. "And they make it possible for others to participate in their advanced level of consciousness, which is far subtler and far more powerful than our ordinary ego-based consciousness. Their aura engulfs others in its fold, at least those who are sensitive enough to be affected by it."

Father stopped talking. He looked over at his wristwatch on the nearby coffee table. "All right, it's been a long evening."

So saying, we took a brief break. Father sipped his herbal tea, while others nibbled on snacks, and some chatted in subdued tones.

Several minutes later Father spoke up, "Okay. Let's still our minds and allow the spirit of God to engulf us. Recall the inspiring words of the Psalmist: 'I have stilled and quieted my soul; I am content like a weaned child.'[220] Likewise, let us place ourselves in a contented state so we may calm our restless thoughts and emotions." Then he fell silent.

Ginny lit the lone votive candle on the altar and dimmed the table lamps.

We sat in silence, in that softly lit room, interrupted only by the rain and the occasional sound of the gentle breeze in the nearby trees. I felt my mind spontaneously come to a stop. An overwhelming wave of pure joy, unspeakable peace, and unruffled calmness flooded my being. I felt a homogeneous part of all that exists. I wasn't fearful anymore. All my various concerns simply didn't matter. My life situations and trivial grousings paled into insignificance. Everything was exactly the way it should be; there was no need to alter anything. I belonged to a benign universe that was entirely perfect.

Prison Term

After a while, Father tapped the meditation bowl, and Ginny turned up the lights. He then bade us goodnight and slowly rose from his chair before disappearing into the kitchen. A couple of people followed him to the kitchen door, hoping for a few private words. But they appeared as phantoms to me, and I talked and moved about unconsciously, as if my body were on autopilot.

Suddenly, I involuntarily found myself having an eerie out-of-body experience. I clearly felt the uncanny sensation of gazing downward from a corner of the ceiling. From that vantage point, I observed myself interacting with others, but I couldn't discern what we were saying. It was an odd feeling of utter detachment, as if I were watching some other person conversing. Then Father reappeared a few minutes later. He called me over, and I woozily snapped back into my body. I walked robotlike into the kitchen. We sat privately at his wooden table, where he began speaking.

"My son, I've been thinking about you, and I wanted to share some thoughts. One of the foremost questions in spiritual life is how to maintain your inner serenity while the outer circumstances of your life are going to pot."

I burst out laughing, which helped to ground me even more.

"At one time in my life, I underwent a prolonged period in which I experienced a seemingly unending series of oppressive situations, betrayals, negative turns of events, setbacks, and losses. You name it. If something were to affect me adversely, it was drawn into my life like a magnet. All my efforts were undermined. My dreams were shattered; my hopes, dashed. I was thrust into situations replete with conflict, confrontation, unwarranted blame, and baseless antagonism. One adverse circumstance followed another." (As far as I could determine from Father's journal and infer from his narrative, this period of conflict occurred from approximately 1940 until sometime in late 1945.)

"This blight affected my dealings with others, both secular and religious. In certain circles I was demonized for my political beliefs—my lifelong pacifism—while in others I was ostracized for my religious eclecticism. I often became a scapegoat. Many of my good intentions backfired. I was frequently chided when trying to help others; my well-meaning interventions were at times viewed as threats. Events were somehow twisted so that I became the unwitting target of others' vitriol. My efforts to clear up misunderstandings seemingly only made matters worse.

"My reputation suffered among colleagues and superiors. I became bitter, disillusioned. I wallowed in despair. I lost a great deal of my faith. Because I couldn't initially cope with all this, I nearly lost my teaching post. The ongoing negativity and ceaseless barrage of problems and unfounded criticism had become relentless and overwhelming. This shook me at the deepest level. I became physically ill several times. My outlook became bleak. I was tormented by a sense of hopelessness. No path opened up to show me a way out. I was altogether powerless to stop this assault, no matter how hard I fought against it. My life seemed utterly futile, and I sank into a profound depression.

"But through it all something was happening, though invisible to me at the time. It finally came to a head one day when I was reading a New Testament passage I had read many times before. It was as though God struck me with lightning when my eyes fell on these words of St. Paul:

> It is on account of Christ that I am content in the midst of weaknesses, insults, hardships, persecutions, and adversities. For when I am weak, then I am strong.[221]

"All of a sudden it hit me: *that* was the solution! Because I couldn't prevent it, I learned a way to accept this adversity. Not to like it—that would have been akin to masochism. But *not to react* to it. To be content no matter what. To remain completely neutral as much as possible by viewing my ordeal not as a torturous endurance test, but as an opportunity for me to grow spiritually. And to undergo these events, and for that matter, all the events in my life 'on account of Christ.'

"From that moment on, I reoriented my focus and began living my life not out of self-centeredness, but from a far nobler and larger purpose: I centered myself in Christ so my whole life revolved around him. I thereby rooted out a hidden pocket of hypocrisy I discovered within myself, because this insight revealed to me that heretofore I had wanted to have my cake and eat it too. Contrary to my vocational calling, I had held back from committing myself fully to Jesus by reserving a little comfort zone for my ego." Father heartily laughed. "But this revelation blew my cover, and I realized I had to relinquish all my personal desires for the love of my life, who is Jesus. And that became my coping mechanism during my trials: giving up my own desires by submitting my ego to God and lovingly carrying the cross I had been handed[222] so I could even more closely follow in the footsteps of Christ.

"I thus learned a way to insulate myself from this onslaught so I could continue to function. But initially I did so mechanically, without feeling. It took some time for me to absorb and meaningfully implement this teaching. I soon saw, however, plain as day: that was the key—not to react. And, at the same time, to maintain a continuous inner connection with Christ. This oppressive steamroller continued to flatten every aspect of my life. It affected my vocation and my career, as well as my ordinary daily dealings. But eventually, upon continually practicing what I had read, I reached a point where I just didn't care. Over time, the ebb and flow of external circumstances gradually ceased to affect me.

"Yet, this was not due to any kind of callous indifference. It was because I anchored my soul in the very heart of Jesus that these adverse situations no longer bothered me. I stopped bracketing off my hardships and labeling them as adversarial; I ceased to view them as detrimental. I surrendered in earnest to God and viewed all things as part and parcel of God's will. This tremendously helped me to navigate this unrelenting tidal wave.

"After a while, the outer world simply stopped causing me any concern. I attained a state wherein I could say in complete joy, along with the Apostle: *I am content; I am undergoing this on account of Christ.* Then, after what seemed to be an eternity spent in hell, my ordeal came to an end. And when it did, I was a transformed man. I ceased to complain about negative events. For that matter, I ceased to rejoice about positive events. The ability to react had been completely squeezed out of me. Yet I remained passionately joyful, no matter what occurred to me externally. I had been stripped of everything I once held near and dear. However, I emerged with a fullness in God that has only multiplied over the years."

Father smiled. "I felt compelled to share this with you in the event some small fragment might prove useful in your own life. The path of cynicism, bitterness, complaining, and regret hurts no one but you. If you allow circumstances to dictate your moods, they will only entomb you."

I sat with my jaw agape. Father, who rarely spoke about himself, shared some of his personal struggles for my benefit. I was filled with somberness upon learning of Father's appalling tale, and equally filled with gratitude for his unexpected help. Even more important, Father's emancipating words, describing how he coped with the adversities of life, burrowed deep into the recesses of my open, receptive mind.

I managed to smile back before asking, "Father, during some of the incidents where you confronted others, were you ever in the wrong?"

"Most of the time I was in the right, but the people with whom I was involved were seemingly blinded from seeing this. When I *was* wrong, they often gloated in smug self-satisfaction, sometimes rubbing it in."

"Didn't this upset you?"

"At first it irritated me, but soon I realized that nothing I could say or do would change their opinion. Even when I was vindicated, they did not and would not credit me. So, many times I would cease arguing my case even though I was right, because I realized the absolute futility of pressing my point."

"What were you criticized for?"

"In so many words, the sin of pride and, more specifically, of personal ambition. I lived honorably and ethically and without a stain on my record, so my superiors couldn't attack my character or behavior." (I was able to confirm from a couple of reliable sources that Father indeed enjoyed an unsullied, irreproachable reputation throughout his life and career, both when serving as priest and professor.)

"But the theme they zeroed in on was that I was a rabble rouser, that I sought to undermine the established order. One time they alleged that I wanted to usurp the authority of a department head—a thoroughly nonsensical and groundless charge, as circumstances bore out, much to their subsequent embarrassment. I was more interested in learning the ways of contemplation than in any kind of power grab, which was the very last thing on my mind!"

"Couldn't you do anything to alter your situation?"

"Not for several years. I felt as helpless as Job when he was visited by his torrent of afflictions. None of the efforts I made could pry me loose from my prison term, so to speak. I was stuck...you might say restrained in solitary confinement until I had served my appointed sentence. However, my frustration at feeling both ineffectual and incapable of changing things soon gave way to a sense of detachment. I just watched the whole thing unfold."

Then the most mischievous grin appeared on Father's face, one that would have put the Cheshire Cat to shame.

"While I never led the insurrection they had assumed of me, it probably didn't help that I was considered somewhat of a whistleblower at the seminary, and also during the times of my regency and investiture, and also when I first began teaching after my ordination. At times I subtly, and sometimes not so subtly, called out a few of my fellow seminarians, priests, and lay teachers alike on their little duplicities, often finding surreptitious means to expose the occasional hypocrisies they tried to suppress." Father laughed. "While none of them had committed any formal infraction, I somehow felt it was my duty to point out the intermittent instances of favoritism, nepotism, closing of ranks, and the general undercurrent of political machinations I had sporadically witnessed. All this took place without any repercussions for those involved, even though these incidents sometimes superseded official policy. Even more egregious to me, some of what I witnessed flew in the face of Jesus' teachings. My whistleblowing tendencies alone got me into a world of trouble.

"Even so, I had to look the other way on more than one occasion rather than directly confront one of my superiors in particular about their periodic double standards and risk a charge of insubordination. This is why I mostly kept to myself. Later in life, I learned that such moral compromises were inherent in many institutions of society, and a few unprincipled persons can be found in every profession. But back then, I was young and idealistic, and that wasn't the reason I requested my transfer from preparatory school to the university where I subsequently served. Nor was I ever given a letter of reprimand, nor was I asked to leave. It was just another of the many confrontational aspects of my ordeal.

"Yet, through it all, I didn't wallow in self-pity or become hateful or vindictive. I held no grudge against anyone; I wished no malice on my oppressors. Nor did I fault others for my circumstances. Just the opposite. I blamed myself, my own shortcomings, and my perfectionist tendencies for these occurrences. This relentless introspection caused me to turn inward and forge a level of faith I had not known before, because I clung to God like never before. I held on to the pillar of spirituality I had carved for myself, which in turn helped me to withstand this bombardment. At the same time, I anesthetized my reactions to outer events. This marked a turning point in my life, and looking back, I believe this period of trials was given as a singular blessing that provided an opportunity for me to grow in the ways of God. As St. James liberatingly exhorts:

> Be exceedingly joyful, my brothers and sisters, whenever you encounter various trials. For when your faith is tested and proven, it produces the ability to endure trials. Allow for this to occur, so that you may become spiritually mature and perfected, lacking in nothing.[223]

"The ability to remain joyful while enduring trials is one of the essential cornerstones when living the spiritual life."

There was no more for me to ask. I simply said, "Thank you, Father." He nodded benevolently, then raised his hands and imparted a palpable Pauline-based blessing that forcefully swept through me: "Let the peace of Christ control your heart!"[224] Then he stood up and motioned to me, saying, "Come." After placing his right hand on my left shoulder and smiling broadly at me, he walked me to the kitchen door where we exchanged goodnights. He then invited some others in for a private meeting. I continued heading straight out of the cabin, where Heather stood chatting with Liz. Upon seeing me, they parted company and Heather drove us home. I didn't tell her of the few timeless moments I had spent with Father Christopher, nor did she ask.

Act Now

I can't recall many events of the next day, a Sunday. The metamorphic effects and my deep spiritual mood from the previous night's meeting persisted, as did the echoing reverberation of Father's private words to me. An overpowering sensation of peace coursed through my being, which was further enhanced by Father's powerful blessing. I felt unburdened of life's cares and centered in my soul. I felt as though I were wandering in a dreamlike haze, as if everything were shrouded in a surreal mist. I felt as I had felt during the autumn of 1974, when I underwent my First Awakening.

Word quickly spread that Father had scheduled another brief talk that evening, which was not typical. Happily, Heather once again drove us to his cabin amid lingering rain showers. We arrived and sat with a slightly smaller group. The following day was a Monday, and I had somehow remembered to contact Jennifer before we left and arranged to take off work that day, as I knew I'd be staying one more night at Heather's and I wasn't ready to be driving just yet. However, I noticed that instead of my usual apprehensions when thinking about my job, I felt my decades-long conflict—pitting my worldly duties against my spiritual aspirations—had all but vanished. It seemed quite feasible that I could integrate the two. On that day, I felt no incompatibility. On that day, I felt they were not two separate activities. Only one.

Fortunately, I thought to bring along my cassette recorder. Father, looking tired, nonetheless started speaking, his eyes seeming to glisten in the softly reflected glow from the gentle lighting.

"I never said that spirituality was an easy path," he began. "The ego resists its own demise at all costs. Yet you must give up all attachment, all hope, and all expectation if you are to succeed. There must not be a trace of anything you call your own. For God to take up residence in you, you must be thoroughly purged of the last remaining vestiges of your ego.

"You are now going through your own dark night—St. John of the Cross' term for that lonely and desolate period on the soul's journey to God in which it is emptied of all that is not God. If you choose to remain on this path, all your emotional baggage and hidden psychological issues will continue to surface until they, too, are purged. So, you must persevere in faith.

"Along with having faith, it is critical to perform your practices wholeheartedly. I'm not encouraging you merely to 'do the best you can.' This is an excuse that lackadaisical aspirants use in order to maintain a status quo of mediocrity. Such practitioners will never progress. On the spiritual path, you must commit to doing better than you've ever done before—to exceed all limitations and break through all barriers. Nothing less than your spiritual welfare is at stake.

"Also, do not allow yourself to become disheartened. This is another insidious trap of the ego, specifically designed to convince you to abandon your spiritual practices. Any time you are in the throes of doubt or find yourself in a crisis of faith, call to mind the stirring words of Paul the Apostle: 'We are afflicted in every way, but not crushed; thwarted, but not without hope; persecuted, but not abandoned by God; struck down, but not defeated.'[225] Because, after you've undergone such crises, you'll find that God had given you the strength all along to endure them, even if you were stretched beyond your limits. As St. Paul confidently affirms, 'God can be trusted and will not allow you to be tested beyond what you can bear ...'[226] Have this same unwavering faith by so trusting in God at all times.

"To surrender fully to God, you must let go of your lower self and follow this path to where it leads. You must unhesitatingly set down your conditions, demands, and planned outcomes. Stop barricading yourself in the fortress of your ego! The troublesome ego will concoct innumerable, elaborate schemes to resist change. But you have the ultimate opportunity to turn the tables and conquer your ego while following this path until every last pocket of its resistance has been vanquished. The choice is up to you. No one is forcing you to walk this path. You must freely choose it without imposed pressure of any kind. But this journey is highly purgative. Nothing of your old self will remain. 'You' will disappear and be made anew as God fashions his will through your mind and body. Your new self—your spiritual self—will then live in everlasting joy, bathed nonstop in the solace and protection of God's loving presence, which you now so ardently seek."

Father collected himself for a moment.

"Yes, you must gain access to the inner Divine without using any outer props or external aids. These can act like opiates that stop your spiritual journey dead in its tracks. Many people become sidetracked by unmindfully turning beads, wearing shawls, taking on Eastern names, and so forth." (Father never opposed the use of rosaries or beads—he himself often used a rosary during his private devotions—but he was against using them inattentively.) "They think that by using the paraphernalia of religion they will get closer to God. Then come the rituals and the nomadic pursuit of truth. They become followers and often feel they will only make progress if they belong to a group. All the while they are developing addictions to the form of religion while missing the point of religion. This is because these outer trappings only serve to divert their attention. They are simply embellishments that fortify the ego and delay a person's spiritual progress. However, when walking this path, a person must be freed from all such dependencies and entirely emptied of their ego. The purpose of following the spiritual path is not to make a career out of being a spiritual aspirant, but to see God.

"By the same token, it is unquestionably supportive to develop spiritual camaraderie with companionable seekers, just so long as this doesn't become a blind dependency or turn into a superficial social gathering that overshadows and prevents true spiritual growth. Once after a peace rally, I asked one of the singers, 'What gives you the courage and inspiration to fight injustice?' He instantly replied, 'Music. It's the music that brings people together.' In our circle, spirituality is the music, and it undoubtedly helps us to maintain company with those pursuing a similar goal and observing similar practices as ours. It is certainly more beneficial than hanging out with reprobates.

"It can also be inspirational to read of others' spiritual struggles and realizations. But is anyone able to tell me whose realization is the most important?"

Ginny, "Your own realization."

"Precisely. We may meet numerous holy people, receive countless blessings, attend an array of religious events, become 'Dharma Bums,' go on pilgrimages, wear flowing robes, set up shrines, burn incense, and make spirituality our lifestyle. But without realization, all this is for naught. You must *internalize* these teachings and make them your own until they resonate within you and become alive in the very core of your soul.

"Bear in mind the perceptive lines of Angelus Silesius, which I'll paraphrase:

> Though Christ be born in Bethlehem
> A thousand times or more
> If he ne'er takes birth inside your heart
> You'll be lost forevermore.[227]

"And so, never forget: every dependency is a blot; every crutch must be discarded. This notion must become an essential part of your understanding. If you truly realize this, your faith will become solid as a rock. You will dispense with external dependencies and become firmly grounded in God, the sole focus of your aspirations. As a result, you will never again feel unsettled or distressed. Jesus emphatically declared, 'Let not your hearts be troubled.'[228] Once you come to embody this rock-solid faith, you will notice a permanent decrease in your level of anxiety and frustration. You will become so infused with God that fear and uncertainty will no longer affect you or govern your life.

"You are now undergoing an inner pruning that will restructure the nucleus of your being so your wondrous soul can luminously shine. You are poised on the brink of the greatest adventure of your life. But first, you must experience the extinguishing of your ego, which will cause you to become nothing. The great Jewish mystics refer to God as *ayin*: 'nothingness.' By becoming nothing, you will merge with the great Nothingness that is God. And yet in that nothingness is everything.

"Remember what we've discussed many times. When you react to your destiny, you only compound the same situation and make it worse. You must learn to swim against the tide of your inner pro-gramming so you can overcome your ingrained tendency to react with emotions to changing events. It is essential to remain detached and retain your evenness of mind no matter what takes place in your life. *Never* lose your composure.

"Right now, you take great pains to avoid many of the very things that confront you each day. You view them as irritants. But the path of least resistance is to accept them, because they will not go away. These events are merely your destiny unfolding. You must learn to bear them good-naturedly and skirt deftly through life, as if walking through a field of land mines. You will succeed if you never once lose your poise.

"Once you master these lessons, then your true spiritual work begins. Once you gracefully cope with whatever occurs to you and accept all situations in life with a spirit of equanimity, you'll be able to see that what you've been practicing so far has been preliminary work. You can then begin to stabilize the deeper states of conscious-ness that you access during meditation and integrate them into your daily activities so that you maintain your connection with God at all times, whether you are 'sitting, moving around, standing, or kneel-ing,'[229] as *The Cloud of Unknowing* declares.

"The situations in life are not to be avoided or hastily gotten through in order to attain some higher state or loftier goal. They all carry equal weight, so you must treat them as though they *are* your life's work, whether advancing your career or cleaning your kitty lit-ter box. There is no part of your life that is not your spiritual life.

"At a more advanced stage, nothing will faze you. As enlighten-ment unfolds, your ability to identify obstacles and problems per se will vanish from your consciousness. You won't even be aware of them. But when you arbitrarily judge what is good or bad, desirable or undesirable, then react emotionally, you automatically set your-self up for failure. And the stress you then experience is entirely of your own doing. And that stress will destroy you. Especially when you could undergo the exact same incidents without reacting to them at all. In which case, you would live with no stress whatsoever.

"I'll give you an example. Two drivers were caught in gridlocked traffic en route to their destinations, making them both late. The first driver threw tantrum after tantrum and cursed at God, fellow driv-ers, and every traffic signal he missed. The second driver remained composed and unperturbed, calmly going along with the flow of events. Which of the two do you think demonstrated more spiritual composure?"

Several replied, "The second driver."

Father nodded. "Similarly, we can teach ourselves not to react emotionally to unplanned, unsought, or unalterable events, and thereby save ourselves a world of grief.

"And so, you must learn these principles: Remain unperturbed no matter what occurs. Never allow situations to upset you. And don't become attached to your own agenda. Make provisional plans, but always be flexible.

"This is the attitude of true surrender—adapting without com-plaint to changing circumstances as they unfold. As Jesus prayed, 'Thy will be done.' You don't know what your destiny is or how it will unfold. Therefore, it's best to let go of all expectations, and the tension you now feel when you plot out your life with a slide rule and caliper will disappear.

"Yes, the path ahead will unfold for you. Have no doubt. Whatever unfolds *is* your destiny. As such, it cannot be altered. Knowing this, give up all worry. Give up all fear. Do not grasp for the future. Surrender to the activity at hand, allowing events to materialize without forcing them. To force or to resist events, then lament your fate, is the hallmark of the ego. Such actions only serve to strengthen its hold. Moreover, ego-based actions constrict your consciousness. You then defeat the very purpose of your spiritual practices.

"So now it is up to you. Have faith. Let go. Perform a self-exorcism. Eliminate the demons in your own mind—fear, desire, and the search for a perpetual love outside of God. Stop resonating with your lower emotions. Stop kowtowing to them. Uproot their tenacious grip by adhering to the far greater attraction of unlimited divine love. Don't brutalize yourself if you falter or err—pick yourself up and begin again. Always keep your sense of humor, which will help sustain you during trying times. Maintain your inner peace moment by moment no matter what happens. Thus, working in lockstep with God, you will readily ascend to another dimension—the dimensionless realm of God. The time is ripe, my dear friends. These are not abstract platitudes, but practical suggestions that will help you overcome your lower emotions so you can abide continuously in God and live a life heretofore undreamt. They can and must be acted upon. Act now."

~~~~~~~~~~~~

Shortly after this, I learned that Father stopped holding meetings. It became increasingly difficult for him to move about. He continued cooking for himself, but Ginny performed grocery runs for him and routinely cleaned his house.

EPILOGUE (April 1992)

I wasn't home when Heather phoned that day. In a shaky voice, she left a two-word message on my answering machine: "He's gone." That's all she needed to say. I knew what she meant. The Lord of Time had taken his leave from this earthly realm.

~~~~~~~~~~~~

Vivid memories of many happy moments I spent with Father Christopher raced through my mind. I recalled numerous life-altering teachings I learned from him while I sat on his living room floor, completely mesmerized by his transformational dialogues. Father's larger-than-life personality had deeply imprinted itself on my mind, my heart, my soul. I remembered his straightforward yet caring manner…his playful sense of humor…his razor-sharp wit…his incisive, often unsparing criticism of the spiritual scene … and his realistic take on every issue. And especially his positive, optimistic attitude. Equally important, I was both captivated and enormously inspired by his gifted intellect, his penetrating insights into and masterly grasp not only of Christianity but all the world's religions, and the seamless manner in which he synthesized diverse mystical traditions and effortlessly explained them. I would never forget his profound insights into our innermost natures and unseen spiritual realities, and his mysterious ability to transmit palpable spiritual blessings. Lastly, and of particular significance to me, because of Father Christopher's immense influence and sage counsel, I had come full circle to find closure to my unfulfilled First Awakening experience of 1974 in the sense of learning techniques that could better help me make mysticism work in my daily life.

But it pointedly sunk in to the depths of my being that I would never see him again, never again be able to spend time in his presence. I felt devastated … numb. I wept unreservedly that evening, mourning the loss of this extraordinary man, who had become and remains to this day a towering figure in my life.

I later learned that Ginny arrived one day to bring groceries and check in on Father, with whom she had briefly spoken earlier that morning. Father was sitting in his favorite chair in the living room, the one where he sat to converse with us. She spotted him from the front window, thinking he was peacefully sleeping. She quietly let herself in through the side door and began unpacking various groceries in the kitchen. On her way out, she stopped by his side. It was then she discovered he was motionless and unbreathing. Yet, she said, his face beamed an expression of fathomless contentment. Despite her haste to phone the ambulance, she noticed his favorite Bible lying on his lap. It was open to 1 Corinthians 13:

> Though I speak in the tongues of men and angels,
> And have not love,
> I have become as a noisy gong or a tinkling cymbal.
> And though I have the gift of prophecy,
> And understand all mysteries and all knowledge;
> And though I have all faith, so that I could move mountains,
> And have not love,
> I am nothing.
> And though I give all my goods to feed the poor,
> And though I sacrifice my body to be burnt alive,
> And have not love,
> It profits me nothing.

Epilogue

Love is patient, love is kind;
Love is neither envious nor boastful;
Love is neither proud nor discourteous;
It seeks not its own gain;
It is not easily provoked; it does not dwell on wrongs;
It takes no pleasure in wickedness, but rejoices in the truth.
Love bears all things, believes all things,
Hopes all things, endures all things.

Love never fails.
But where there are prophecies, they shall fail;
Where there are tongues, they shall cease;
Where there is knowledge, it shall pass away.
For we know in part, and we prophesy in part.
But when that which is perfect comes,
Then the imperfect shall pass away.

When I was a child, I spoke like a child,
I understood like a child, I thought like a child.
But when I became a man, I set aside my childhood ways.
For now we see through a glass, darkly;
But then we shall see face to face.
Now I know in part; but then I shall understand fully.

So now these three abide: faith, hope, and love.
But the greatest of these is love.

FATHER CHRISTOPHER'S JOURNAL

I have gathered together several dozen entries from Father Christopher's two thin notebooks, which Ginny gave me for safekeeping once she learned I'd be writing about him. These notebooks encompass the years 1938 through 1952. The earlier entries were generally shorter, while the later ones tended to be longer. While many entries addressed nonspecific personal issues in Father's life, the teachings were universally applicable, and so I included them. I have minimally edited these excerpts for textual clarity, and I added brief titles based on their content.

Curiously, this was not a diary in the sense of a personal history. There are virtually no references to Father's outer conditions of life at any given time. Little or no mention is made of his family, his early priesthood years, World War II, university life, his various travels, his Civil Rights–era involvements, or his retirement. The entries aren't even written in a typical first-person manner. They are almost always written from the perspective of someone talking to him, although a few are written in dialogue format. There are numerous instances wherein he is addressed simply as "my son."

When I perused these writings, it became evident that many of Father's oral teachings strikingly corresponded to several of his journal entries. A number of entries uncannily paralleled the style in which Father would speak to us in his otherworldly state. Perhaps they were what Catholics call *locutions*—inner, spiritual revelations from a beneficent spiritual source. It may seem reasonable, or even obvious at times, to attribute these revelations to Jesus or to God, especially when reading utterances such as, "Trust in me exclusively. Love me with all your heart." But I hesitate to do so because the true source will never be known. However, regardless of their origin, these inspired maxims and teachings were penned by a man whose spiritual counsel profoundly influenced a dedicated group of like-minded spiritual seekers.

Learn to Forgive

Why dwell on wounds inflicted by those from the past? Just quietly forget. Inject no venom of your own. Learn to forgive others' shortcomings. Do not be vengeful. Let go.

Avoid bringing suffering upon yourself. Suffering means you are going against God. That is the test.

This is the highest discipline: surrender your life to God. Hold on to nothing. Then you will have the peace you wish for.

June 28, 1938

Patience

My son, you are on the right course. I have placed you there myself and am watching over you and am guiding and protecting you.

You must learn patience. Everything will happen at the right time. Continue coping with whatever comes your way. Do not be distressed. Your path has been set.

October 19, 1938

Free Yourself

Father wrote: "Free me from the shackles of my mind."
    Free yourself.
"Help me."
    You need to help yourself.

May 22, 1939

Do Your Duty

Father wrote: "Dear Lord, I don't want this!"
    You are obliged to do your duty. I have chosen this work for you at this time.

August 1939

Shake Off the World

Father wrote: "Should I stay in this place?"
    Yes.
"How long?"
    As long as I want you here.
"This is difficult."
    Persevere, my son. I will guide you. Turn inward to me. Follow me alone. Shake off the world. Do not allow your plans to usurp your soul. Do not worry.

February 13, 1940

All These Situations Are Tests

All these situations are tests to mold and strengthen your character. They are intended to lead you back to God.

June 1940

Let Go

My son, give up controlling your time and attempting to manage every detail of your life. Let go. Do not allow yourself to become anxious, perturbed, or agitated by any event. Never. Even if you are one hour late for a meeting with a king. Do not react. It is as simple as that.

September 14, 1940

Do Not Force Any Event

This recent situation caught you off guard. You felt attacked, betrayed. It came to you unprovoked, assailing you without warning. The situation will resolve itself. Therefore, be patient. Do not force any event.

Look on this situation as your teacher; view it as your friend. Use it to transform your mind. Such events serve to expose your deficiencies and weaknesses. This incident brought out your fear, pride, and jealousy. So long as these emotions reside in your mind, you remain in their grip. You are then far from the goal. When they no longer overshadow your inner peace, you will succeed in attaining spiritual freedom. You must watch your mind and see which holds the upper hand: your emotions or your soul.

January 1, 1941

Do Not Be Anxious

Do not be anxious. Your task will get done. Remember, God is more important than all this.

November 19, 1941

I Am With You Always

Remain calm and fearlessly cope with every situation. I am with you always and am guiding you through these different experiences. You must gracefully accept your present state of affairs and courageously deal with all these circumstances.

Practice forbearance and carry out your plans for the year. You will sense my presence more strongly than in many a year past. You are changing. I am drawing you to myself.

Continue with your duties at hand and all will be right. Your contemplations will be deep and your love will grow. Part of your dissatisfaction is an eruption from within. Recall what your confessor said: you are being purged of all dross so that Spirit alone will shine. Never doubt this.

February 15, 1942

What You Seek Is Me

Father wrote of...“My unassuageable longings for love.”
What you seek is me. I am your soul's inner companion.

March 30, 1942

Pray With All Your Heart

Your prayer must be so intense, so heartfelt, that it forges an unbreakable connection with God. My son, pray with all your heart. Pour your soul into your prayer. Establish a bond with God you have never known before, a bond so strong that nothing can disturb it. Intense, incessant prayer will take you straight to the very core of God, where you will be embraced by God's loving arms.

June 2, 1942

Never Succumb to Distress

You must face each event that presents itself before you with a calm, unperturbed mind. Once you react to external conditions or worry for any reason, you are cut off from your soul. It does not matter in the slightest what activity you are engaged in—walking, eating, praying, work, rest. The sole requirement is that you maintain your peace of mind throughout that activity, whatever it may be.

You are consumed with worry because you so easily forget these truths: love unconditionally, trust in God ceaselessly, and have unshakable faith. Never succumb to distress. You can maintain your spiritual consciousness and perform your work at the same time. The secret is never to worry and never to react. Practice these truths.

October 14, 1942

This Is Your Life

My son, the matter is out of your hands. It is not for you to decide. You have little control over it. You are undergoing severe trials and misfortunes. Remember, this is no theory. This is your life. Find joy in the midst of it all. Most important, do nothing that would extinguish your love or diminish your faith in God.

May 12, 1943

A Perfect Opportunity

This situation is a perfect opportunity for you to grow. Look on this seeming hardship as the greatest of blessings. It is pointing your way to God. Use it to go directly to God.[230] You must overcome your wavering faith and your uncertainty. Do not fall prey to a doubting mind or a heart filled with distrust. Be like a child in spirit.[231] Truly, this is the key to your salvation. Maintain childlike faith even while the structures of your life crumble around you.

September 1943

These Events Are Tests

Cling to God always. Do not divide your mind with doubt. When you can do this and remain firmly established in your soul, neither your lower emotions nor the world will disturb you. At present, you allow the clatter of this world to affect you. But you must remain anchored in your own blissful soul. Then you can shrug off all external matters in an instant.

All these events are tests for you. They will keep appearing until you remain unaffected by them. To react is your greatest weakness. God in his mercy will help remedy your weakness by testing you. Once you remain unaffected by the external world, you will be fit to walk the spiritual path. These outer situations are indicators that measure how far you have progressed. My son, you still have a long way to go. Therefore, persevere in your practices. Have faith in the words I speak, then act on them.

February 13, 1944

Give Unceasingly

It is your duty to give of yourself unselfishly, unquestioningly as the need arises. You must maintain your attitude of selflessness even if it inconveniences you, even if you are deceived, betrayed, mistreated, or taken advantage of. Recall the words of Paul you recently read. [Ed.—This likely refers to Father's revelatory reading of 2 Corinthians 12:10, which proved a life-changing event for him, as recounted during the Sixth Visit.] Your responsibility is not to react; to remain untainted by the world;[232] and to continue embodying an attitude of giving, unaffected by others' responses, be they positive or negative.

Open your heart. Keep your spirit free from all constraints. Do not revert to your walled-up, fearful self. Such an attitude kills your soul. Give unceasingly, unconditionally. Surrender continuously. I am allowing you to be knocked around solely to bring about the state of perfection in you. Learn these valuable lessons. You will benefit from the fruits of your ordeal. But first, you must forge an unbreakable inner link with me. This is easily accomplished. My grace is with you always. Feel my loving presence inside your soul; look within to find me there.

July 1944

Develop Inner Faith

It is essential to develop inner faith and fortify yourself so you do not react to any event, person, or circumstance. You must be hoisted to the next level where you will be able to remain neutral and indifferent to the winds of change. Right now, you are caught in a vicious circle. You are easily tossed about by outer events. You react by expressing emotions, which only chain you to your lower mind. You then become sad or happy, fearful or courageous, depending solely on outer circumstances. You must instead find the strength and courage to anchor yourself inwardly in your soul where there is no change. You will then overcome your variable moods. Once you accomplish this, you will not be shaken by any external circumstance.

September 12, 1944

Do Not React

Your job is not to react when adverse destiny unfolds. By reacting, you paralyze your soul by polluting your mind with anger, regret, fear, and other harmful emotions. You must free yourself from this pattern. Why should such seemingly negative incidents affect you? A spiritual aspirant must remain unmoved in situations of loss or gain alike. Yet, you sulk over such paltry things. You must regain your poise and face whatever occurs with equanimity. Be detached from any outcome. Do not react. When you can succeed at this, you will begin to progress.

October 11, 1944

Keep Your Mind Free From Worry

Keep your mind free from worry. Trust in me exclusively. Love me with all your heart. Never once allow negativity to enter your mind and drag you down. Smother all gloom and despair in the radiance of limitless divine love.

Never compromise your resolve by allowing your mind to wallow in fear. Fight your inner battle. Do not give in to lower emotions.

You have learned inestimable, priceless lessons. These lessons could not have been gained by any other means. Never slacken in your practices, but do not be so hard on yourself. Focus on your goals rather than your shortcomings. Then let go of everything.

October 25, 1944

Be More Gentle With Yourself

The circumstances of life will come about whether or not you create deadlines or pressure yourself to achieve your various goals. Therefore, do not be attached to your own plans. Learn to be more gentle with yourself. Keep up your spiritual practice, but apply it lovingly.

November 2, 1944

Situations Will Keep Repeating Themselves

When you arrive at a place within yourself where you do not complain about anything and do not even notice if a given situation is good or bad for you, you will have taken the first step toward spiritual progress. Until that time dawns, these situations will keep appearing in ways you least expect them. They are giving you the opportunity to advance beyond the point of reacting. But you choose to remain where you are. And so, the situations will keep repeating themselves until you choose differently.

December 3, 1944

Always Abide in Me

Father wrote: "How can I be rid of anxiety?"

When you navigate through the traffic of life, cling to me and you will never lose your poise. Avoid attachments to worldly situations. Do not be agitated by the circumstances of life. If you cannot fully control your reactions, then for now avoid situations that provoke your lower emotions.

Learn to detect when the world encroaches on your spiritual citadel. At the very moment it intrudes, you forfeit your inner peace. Spiritually speaking, the answer is simple, my son. Always abide in me. There is nothing more you need do.

December 20, 1944

Your Fears Are Unfounded

Your fears are unfounded. Along with dwelling continuously in my presence, one solution will cure you of all fears. You must have unwavering faith. You have read of many saints whose faith was severely tested. Yet they won out, passing the harshest of trials solely by the courage of their convictions. It is essential to have faith in things unseen.[233] Otherwise, what is the point of developing yourself spiritually?

December 24, 1944

Cease Demanding Proof

My son, cease demanding proof. No amount of proof will convince a doubting mind. Only faith will comfort the yearning of the heart. Find that faith within.

January 25, 1945

Engage Your Inner Demons

Father wrote: "I feel pressured again!"

Abandon your preoccupation with self-imposed goals. Do not become consumed with plans. Engage your inner demons with fortitude; meet them head on. Doing this will imbue you with courage, which will mobilize you to perform your work unperturbed by doubt or fear.

You have your path, your practice, and your work. Perform them with diligence. Employ skillfulness. Be industrious. Do not become impatient. Moment by moment, never lose your inner serenity. It is not worth the price you pay, which is your spiritual peace.

February 9, 1945

Remain Inwardly Unaffected

The onslaught will continue—relentless and unabated—until which time you accept and embrace it and remain inwardly unaffected by it. It will not stop if you wish it away, curse it, attempt to alter it, or in any way refuse it. You cannot defeat it; it merely changes its form and reappears elsewhere. The only solution that will preserve your inner peace is to cling to God incessantly as it occurs.

Your chief fault is paying attention to it when it erupts. By even noticing it, your consciousness remains steeped in duality. It then becomes a "you versus it" relationship. Your second fault is reacting to it. By reacting to it, you feed it, and by such continual feeding it continually breeds. Thus, it perpetuates itself. All at the expense of your soul.

March 19, 1945

Let Nothing Disturb Your Inner State

Always remain fully poised in your soul. Be content, peaceful, and calm. Let nothing disturb your inner state. Infinite, unruffled tranquility can be yours in an instant if you let go of the worrying mind. Drop it into the abyss of your boundless soul. You will then be established in your own true nature, in which there is no change, in which there is unfathomable peace.

June 30, 1945

Your Dream Life Does Not Exist

Listen, my son. This is your life. This is your fate. Your dream life does not exist. It exists only in your imagination. What you are fighting is reality. But nothing can alter these events. Yet, you somehow wish them away, and this sets up ongoing conflict within you. You thus create your own tension and manufacture your own distress. You yourself thereby harm your own soul. No one is causing this except you.

However, all this conflict is unnecessary. You must face reality. There is no escape. Do not torture yourself with escapist fantasies that do not exist. Be infinitely content. Approach each day with unlimited joy. Never for one moment think that life is burdening you.

August 20, 1945

No One Can Enter Your Inner Domain

My son, no one can enter your inner domain. Point to an actual person who is residing inside your head. It is you alone who carry these memories. By continuously revivifying them, you torment yourself.

You would deny yourself access to your own soul because you allow other people's reactions to affect you. You let these trifles disturb your spiritual bearing. What little faith you possess![234]

Where is your mettle? Where, too, your resolve, your conviction? You fear this person or that incident will intrude into your mind and taint your soul, so you mentally guard against them. You feel a need to safeguard yourself with imagined defenses. But in reality, there is no need. Your anticipation of the future and your concern about various unknown, speculative outcomes dictate your behavior.

Until you remove this inner protective armor, your spiritual progress will remain at a standstill. You need the sanction of your own mind to dispense with this imaginary shield. At present, you are victimized by your fears. You and you alone allow self-created ghosts to inhabit your inner sanctum, where you invest them with life and permit them to haunt you, where they constantly strike at you like a snake.

Look squarely at these apparitions. Track them down or they will continue to stalk you. Find out who has lowered your inner drawbridge, which allows this fictional army inside. Who is it that so readily betrays the sanctity of your inner kingdom? Work to uncover this mystery. Much is at stake.

September 23, 1945

Never Outside Your Own Mind

My son, do not allow your mind to control you. Practice wholeheartedly, undaunted by any adversity. Overcome every obstacle. Never give in to fear. Do not allow worry to destroy your connection with your soul. Remember: Every obstacle, every adversity, every fear resides within you; they are never outside your own mind. Conquer your mind by means of single-minded determination. The grace is there. And the path for you is then very, very easy.

October 19, 1945

What Is This Fear?

Love and fear cannot exist together.[235] I am exposing and rooting out the fear buried deep inside you. This fear was wrought when you closed your heart long ago because of wounds from your past. And what do we see now? A man stymied by a multitude of concerns—all stirred up in the depths of his own mind.

You lack the courage to grab hold of the faith you need to make the final leap into God. Yet, you must find that faith and take that leap. You experience spiritual bliss and rapture, but all the while

254

your lower mind is tethered to a great fear. What is this fear? How did it originate? Why is its hold so powerful today?

December 2, 1945

Love Unconditionally

Never compromise your spiritual outlook. Break this pattern of worry and self-doubt. Most important, keep up your practice. You must come to embody selfless, unconditional love in all your thoughts and actions.[236] This is your main path.

Love unconditionally, regardless of how others treat you. Love is the strongest force. Never allow outside influences to affect your love. Let the flame of unconditional, nonjudgmental love burn brightly in your heart at all times. Never extinguish it with condemnation, envy, or anger—these emotions only imprison you within their confining walls. Be a walking, living, breathing pillar of love, a blazing reservoir of divine solace and compassion. Never allow your mind to partake of even one angry or malignant thought. You thus poison your own practice. You pollute your heart and cut off all blessings.

January 13, 1946

Fully Reside in God

Remain inseparably bound to God. When you fully reside in God, nothing in this mortal realm matters in the slightest. Which is why you must follow this counsel. You have no choice. The sooner you take up residence in God, the quicker you will progress. Your anxieties will cease. You will forever be immune from the vicissitudes of change. Step aside from the passing spectacle of this fleeting life and plunge headlong into God. Abide there without worry. Reside there in joy.

February 8, 1946

Be Fearless

Be fearless, my son. Once you rid yourself of fear, the deep spiritual realizations will dawn.

April 2, 1946

Think of God Always

Cling to God tenaciously. Think of God always. Forge your path forever in God's direction. Cry out to God incessantly. Focus your spiritual work on uniting with your own soul. Free your mind from all impurities. Then you will know that God perpetually lives inside you. Then you will come to see God.[237] Then you will be free.

November 12, 1946

Forget All Other Concerns

Center your life in God. Forget all other concerns. If something needs to be accomplished, have faith that it either will or will not occur. It does not matter in the least what happens. It is your destiny coming to fruition and nothing more.

Do not try to force reality to conform to your wishes. Let go of your agendas. Give everything to God. All else is a passing dream, a mirage of transient illusions.

This, my son, is an essential teaching. It holds the key for you, especially at this time, which is ripe with blessings. Make use of these blessings, and follow this simple instruction. It will yield fruits beyond what you could possibly conceive.

May 1947

Work Without Pressure

Work without pressure, without worry. You are a spiritual aspirant. Answer only to God. Do not make an idol of your earthly tasks. You only tyrannize yourself and lose your inner composure. When you muddle your mind with assorted plans and frenzied mental activities, you immediately lose touch with the moment-to-moment bliss of your soul.

Engage in one activity at a time. Be fully present to it. Have no anxieties about your future plans.[238] This creates distress, which is self-perpetuating, rolling over from one moment to the next, completely obscuring your soul.

When you are fully poised and aware in the moment, boundless energy arises that otherwise is spent in worry. Worry saps your energy, and the continuous sustenance of speculative thought consumes tremendous energy. Whereas surrendering to the moment frees it up.

July 8, 1947

Remain Fixed in Your Soul

You feel agitated because of your deep meditation. It brought many images from your past to the surface—memories and feelings that still lurk in your mind. These images are now actively playing themselves out in your imagination. But by paying attention to them, you allow them to wrench you away from your soul.

Do not be lured by these phantoms. Be detached as they work themselves through your mind. They will soon exhaust themselves. It is up to you to ignore them. By so doing, you will remain fixed in your soul at all times.

September 5, 1947

Total Surrender

Your only choice is total surrender. You keep fighting this, but surrender is the only practice that will take you where you ache to go. Let go of all planning, all agendas. Live fully in the moment. Love fully in the heart. Do not allow the calculating, worrying mind to gain a foothold. You must master this.

September 29, 1947

Forget About the Future

Instead of focusing your mind on the activity at hand, you clutter it with countless thoughts about upcoming plans. This keeps you in a constant state of tension.

Divest yourself of all cares, all strategies. Forget about the future. It will unfold of its own accord, regardless of your plans.

November 5, 1947

The Only Cure for the Mind

My son, the only cure for the mind is to transcend it. Beyond the mind is the soul, where memories of the past and thoughts of the future do not intrude. Once you still your mind and calm your emotions, you will contact your soul. There, you will find immutable peace. Once established in your blissful soul, you will be free from lower emotions, fear, likes, and dislikes. Psychological studies can only reveal so much. The ultimate remedy is to live in God.

December 24, 1947

Cast Your Anchor in God

Never harbor any worry or concern over any incident or event. Remain firmly centered in your soul. Pay no heed to changing external events, which rise and subside, rise and subside. Cast your anchor in God, the one unchangeable reality. Continue your practice of not reacting to changes that occur to your senses and mind—view them in their true light: as fleeting, temporal phantasms. You must constantly strive to accomplish this.

Once you make your home in your soul and steadfastly remain there, nothing will sway you from this inner sanctuary. Your lesson is to ignore completely any intrusions that would breach the abode of your soul. You must dismiss them, viewing them as transitory images that pull you away from your spiritual home. It is essential that you fortify yourself so these passing apparitions do not touch you. By not doing so, you become a stranger to your own soul.

January 3, 1948

Imperturbable Joy

You can maintain an inner state of imperturbable joy in the midst of any situation—activity, illness, conversation, rest. In waking or sleep. Anytime, all the time. The interruptions that block this state arise from two sources. First, the deeply etched personality traits in your mind, which cement your behavior into fixed patterns that obstruct your soul. These patterns are like clouds in the sky that cover the light of the sun. Once these clouds disperse, the sun shines with utmost clarity.

Second, and this particularly applies to you: taking the outer world as real. You are easily overwhelmed by many activities and sensations perceived by your mind and senses. This causes you to become guarded, which keeps your mind constantly unsettled. You cultivate this guardedness to protect yourself from upsetting interactions, both imagined and real. You pay too much attention to external events, which take you away from your spiritual center. This is because you are not fully stationed in your soul. Once you set your sights on your soul alone and moor yourself there, you will no longer be shaken by external events. You will remain forever established in the infinite peace of God.

January 23, 1948

Make Determined Efforts

Walk this path confidently, my son. Increase your aspirations. Burn away the negative residue of your lower emotions through fervent prayer. Make determined efforts to succeed. Break through the shrouds of your finite mind. The path will then unfold for you in the twinkling of an eye.

February 1948

The Highest Teaching

I will give you the highest teaching of all. You learned that the key to your healing rests with you, not anyone else. In the same way, the key to your spiritual transformation rests with you alone. You must change yourself. Do not try to change others. Become love and compassion incarnate, and those in need will find a way to your abode. They will derive a fountain of solace from you.

To have devotion, become filled with undying faith. To trust, eliminate suspicion within. To give unstintingly, destroy all vestiges of selfishness. To forgive unconditionally, open your heart to everyone. For others to look on you as loving, rid yourself of animosity and ill will. To walk in the footsteps of God, radiate limitless love unceasingly.

February 17, 1948

Remedying All Your Deficiencies

I am remedying all your deficiencies. You must have a strong ethical grounding if you are to succeed in your spiritual blossoming. It is indispensable to practice what you profess by freeing yourself from all hypocrisy, all double standards.

March 19, 1948

Do Not Shut Down

Do not shut down one iota of the love, the openness, and the vulnerability you feel. Do not withhold your love from others or barricade yourself inside a wall of fear. Do not destroy the link you are forging with your soul and with God.

July 1, 1948

None of These Matter

Remember, it does not matter how your destiny unfolds as long as you are grounded in God. The key is to remain detached in the midst of whatever situation you find yourself. Whatever goals you achieve, whatever dreams you dream, whatever life you live—none of these matter in the slightest. The only thing that matters is fully residing in God at all times.

August 21, 1948

The Religion of Love

Focus on the religion of love, my son. That is the point of it all. Recall what Father Petros taught you—without love, religion is heartless, meaningless. [Ed.—Father Petros was the Greek Orthodox priest whom Father Christopher met on his spiritual travels in the late 1940s, most likely 1949.]

December 5, 1950

Examine Your Motives

Never pollute your acts of helping others with your own selfishness. This is a hard and fast rule you must not violate under any circumstances. Otherwise, you will suffer terribly, because the memory of your hypocrisy will haunt your conscience.

Examine your motives. Always maintain the highest aspirations. Do not fall prey to selfish desires. Become the finest aspirant of which you are capable. Never settle for mediocrity. This is the ideal you must follow.

God looks into your heart and knows your true intentions.[239] Your untainted motives will act as your shield, helping you to remain completely selfless at all times.

January 16, 1951

Worldly Attachments

Worldly attachments must never dictate your decisions in life. If a worldly attachment or involvement of any kind pulls you away from your spiritual pursuits, you must cut it off decisively, regardless of consequences.

Never allow yourself to be led by desire. If any worldly desire gains the upper hand and displaces your spiritual goal, you will have compromised your soul. You must continually renew your spiritual focus to ensure that God is forever your top priority.

January 29, 1951

God in Disguise

Do not think that any person or situation is causing you distress. In reality, each person and every situation is God in disguise. Look beyond their outer forms to see God within them, no matter how thick the apparent covering.

March 9, 1951

Maintain Your Inner Poise

My son, do not worry about anything. Maintain your inner poise uninterruptedly. Never become seized by apprehension. Do not become impatient. Remain calm, come what may. Center yourself in God. Once you react to nothing, then you will fear nothing.

April 24, 1951

All We See and Experience Is God

Cut off the tentacles of your mind that extend into the world of people and things. Like a tortoise, withdraw your curiosity from outer phenomena. Subdue your thoughts and quell your tendency to brood over events that befall you. Extinguish these mental activities entirely in the infinite expanse of God.

Let events unfold of their own accord. Be neither attached to nor repulsed by them. Never feel distressed, for all we see and experience is God; there is nothing that is not God. God's radiant presence fills the entire creation, permeating every fiber of matter, each atom, all creatures. These are all expressions of God. They are not different from God. There are not two gods; there is only one God. Never differentiate "this" from "that"—such is the confusion of a divided mind.

Release all attachment to the results of your efforts, to forcing your own agenda, to altering events so they unfold in ways that are beneficial to your ego. Let go of all desire. Never once remove your mind from God for anything. Sever all umbilical cords of attachment that connect your mind to this mundane world. By so doing, you are giving up nothing and gaining everything. For your loss is your ego and your gain is God.

June 11, 1951

Re-Establish Your Priorities

I tell you truly—you are frustrated solely because you cannot tap into the well of inexhaustible love that exists within your own heart. You mistakenly look to outer sources to provide you with this love. But you can never rely on others or external objects to supply this love. Only God can provide this unfailing love—a love that comes from within your own soul, never from the things or people of this world.

So I advise you, my dear son: Re-establish your priorities. Make God your one true everlasting relationship. Seek his love unfailingly. Disregard what others say or do; remain unaffected by their actions. You will discover the source of your dissatisfaction if you follow this counsel. And this will solve your spiritual search. You will find what you now but halfheartedly seek.

August 15, 1951

Overcome Your Mind

You must become a living example, twenty-four hours a day, of all you aspire to attain and will attain if you but diligently apply yourself. My grace is always there. Obstacles only occur in your mind. Overcome your mind and you defeat the only obstacle that exists.

October 30, 1951

The World Is a Mirror

Many times you are presented with adverse situations during your weakest, most vulnerable moments, when you least expect them. These are the very situations that trigger your lower emotions. You cannot hide from them in order to avoid them; they will await you in one form or another.

Outer events activate the emotions that dwell in your mind. These emotions reside within you, never outside you. If an external event causes you to react, it merely stimulates an emotion that already exists in your mind. The world is a mirror, as are people. That which we encounter outside is simply a reflection of what resides inside. Once you clearly understand this, all emotions will loosen their grip on your soul.

December 18, 1951

Immerse Yourself Solely in God

My son, you are finally putting into practice the counsel I have been giving you. Cut off all attachment to the things of this world. Immerse yourself solely in God. Pay no heed whatsoever to the fluttering images of this mundane, finite sphere. Enshroud yourself with the mantle of God's loving presence. Forget the attractions of this earthly realm; take your mind from them. They are solely presented to ensnare you and distract you from your goal.

At all times, without exception, remain absorbed in God. Dive deep into the ocean of God's infinite presence. Only God is fully alive, pulsating with vibrant love. Cleave to him, the very source of your being.

March 18, 1952

Love Is the Balm

Transform all negativity into boundless joy through the elixir of divine love. Love is the balm; love is the tonic. Love alone will free you from all things harmful. Fill yourself with limitless love, and you will forever be shielded from all negative influences. The cloak of divine love is your eternal protection. Wear it always, and lower forces and negative energies can never touch you, never get near you.

This is a most secret teaching. Love alone will transform your relationship with any situation, any person—even your environment. Only the greatest of teachers teach this. Love is the sovereign cure for every shortcoming, every weakness. It has no residue attached to it. Its effects are far ranging; its benefits, long lasting, even if you do not perceive them on the physical level.

Love never fails.[240] Love is the invisible glue that binds the universe together. For you to master this sublime instruction, you must practice it every moment. Apply it regardless of circumstances. Hoist yourself up to the next plateau by embodying this perfected state of divine love. This alone will remedy your shortcomings. This alone is the sole ingredient you need if you are to grow spiritually. Become a wondrous being of pure love.

April 13, 1952

APPENDIX

Father Christopher's Meditation Practice

Father Christopher taught that the focal point of one's meditation—the home object—could be a scriptural passage; a short prayer or invocation, such as the Jesus Prayer; an image of a holy being; a noble virtue, such as love or peace; a visualization of the infinite, formless God; one's breath or heartbeat; or audible sounds, such as the ticking of a clock, or even (based on my specific question) agreeable music. He considered acceptable whatever consistently captivated one's attention and induced deep concentration. He once said, "You can focus on anything that will suspend the workings of the mind." But he most often recommended meditation conjoined with devotion. Otherwise, one's practice can become dry and mechanical. "Meditate regularly," he counseled, "and pray to God with a yearning heart."

To bring the mind quickly into a deep state of concentration, he further taught that a person could simultaneously focus on the home object and monitor their breath. Because it is impossible for the mind to concentrate on two objects at the same time, Father held that by attempting to do so, the mind, now doubly occupied, would become inwardly absorbed all the more rapidly.

In addition, Father recommended centering one's awareness in one's spiritual heart during meditation. He once remarked, "I prefer to meditate in the spiritual heart, which is the seat of divine love."

Father suggested early evening as the best time to practice meditation, especially for those working in the world, as suspending the operations of the mind through prolonged deep meditation in the early morning hours could present problems for householders need-ing to engage their minds when commuting to work or occupied at their jobs. He advised sitting for approximately thirty to forty minutes per session on a daily basis. However, he also advocated a brief morning routine of prayer and quiet time in order to renew one's spiritual focus, center oneself in God, and reaffirm one's ethi-cal foundations, the latter of which he invariably summarized in two words: integrity and selflessness. At the conclusion of one's medita-tion and prayer sessions, Father advised mentally dedicating the love, joy, and peace that one experiences to the welfare of all beings, which he said helps to reinforce one's attitude of altruism.

Rather than trying to control thoughts racing through the mind, Father instructed us to concentrate solely on the home object. By so doing, wandering thoughts will subside of their own accord. The goal, he stated, is to immerse oneself in the divine Presence so thor-oughly that all mentations cease and the mind becomes completely still and filled with unflappable tranquility. When coupled with de-votional outpourings, a dedicated practitioner will soon be overtaken by a deep spiritual mood. Father maintained that the re-sultant transcendent state is inexpressible and overflowing with tremendous joy and peace. Through repeated practice, this sublime state incrementally adheres over time until it overshadows one's ego-based consciousness. Soon, an aspirant comes to feel a tangible Presence even as they are engaged in worldly activities. Eventually, this spiritual consciousness becomes part and parcel of their normal waking state.

Father correspondingly encouraged practitioners to integrate the transformative effects of their meditation practice with their eve-ryday activities. He never advised shunning one's active participation in the world while practicing spiritual disciplines, but rather he advo-cated merging both the inner and outer facets of one's life. As with religious approaches that are geared toward householders, Father recommended employing *spiritualized actions* as a pathway to God. This requires an aspirant to maintain the same interior state of spir-itual detachment and the same inner link with their spiritual self that they establish during meditation while they perform their work and discharge their duties in the world.

Finally, Father maintained that the best way to learn how to meditate is simply to meditate, that is, practice the actual technique. And, he emphasized, practice with a dedicated heart. One should never abandon their spiritual routine during dry spells or amid times of adversity, but continue their practice at all times, motivated by their resolute intentions and undaunted aspirations. "It's when you struggle the most that you need to tap into the limitless reservoir of your deep-seated faith," he advised. Father Christopher repeatedly stated the formula for success in spiritual life: "Always remember— incessant longing for God and yearning for spiritual liberation are the keys to realization."

NOTES

The Epigraph is from *An Autobiography by Ansel Adams* (New York: Little, Brown, 1996), p. 323.

[1] Koran 2:152.

[2] Luke 17:21.

[3] Matthew 7:7.

[4] Ezekiel 18:31.

[5] Galatians 6:7.

[6] Matthew 7:24.

[7] Mark 10:27.

[8] Luke 12:15.

[9] Matthew 6:6.

[10] Brother Lawrence, *The Practice of the Presence of God* (New York: Fleming H. Revell, 1895), Second Conversation, p. 12. (Hereafter, *The Practice of the Presence of God*.)

[11] Romans 12:2.

[12] Ephesians 4:24.

[13] Bhagavad Gita 8:12.

[14] Margaret Smith (trans.), *Readings from the Mystics of Islam* (London: Luzac & Company, 1972 reprint of the 1950 edition), p. 89. (Hereafter, *Readings from the Mystics of Islam*.)

[15] John 4:48.

[16] Yogasūtra 3:38.

[17] John 13:34.

[18] Haṭha Yoga Pradīpikā 2:76.

[19] Haṭha Yoga Pradīpikā 4:78.

[20] Matthew 6:33.

[21] 1 Peter 5:7.

[22] Matthew 8:20.

[23] Jeremiah 29:13.

[24] Sirach 2:4–6.

[25] 1 Corinthians 3:18–19.

[26] Plotinus, *The Enneads*, Sixth Ennead, Ninth Tractate: "On the Good, or the One" VI.9.11.50–1.

[27] William Barrett, *Irrational Man: A Study in Existential Philosophy* (Garden City: Doubleday Anchor, 1962), p. 169.

[28] Ephesians 4:6.

[29] Matthew 14:23, Mark 1:35, Luke 5:16, Luke 6:12.

[30] Mark 6:31.

[31] Khaggavisāṇa Sutta, Verse 8.

[32] Henry David Thoreau, *Walden; or, Life in the Woods* (1854), "Economy."

[33] Ralph Waldo Emerson, "Self-Reliance" (1841).

[34] Luke 8:14.

[35] John 16:33.

[36] Tao Te Ching, Chapter 20.

[37] Matthew 7:7.

[38] Isaiah 43:18.

[39] Oscar Wilde, *A Woman of No Importance* (1893), Third Act.

[40] Psalm 51:10.

[41] Psalm 19:12.

[42] Jan van Ruysbroeck, as cited in *The Sparkling Stone*, in Dom C. A. Wynschenk (trans.) and Evelyn Underhill (ed.), *John of Ruysbroeck* (London: J. M. Dent & Sons, 1916), p. 211. (Hereafter, *The Sparkling Stone*.)

[43] Matthew 23:9.

[44] H. A. Reinhold (ed.), *The Soul Afire: Revelations of the Mystics* (New York: Pantheon, 1944), p. 304. (Hereafter, *The Soul Afire: Revelations of the Mystics*.)

[45] Isaiah 25:7.

[46] Ralph Waldo Emerson, *Essays: Second Series* (1844), "Nature."

[47] Matthew 5:8.

[48] 2 Corinthians 3:18.

[49] Bhagavad Gita 6:29.

[50] John 4:24.

[51] Proverbs 8:17.

[52] Mark 8:33.

[53] Mark 7:15.

[54] Matthew 6:24.

[55] James 1:13–14.

[56] John 16:33.

[57] Psalm 33:10.

[58] *The Lion in Winter* (directed by Anthony Harvey, AVCO Embassy Pictures, 1968).

[59] Matthew 6:25, 6:31, 6:34.

[60] 1 Corinthians 7:32.

[61] Philippians 4:6.

[62] Matthew 6:27.

[63] Ephesians 4:31.

[64] Galatians 5:22–3.

[65] Matthew 7:16.

[66] Sirach 2:1–3.

[67] Matthew 7:15.

[68] Tao Te Ching, Chapter 66.

[69] Philippians 2:3.

[70] Hebrews 6:11–12.

[71] Timothy Ware (ed.), Igumen Chariton (comp.), E. Kadloubovsky and E. M. Palmer (trans.), *The Art of Prayer: An Orthodox Anthology* (London: Faber and Faber, 1976 reprint of the 1966 edition), p. 183. (Hereafter, *The Art of Prayer.*)

[72] 2 Thessalonians 3:16.

[73] John 12:49.

[74] 1 John 4:5.

[75] Matthew 23:23–24.

[76] Matthew 23:3.

[77] St. Augustine, *Sermons on Selected Lessons of the New Testament*, Sermon 117:3: "On the Gospel of St. John 1:1."

[78] Matthew 7:24.

[79] Matthew 7:15.

[80] *The Cloud of Unknowing*, Chapter 70.

[81] Swami Prabhavananda, with the assistance of Frederick Manchester, *The Spiritual Heritage of India* (Hollywood: Vedanta Press, Second Paperback Edition, 1969), p. 354.

[82] Tao Te Ching, Chapter 32.

[83] *The Practice of the Presence of God*, Second Conversation, p. 12.

[84] Jeremiah 17:10.

[85] Bhagavad Gita 6:8.

[86] *Readings from the Mystics of Islam*, p. 11.

[87] Psalm 63:1.

[88] Hebrews 5:7.

[89] St. Anthony, from the *Ninth Conference* of St. John Cassian, Chapter 31, as cited in Rt. Rev. Dom Vitalis Lehodey, *The Ways of Mental Prayer* (Dublin: M. H . Gill & Son, 1960 reprint of the 1924 edition), p. 345. (Hereafter, *The Ways of Mental Prayer*.)

[90] John Bunyan, "A Discourse on Prayer" (1662), in *The Complete Works of John Bunyan* (Philadelphia: Bradley, Garretson & Co., 1873), p. 664.

[91] Luke 18:1.

[92] 1 Thessalonians 5:17.

[93] Swami Prabhavananda, *The Eternal Companion* (Hollywood: Vedanta Press, Third Edition, 1970), p. 5.

[94] Bhagavad Gita 5:12.

[95] Matthew 16:26.

[96] Bhagavad Gita 4:20.

[97] Tao Te Ching, Chapter 37.

[98] Bhagavad Gita 2:62–63.

[99] Matthew 6:10.

[100] *The Practice of the Presence of God*, Second Conversation, p. 11.

[101] Thomas à Kempis, *The Imitation of Christ*, Book One, Chapter 19.

[102] Adapted from *The Gospel of Râmakrishna* (New York: The Vedanta Society, 1907), pp. 90–92.

[103] Matthew 6:6.

[104] Luke 10:42.

[105] Luke 17:21.

[106] Psalm 143:8.

[107] Shaqīq al-Balkhī, as cited in Reynold A. Nicholson, *The Mystics of Islam* (London: G. Bell and Sons, 1914), p. 43.

[108] Paul Jackson, S.J. (trans.), *Sharafuddin Maneri: The Hundred Letters* (New York: Paulist Press, 1980), p. 35.

[109] Matthew 6:21.

[110] Exodus 20:3.
[111] Bhagavad Gita 4:22.
[112] Jeremiah 1:17.
[113] St. Teresa of Ávila, *The Way of Perfection*, Chapter 31.
[114] Matthew 21:12.
[115] Luke 6:29.
[116] Luke 16:10.
[117] Matthew 18:21–22.
[118] Matthew 6:12.
[119] Sirach 28:2.
[120] Matthew 6:14.
[121] Matthew 22:39.
[122] Matthew 5:44.
[123] Proverbs 15:17.
[124] Luke 6:27–28.
[125] Romans 10:12.
[126] Matthew 6:33.
[127] John 4:24.
[128] 1 John 4:8.
[129] Luke 17:21.
[130] Mark 12:30–31.
[131] Matthew 6:21.
[132] Matthew 7:24.
[133] Matthew 4:19.
[134] Lewis Carroll, *Alice's Adventures in Wonderland* (1865), Chapter V, "Advice from a Caterpillar."
[135] Elizabeth Barrett Browning, *Aurora Leigh* (1856), Seventh Book.
[136] Matthew 7:1–2.
[137] Matthew 14:28–30.
[138] Matthew 14:31.
[139] J. M. Barrie, *Peter Pan in Kensington Gardens* (1906), Chapter II.
[140] Robert Frost, *The Road Not Taken* (1915).
[141] Shunryu Suzuki, with Trudy Dixon (ed.), *Zen Mind, Beginner's Mind* (New York: Weatherhill, First Paperback Edition, 1973), p. 47.
[142] Psalm 118:8.

[143] Robert William Service, *The Spell of the Yukon* (1907).

[144] Matthew 6:34.

[145] Tao Te Ching, Chapter 3.

[146] Isaiah 64:8.

[147] *The Wizard of Oz* (directed by Victor Fleming, Metro-Goldwyn-Mayer, 1939).

[148] Galatians 5:18.

[149] Philippians 3:19.

[150] 1 John 2:6.

[151] See also Matthew 23:3.

[152] Matthew 5:44.

[153] 1 Cor. 4:12–13.

[154] Proverbs 11:3.

[155] J. S. (trans.), *The Spirit of St Francis de Sales* (London: Burns Oates & Washbourne, 1925), pp. 286–287.

[156] Wisdom 11:22.

[157] Bhagavad Gita 4:7.

[158] John 3:16.

[159] Philippians 2:14.

[160] Tao Te Ching, Chapter 52.

[161] St. John of the Cross, *Dark Night of the Soul*, Book 1, Chapter 6.

[162] *The Art of Prayer*, p. 160.

[163] Matthew 6:6.

[164] 1 Corinthians 7:9.

[165] Matthew 7:13.

[166] Jan van Ruysbroeck, as cited in *The Adornment of Spiritual Marriage*, in Dom C. A. Wynschenk (trans.) and Evelyn Underhill (ed.), *John of Ruysbroeck* (London: J. M. Dent & Sons, 1916), pp. 69. (Hereafter, *The Adornment of Spiritual Marriage*.)

[167] St. John of the Cross, *Living Flame of Love*, E. Allison Peers (trans. and ed.), (Garden City: Image, 1962), p. 193.

[168] St. Teresa of Ávila, *The Interior Castle*, The Benedictines of Stanbrook (trans.), Very Rev. Prior Benedict Zimmerman (ed.), (London: Thomas Baker, 1921, Third Edition), p. 270. (Hereafter, *The Interior Castle*.)

[169] 2 Peter 1:4.

[170] Romans 8:17.
[171] 1 Corinthians 6:17.
[172] Luke 17:21.
[173] 1 Corinthians 3:16.
[174] 1 Corinthians 2:14.
[175] *The Adornment of Spiritual Marriage,* pp. 68–69.
[176] Old English version of Romans 12:2.
[177] *The Interior Castle,* p. 271.
[178] *The Interior Castle,* pp. 271–272.
[179] *The Interior Castle,* p. 271.
[180] Luke 21:36.
[181] Ephesians 1:3.
[182] Charles Dickens, *A Christmas Carol* (1843), Stave One: "Marley's Ghost." (Hereafter, *A Christmas Carol.*)
[183] 2 Timothy 4:5.
[184] St. John of the Cross, *The Ascent of Mount Carmel,* Book Three, Chapter II, Section 4.
[185] Tao Te Ching, Chapter 64.
[186] See also Matthew 16:26, Mark 8:36.
[187] 1 Corinthians 10:31.
[188] Jonathan Swift, "Thoughts on Various Subjects" in *The Works of the Rev. Jonathan Swift, Volume V,* Thomas Sheridan (ed.) and John Nichols (ed.), (London: H. Baldwin and Son, 1801), p. 465.
[189] Philippians 4:11–13.
[190] Tao Te Ching, Chapter 20.
[191] Acts 17:28.
[192] Wisdom 9:13–14.
[193] Proverbs 3:5.
[194] James 4:14.
[195] Bhagavad Gita 18:61.
[196] Galatians 6:7.
[197] *A Christmas Carol,* Stave Four: "The Last of the Spirits."
[198] Bhagavad Gita 6:5.
[199] Bhagavad Gita 6:29.
[200] Psalm 139:8.
[201] Philippians 4:7.

[202] Adapted from *The Gospel of Râmakrishna* (New York: The Vedanta Society, 1907), p. 109; and from *Gospel of Sri Ramakrishna, Vol. II* (Madras: Sri Ramakrishna Math, Second Edition, 1928), p. 33.

[203] *The Ways of Mental Prayer*, p. 345.

[204] 1 John 3:2.

[205] *The Sparkling Stone*, pp. 209–210.

[206] Swami Prabhavananda and Frederick Manchester (trans.), *The Upanishads: Breath of the Eternal* (Hollywood: Vedanta Press, 1947), pp. 65–66, citing the Mundaka Upanishad 3.1.1.

[207] Bhagavad Gita 4:18.

[208] Luke 10:38–42.

[209] Mark 8:36.

[210] 2 Corinthians 4:18.

[211] Yogasūtra 1:2.

[212] Mark 12:30, based on Deuteronomy 6:5.

[213] Mark 12:31, based on Leviticus 19:18.

[214] Job 19:26–27.

[215] *The Soul Afire: Revelations of the Mystics*, pp. 286–287.

[216] Adapted from *The Life of St. Mary Magdalene of Pazzi, Carmelitess* by Virgilio Cepari, S.J., F. W. Faber (trans.), (London: Thomas Richardson and Son, 1849), p. 236; and from *The Life and Works of St. Mary Magdalen De-Pazzi* by Rev. Placido Fabrini, Rev. Antonio Isoleri (trans.), (Philadelphia: St. Mary Magdalen de-Pazzi Italian Church, 1900), p. 163.

[217] James 4:8.

[218] Mark 10:44.

[219] Romans 1:25.

[220] Psalm 131:2.

[221] 2 Corinthians 12:10.

[222] Matthew 16:24.

[223] James 1:2–4.

[224] Colossians 3:15.

[225] 2 Corinthians 4:8–9.

[226] 1 Corinthians 10:13.

[227] Angelus Silesius, *The Cherubinic Wanderer* (1657), Book One, Couplet 61.

228 John 14:1.
229 *The Cloud of Unknowing*, Chapter 71.
230 See also Acts 14:22.
231 See also Matthew 18:3.
232 See also James 1:27.
233 See also Hebrews 11:1.
234 See also Matthew 6:30.
235 See also 1 John 4:18.
236 See also 1 John 3:18.
237 See also Matthew 5:8.
238 See also Matthew 6:34.
239 See also 1 Chronicles 28:9.
240 See also 1 Corinthians 13:8.

ABOUT THE AUTHOR

John Roger Barrie is the literary executor of influential author, historian, and philosopher Gerald Heard (1889–1971), and the creator and publisher of geraldheard.com. He has overseen reissues of eighteen classic Gerald Heard titles, both nonfiction and fiction. He served for many years as a regional freelance writer and editor.

For nearly five decades, Mr. Barrie has practiced spiritual disciplines from many different religious traditions, and he has studied with and received blessings from numerous spiritual teachers. Raised a Catholic, he has intentionally followed the spiritual path since 1974, branching out thereafter to embrace an interfaith approach while maintaining his Christian roots. His interfaith approach incorporates teachings and practices from several spiritual paths, including the rich mystical traditions from his native Catholicism, and the universal principles advanced by the respected, interfaith-oriented Ramakrishna–Vedanta tradition, of which he is an authorized lay instructor. His emphasis on experiential spiritual realization and his firsthand familiarity with diverse spiritual traditions has imbued him with a fluent knowledgebase and practical outlook when addressing the subtleties of the mystical path.

Mr. Barrie's first spiritual article appeared in 1981, and *Dialogues With the Lord of Time* is his first book. For more information, visit johnrogerbarrie.com.

John Roger Barrie lives in Northern California with his wife.

www.ingramcontent.com/pod-product-compliance
Lightning Source LLC
Chambersburg PA
CBHW020436130626
46549CB00001B/176